The Gen X Series

CYBER OLYMPIAD 7

Useful for Cyber Olympiads Conducted at School, National & International Levels

Authors

Atul Bhardwaj
Mohd. Arif Siddique

Peer Reviewer
Navneet Mehra
[M.Sc. (IT), B.Tech. (CSE), B.Sc. (IT)]

Strictly According to the Latest Syllabus of Cyber Olympiad

Published by:

V&S PUBLISHERS

F-2/16, Ansari road, Daryaganj, New Delhi-110002
☎ 23240026, 23240027 • *Fax:* 011-23240028
✉ info@vspublishers.com • ⊕ www.vspublishers.com

Online Brandstore: amazon.in/vspublishers

Regional Office : Hyderabad
5-1-707/1, Brij Bhawan (Beside Central Bank of India Lane)
Bank Street, Koti, Hyderabad - 500 095
☎ 040-24737290
✉ vspublishershyd@gmail.com

Follow us on:   

BUY OUR BOOKS FROM: | AMAZON | | FLIPKART |

© Copyright: V&S PUBLISHERS
ISBN 978-93-579406-5-8
New Edition

Publisher's Note

General Trade and Mass Appeal books across various genres have helped **V&S Publishers** to gain widespread popularity. In a short span of 10 years, we have successfully published more than 1000 titles across 9 languages in our 50 subject categories. Being into the publishing business for about 40 years, we have always been a dynamic publishing house, with a massive distribution network, across India; including E-commerce platforms.

Understanding the need of inculcating knowledge and developing a spirit of healthy competition amongst students to make them ready for the world outside schools and colleges; we created Olympiad Series under the **GEN X SERIES Imprint** which, owning to its rich content and unique representation became popular amongst students, in no time. The motivation is not to improve marks in terms of numbers, but is to make sure that the students are already prepared to face competitive environment with respect to college admissions and cracking various entrance examinations, while ensuring their conceptual clarity.

Published for classes 1-10 across subjects English, Mathematics, Science, Computers, General Knowledge, the books are unlike any other in the market and are written in a guidebook pattern and exhaustively include examples and Multiple-Choice Questions.

Here, we present the latest Edition of **CYBER OLYMPIAD CLASS 7.**

Unique Features of the book are as follows:

- ☞ Authored by Subject Matter Experts' and Peer reviewed by School Principals and HOD's for the respective subjects
- ☞ Books based on principles of Applied Psychology and Bloom's Taxonomy
- ☞ Suited for Olympiad Examinations held at School level, National level & International Level irrespective of organizing body.
- ☞ The only Olympiad Book in India written in Guidebook Pattern with Concise Theory, images and illustrations.
- ☞ Exhaustively include Examples, MCQs, Subjective Questions, and HOTS with Answer Keys & Solutions.
- ☞ Multiple Model Papers for thorough practice also given inside the book with solutions.
- ☞ OMR sheets appended at the end of the book for simulating exam environment.

Besides, we are also planning to launch an App very soon for the Olympiad preparation which further testifies our constant endeavor to keep up with student demands. We have made sure to closely follow syllabus patterns of not only Olympiad conducting bodies but also education boards & organizations like CBSE and NCERT, to make sure that our books prove useful to students; helping them to boost their academic performance in schools as well.

P.S. While every care has been taken to ensure the correctness of the content, if you come across any error, howsoever minor, do not hesitate to discuss with teachers while pointing that out to us in no uncertain terms.

We wish you All the Best!

DISTINCTIVE

01 — LEARNING OBJECTIVES

They list the whole chapter as subtopics, helping the teachers to guide children in a step-by-step manner.

02 — DID YOU KNOW

Enhance your knowledge by getting acquainted with some amazing facts across various subjects like science, Mathematics and English.

03 — MULTIPLE CHOICE QUESTIONS

MCQs act as an excellent learning aid, helping you to understand and work on your mistakes.

04 — THINGS TO REMEMBER

A quick recap of the chapter in a summarized format helps in faster revision along with conceptual clarity.

05 — HOTS

The High Order Thinking Questions aim to help the student to solve Application-based questions and gain practical understanding of the subject.

FEATURES

SUBJECTIVE QUESTIONS

06 Help to place the knowledge gained in orderly fashion by using **"WH"** questions, mostly in the form of bullet points.

ACHIEVER'S SECTION

07 Offers a quick revision of the book along with some new facts for the students to discover.

A SET OF OMR SHEETS

08 To allow the student to practice question in an exam-like format which would help them to get the "feel" of how Olympiad exams take place.

MODEL TEST PAPERS

09 Two model test papers are provided at the end of each book, which help the student to test the knowledge which they have gained after thorough reading of all chapters.

ANSWER KEY & SOLUTION

10 Detailed Answer Key along with explanations aid the pupil to indentify, understand the mistakes they make during the course of Olympiad preparation.

COMPLEMENT SCHOOL SYLLABI

The syllabi across all Olympiad examination closely follow the pattern of academic books. Hence, they not only provide a competitive examination experience, but also help to revise topics for school examinations as well, while strengthening conceptual precision.

ENHANCEMENT OF ANALYTICAL & LOGICAL REASONING

Practicing analytical ability questions, not only helps in developing intellectual ability but also plays a vital role in building critical thinking ability which helps an individual to think about a question or a crisis like situation in day to day life; from all aspects and directions.

Note to Parents

Dear Parents,

Olympiad examinations come with a plethora of advantages. First and foremost among such advantages is the application of knowledge studied, in the form of multiple-choice questions. It helps the child not only to step away from rote learning, but also helps them to exhibit their competencies across various subjects.

In addition to this, Olympiads help the student to understand the importance of revision and practice, and to imbibe upon these practices; which also prove useful in academic performance of the child.

The Olympiads are conducted across multiple subjects, and help the child to recognize their field of interest, thereby encouraging the students to make a career in the field where they can excel the most.

However, cognitive development of a child is not just limited to the four walls of classroom. Following steps can be encouraged by you, to ensure their ward is able to grasp various concepts with ease or lesser difficulty:

- **Eat a balanced diet:** Ensure intake of vitamins and minerals to keep you active. Include fruits and super foods like millet in your diet to ensure healthy functioning of organs. Huge intake of junk food should be avoided.

- **Indulge in outdoor activities:** Outdoor games break the monotony of life. Play your heart out in greenery to keep yourself alert, active and fit.

- **Sleep well:** A sound sleep of 7-8 hours refreshes the brain and makes it ready to understand new topics with more clarity. A sleep derived person faces difficulty in doing even the simplest tasks of day to day life.

- **Reduce your Screen time:** More screen time leads to not only weakening of eyesight but decreases concentration span. Regulated Screen time should be encouraged

- **Do not hesitate to raise a hand:** Having a doubt in class? Do not hesitate to ask your parents or teachers. This ensures more Conceptual Clarity and hence leads to Application based understanding of various subjects and topics.

- **Teach and Learn:** No need to do rote-learning. Once you understand a topic teach or explain it to your friends, siblings and parents. It brings clarity and ensures the child does his revision this way.

- **Keep smiling:** A positive attitude promotes a growth mindset and encourages the child to be more inquisitive and try to learn something new, everyday!

HAPPY LEARNING!

Contents

SECTION 1
COMPUTERS AND IT

Fundamentals of Computer

Learning Objectives : In this chapter, students will learn about:

- ✓ Hardware components
- ✓ Input Devices
- ✓ Output devices
- ✓ Software concepts
- ✓ Using Internet Explorer
- ✓ Using Windows

CHAPTER SUMMARY

A computer is an electronic device and in today's world an indispensable invention. Information Technology (IT) is the broad subject related to computers and it mainly focuses on managing and processing information.

Hardware

A computer's hardware is a computer item you can physically see or touch. A computer hardware consists of three main parts. They are the input devices, the central processing unit and the output devices. These components of the computer work together in an IPO cycle i.e., Input-processing-output cycle.

The hardware components of a modern computer system is shown in the picture given below.

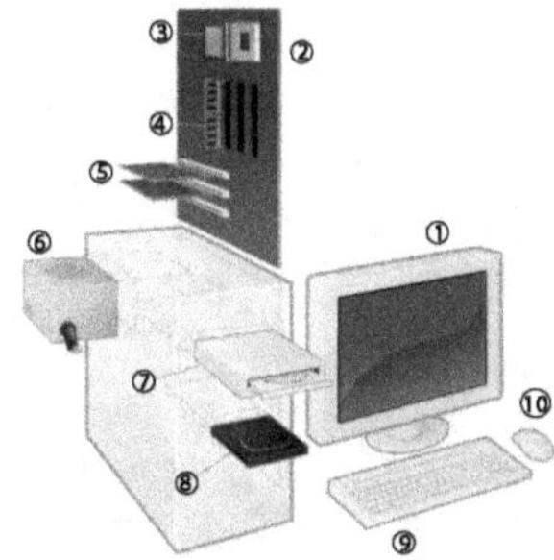

1. Monitor
2. Motherboard
3. Microprocessor
4. RAM
5. Expansion card
6. Power Supply
7. CD/DVD Drive
8. Floppy Disk Drive (Obsolete now)
9. Keyboard
10. Mouse

Input Devices

Input devices are those that are used to give instructions to the computer or to make an entry into the system. Some of the input devices are keyboard, mouse, scanner, light pen, joystick, etc.

Mouse

A mouse acts as a hand-held pointing device and controls the actions of the pointer blinking on your computer screen known as a cursor.

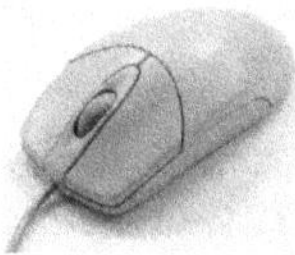

Keyboard

A keyboard let you enter information and commands into a computer.

Digital Camera

A digital camera lets you take pictures and transfer them to a computer.

Central Processing Unit (CPU)

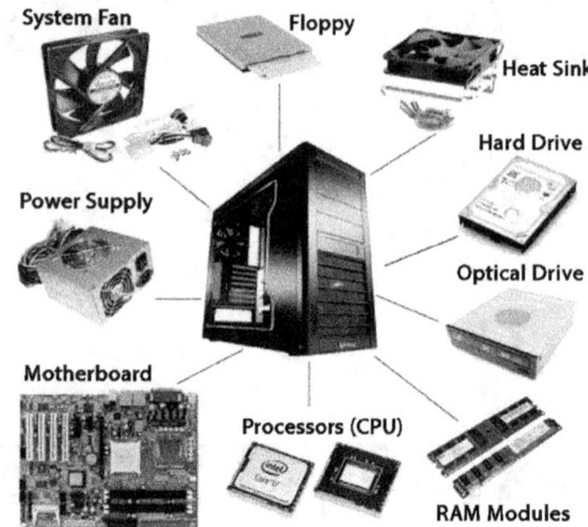

The computer's brain CPU is a computer's main chip. It calculates and processes information, and its speed is measured in Megahertz (MHz) and Gigahertz (GHz). The software is a computer program that tells computer hardware how to operate. After processing, the input data are converted into meaningful information and given as output. The cabinet that holds the central processing unit have the parts shown in above figure.

Output Devices

Output devices are those that display results. Some of the output devices are monitors, printers, speakers, etc.

Monitors

A monitor looks and works a lot like a TV screen. The monitor is really only half of what makes text and images appear on the screen. The other half is the graphics card. The monitor plugs into the graphics card in the back of the computer.

Printers

A printer transfers processed information to printed page. Main types of printers are: InkJet; Laser and color laser; Multifunction; Dot matrix; and Plotter.

Speakers

Speakers allow you to hear the sounds produced by the sound card.

Software

Graphical User Interface (GUI): Makes computers easier to operate by using pictures and icons to represent files and programs.

An Operating System: Loads automatically and controls just about everything on your computer.

Application Program: Helps you accomplish a certain task, such as writing a letter, browsing the Internet, or playing a game.

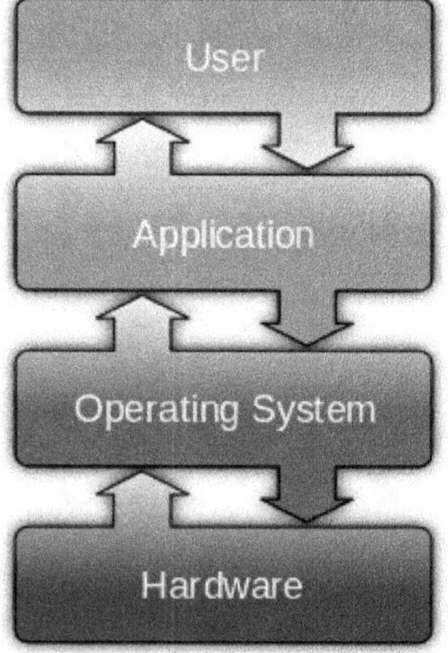

New Software Versions and Releases: Come out periodically and add new features and improve components of a program. New versions also take advantage of ever-improving technology.

The flowchart shows how the operating system software and application software are layered on a typical desktop computer. The arrow shows the flow of information.

Memory
It is computer's temporary storage place where it stores its information and data.

There are two main types of memory on your computer: They are RAM and ROM.

RAM (Random-Access Memory)
Computer's main memory, which is used to process information also called primary memory is the RAM (example: work with a file). This memory is volatile, which means unsaved data disappears when you shutdown the computer.

ROM (Read-Only Memory)
Computer's low-level memory, which is used to perform its most basic functions is ROM (example: start the computer). This memory is non-volatile, which means data remains even when you shutdown the computer.

Measuring Memory
Bit: Short for *binary digit*, a bit is the smallest memory unit. Eight bits equal one byte.

Byte: Short for *binary digits eight*, one byte equals one character (letter, number, or symbol).

Kilobyte (K or KB): 1,024 bytes

Megabyte (M or MB): 1,048,576 bytes

Gigabyte (G or GB): 1,073,741,824 bytes

Terabyte (TB): 1,099, 511,627,776 bytes

Storage Devices or Memory Devices
Memory devices are very useful for sharing or transporting information. They are also useful for backing up your information.

Computer Performance
CPU Speed: Arguably the single most important factor that determines a computer's performance is the speed of its CPU.

RAM: The more RAM a computer has, the better its performance.

Multitasking: Microsoft Windows can run more than one program at a time.

The more programs or tasks being done at a time, the longer it takes to complete each one, and hence a drop in computer performance.

Networks and the Internet
LAN: Stands for Local Area Network and connects computers in the same geographic area or building, using cables.

Internet: The Internet is the largest computer network in the world, connecting millions of computers. People use it for many reasons, such as to make purchases finding, research information, or send e-mail.

World Wide Web: The World Wide Web is a hypertext system that operates over the Internet. The hypertext is read by browsers, which display the web pages from web servers.

Parts of Typical Window

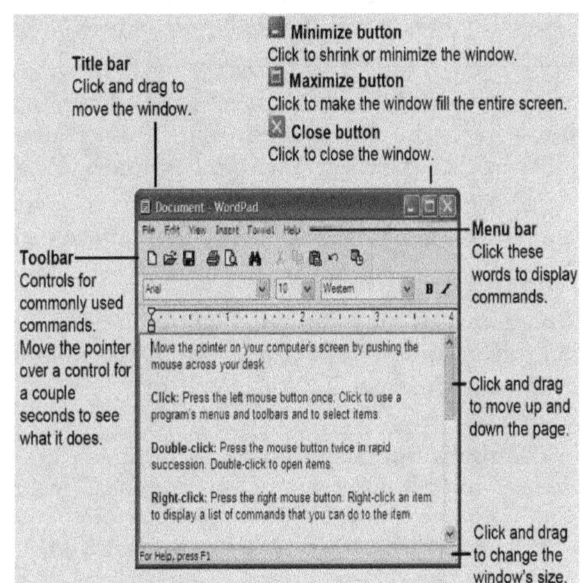

The password of the computers in charge of controlling the nuclear missiles of the United States Army for years was 0000000000.

Windows Tips
The Windows Start menu displays your most frequently used programs.

What a toolbar button does? Place the pointer over the button for a second; a helpful description will usually appear. This will tell you the function of the button on which you have placed the mouse pointer.

Right-clicking an icon: Clicking the object with the right mouse button shows you a list of what you can do to the object.

What do to when you make a mistake? Try using the undo command by selecting Edit → Undo from the menu, or by pressing Ctrl + Z.

Using the menu without using the mouse: Press Alt and the underlined letters of the menu item you want to open. In a dialog box, you can press Enter instead of clicking OK, and you can press Esc instead of clicking Cancel.

What to do when you need help? Press <F1>. Pressing F1 will open a help window with information about the program.

Control in a dialog box: Click the ? What is this button in the upper right corner of the window and then click the control with the pointer.

To see what programs are running: Look at the names on the taskbar along the bottom of the screen.

Internet Explorer

To Connect to the Internet: Click the Start icon and select Internet Explorer from the menu, or click the Internet Explorer icon on the Quick Launch bar.

To Display a Specific Web Page: Type the Web address in the Address bar and press Enter, or press Ctrl + L, type the Web address, and click OK.

To Use a Hyperlink: Click the hyperlink with the pointer.

To Go Back to the Previous Page: Click the Back button on the toolbar. To Return to a Web Address you typed in the Address Bar: Click the Address bar list arrow and select the Web address.

To Refresh a Web Page: Click the **Refresh button** on the toolbar.

To Stop the Transfer of Information: Click the **Stop button** on the toolbar.

When using your Windows 10 system to create information, we accumulate many files that store on our hard disk over time. A critical part of how Windows 10 (and Windows in general) organizes this is using a File System that manages how files are stored and accessed on your computer. When we interact with the records that we create on our computers, such as documents, audio files, pictures, and videos, the part we see is the File Manager.

Formerly File Manager

In the case of Windows, it's File Explorer. Over the years, this essential part of the Windows experience has evolved from its roots as File Manager in early releases, then Windows Explorer, and now called File Explorer, first introduced in Windows 8.

Using File Explorer in Windows 10

To see into your computer's storage vault, click the File Explorer icon located on your Taskbar or click *Start > File Explorer.*

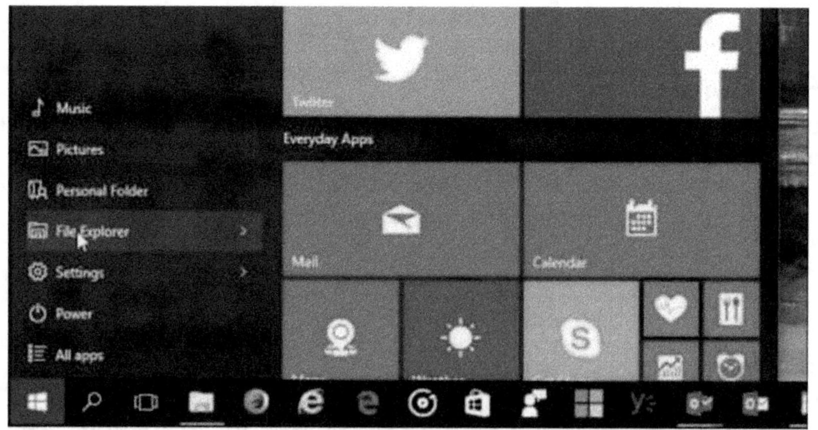

When you launch File Explorer in Windows 10, you get the Quick access window. Formally called Favorites in previous versions of Windows, here you will see your most frequently accessed folders and files you created.

You can use File Explorer for a variety of tasks. In addition to the management and organization of files and folders, it's also used to view and manage the resources of your computer, such as internal storage, attached storage, and optical drives.

What Everything Means on File Explorer

Quick Access Toolbar	Here you can pin your most frequently accessed commands. Quick Access also automatically pins your most frequently accessed folders.
Ribbon Toolbar	If you are familiar with Microsoft Office or apps such as Paint and WordPad, the Ribbon toolbar command is used to manage your files and often reveals hidden commands quickly. When you select a file or folder, this will display a contextual tab with additional options. You can copy, move, delete, rename, and do a host of other tasks using the Ribbon.
Navigation and Address Bar	You can use these to navigate smoothly through a folder's hierarchy or back and forward between folders. The Address bar also has a breadcrumb menu that makes it easy to navigate to a different folder path.
Quick Access	Here you can find your most frequently accessed folders, and the ones you have pinned show up here, which is a new feature in Windows 10.
OneDrive synced folders	If you have a Microsoft Account setup with your Windows 10 PC, you can have your files stored in the online storage service and have them synced to your computer.
This PC	In previous versions of Windows, this was called Computer Explorer. Here you can view and manage your internal storage and attached storage devices, including optical media.
Search	Use the search command to find files stored in the current folder.
Status bar	Displays information about the contents stored in the window, such as the number of files, size, file selection, and quick access to folder layout.

This PC

If you would rather see your computer environment now called *This PC,* click it in the left pane, or you can change it to the default from the Folder Options dialogue. To do so, select the View tab on the Ribbon and click *Options* under *Show/Hide* group.

Click in the *Open File Explorer* to list box, choose *This PC,* and then click *Apply* and OK.

If you don't like to see your most frequently accessed folders and recently accessed files, you can adjust those settings from the same dialog. Under Privacy, uncheck the following:

■ Show recently used files in Quick access

■ Show frequently used folders in Quick access

Or you can choose to erase all traces by clicking the Clear button.

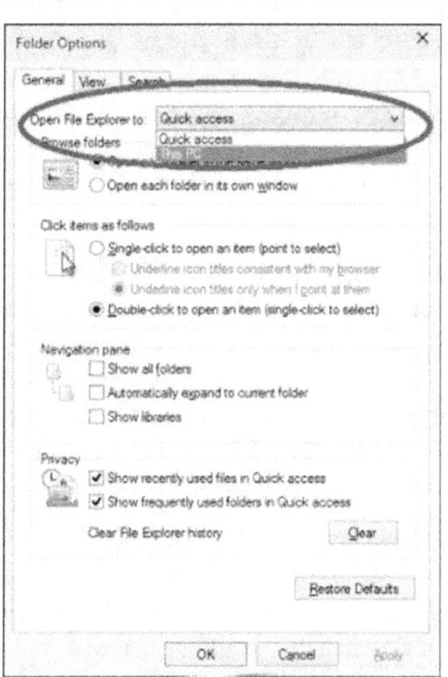

User Folder

In Windows 7 and earlier versions, you had a User folder directory used to store and organize your files in folders by content, such as Documents, Audio Files, Pictures, Videos, and other types of data. Some of these folders will still be available from **This PC**. Other folders that might be part of your User Folder created by third-party applications are accessible from within your user directory from the Bread Crumb menu.

Change how Files Display in Windows 10 File Explorer

You can change how your files look by using the View tab. When you activate this tab, you will see various groups for changing the window's layout, files, current view, or hide certain things you see onscreen. Within the Layout group, click one of the available options to change how your files display onscreen. You can also preview the layout before confirming by hovering over one of the available options.

Go Back to a Previous Folder

If you would like to navigate to a previous folder, you can do this a couple of ways efficiently using either the Recent Locations button or the Bread Crumb menu. When you click the Recent Locations menu, you can go back to a previously working directory quickly without going through multiple directories along the way.

The Bread Crumb menu introduced in Windows Vista provides similar capabilities; for instance, you can easily navigate to a folder with a folder path. So, if there are subfolders within a folder, you can quickly jump to any folder within that path.

Organizing Files and Folders

If you have many files on your Windows 10 system computer, you'll want to organize them. So if you need to see recent files created or older files, or you need to archive certain files elsewhere, you can easily do so. The View tab provides options for sorting how files are displayed.

Copy, Pasting a File or Folder

One of the most common operations for users is copying, which creates a replica of an original file. To copy a file, select the file you want to copy and click Copy under the Home tab.

You can just as easily copy or move a file without leaving your current location. Under the Home tab within the *Organize* group, click the 'Copy to' or 'Move to' button, choose the location if it's listed, or click the *Choose Location* button and select the location.

Customizing Windows 10 File Explorer

If there are folders you commonly access, you can have them pinned to the Quick Access pane. Right-click the folder you want to be pinned and select *Pin to Quick Access* or select the folder and then *Pin to Quick access* under the Home tab.

If you don't always want to see the Ribbon in Windows 10, you can minimize it by clicking the Minimize button or press **Ctrl + F1** on your keyboard.

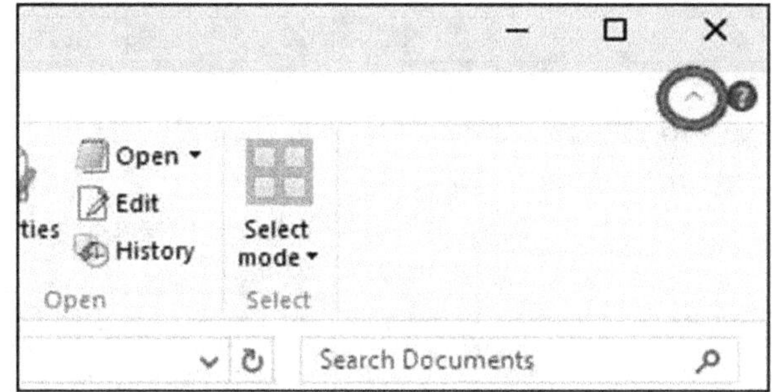

Algorithm and Flowchart

Algorithm is a sequence of activities to be processed for getting desired output from a given input. Once an algorithm is designed, a flow chart is used to show the step by step representation of it. A flowchart is a graphical representation of a process in which each step is represented by a symbol.

The flowchart always starts/ends with an oval shaped symbol. Whenever any decision is required to be taken based on some condition, then the diamond symbol is used. All operations representing processing, computations are written inside the rectangular shaped symbol. Some commonly used flowchart symbols are terminal symbol, input/output symbol, processing symbol, decision box and flow lines.

The oval shaped symbol is a terminal symbol which is used to represent the beginning and end of a program. A parallelogram symbol is used to represent input of data to a device or output of data from a device. A rectangle shaped is used as a processing symbol.

A processing symbol is used to represent processing of data. A diamond shape in a flowchart is a decision box which is used to represent conditional statements. The arrow symbol is used to show the direction of a flowchart and to connect various flowchart symbols.

Let us see some of the common flowchart symbols and their shape:

Shape	Symbol
	Flow Line
	Terminal
	Processing
	Decision
	Connector
	Document

Sample Flow Chart

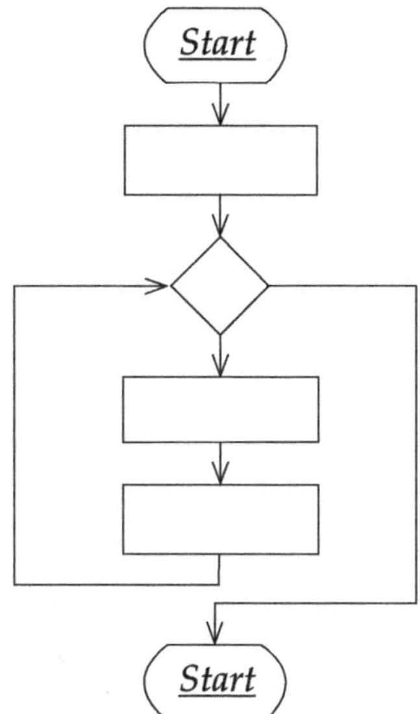

- ➡ A mouse acts as a hand-held pointing device and controls the actions of the pointer blinking on your computer screen known as a cursor.
- ➡ CPU calculates and processes informtion, and its speed is measured in Megahertz (MHz) and Gigahertz (GHz).

1. Which of the following is an example of mobile computers?
   (a) Laptop
   (b) Desktop computers
   (c) Cray-1
   (d) SDS 92

2. Which is the supercomputer developed in India?
   (a) Param
   (b) Anurag
   (c) Abacus
   (d) Both (a) and (b)

3. What is the given strips of black lines called?

   (a) Strip code
   (b) Bar code
   (c) Line code
   (d) Bill code

4. What device is used for reading cheques in India?
   (a) Scanner
   (b) OMR
   (c) Bar code reader
   (d) MICR

5. Find the correct statement(s).
   (i) Supercomputers are used for weather forecasting.
   (ii) Supercomputers are used for rocketing and plasma physics.
   (iii) Processing speed of microcomputer lies in the range of 10-30 MIPS.
   (iv) Mainframe computers are less powerful than the mini computers.
   (a) Only I & II are correct
   (b) I, II & III are correct
   (c) III & IV are correct
   (d) All are correct

6. Which device is used to scan the input and convert it into a computer file?
   (a) Key board
   (b) Mouse
   (c) Scanner
   (d) Microphone

7. Which is the device used for checking a multiple answer sheet?
   (a) OMR
   (b) OCR
   (c) MICR
   (d) Light pen

8. What is meant by double click?
   (a) Pressing the left button of the mouse.
   (b) Holding the left button and moving.
   (c) Pressing the right button of the mouse twice.
   (d) Quickly clicking left mouse button twice.

9. Web camera is a/an _______ device.
   (a) Input
   (b) Output
   (c) Memory
   (d) Both (a) and (b)

10. OCR stands for _______.
    (a) Optical Card Reader
    (b) Optical Calculator Reader
    (c) Optical Card Reader
    (d) Optical Character Recognition

11. Which card contains a magnetic strip and can store information magnetically?
    (a) Smart card
    (b) PAN card
    (c) Credit card
    (d) Grocery cards

12. Which is specially used for printing graphs, maps, and charts?
    (a) Printer
    (b) Plotter
    (c) Modem
    (d) Speaker

13. Which device is used for transferring files to other computers (of the network) without any damage?
    (a) Speaker
    (b) Mouse
    (c) Plotter
    (d) Modem

14. What is the result displayed on the monitor called?
    (a) Soft copy
    (b) Hard copy
    (c) Duplicate copy
    (d) Inkjet printer

15. Which printer gives output in Braille text?
    (a) Impact printer
    (b) Laser printer
    (c) Braille printer
    (d) Inkjet printer

16. Modem is a/an ____ device.
    (a) Input   (b) Output
    (c) Recording   (d) Both (a) and (b)
17. Microphone accepts ____ as input.
    (a) Sound   (b) Pictures
    (c) typed data   (d) video
18. Which kind of software performs the maintenance work of computer?
    (a) Packages   (b) Utility software
    (c) Computers   (d) Assembler
19. Which of these was an operating system?
    (a) MS DOS   (b) MS Paint
    (c) MS Office   (d) MS Front page
20. Which computer hardware do you require to type the input?
    (a) Mouse   (b) Keyboard
    (c) Monitor   (d) Printer
21. Which of these software will you install before you execute assembly language program?
    (a) Interpreter   (b) Compiler
    (c) Assembler   (d) Both (a) and (b)
22. The last statement of the source program should be ______
    (a) Stop   (b) Return
    (c) OP   (d) End
23. What is the program written by the user called?
    (a) Object code/program
    (b) Machine code
    (c) High language
    (d) Source code/program
24. Name the software that translates high level language to object code line by line.
    (a) Operating system
    (b) Compiler
    (c) Interpreter
    (d) Assembler
25. Which software translates the entire user written, high level language program to object code at once?
    (a) Operating system
    (b) Compiler
    (c) Interpreter
    (d) Assembler

26. Which kind of software includes programs to perform a particular task?
    (a) Application software
    (b) Operating system
    (c) Computer
    (d) Interpreter
27. BASIC, COBOL, LOGO, FORTRAN, etc. are some examples of ______.
    (a) Low Level Languages
    (b) High-level languages
    (c) Machine languages
    (d) Both (a) and (b)
28. Which one of the following is a low-level language?
    (a) Logo   (b) BASIC
    (c) Assembly language   (d) Pascal
29. What is the program written in high-level language called?
    (a) Object program
    (b) Source program
    (c) Assembly program
    (d) Machine language
30. Identify the false statement from the following.
    (a) Mobile computers are smaller than microcomputers.
    (b) Minicomputers are larger than micro-computers.
    (c) Supercomputers are bigger in size.
    (d) Mainframe computers are larger than supercomputers.
31. Desktop computers are generally referred to as ______.
    (a) microcomputers   (b) minicomputers
    (c) mobile computers   (d) mainframes
32. What is meant by physical components of a computer?
    (a) Software   (b) Memory
    (c) Hardware   (d) Both (a) and (c)
33. What set of instructions is used for developing software of a computer?
    (a) Computer language
    (b) Programming language
    (c) Both (a) and (b)
    (d) Command

34. Which of the following programs directs the operation of a computer system?
    (a) Hardware   (b) Instruction
    (c) Software   (d) Command

35. Which symbols are used for storing information in the memory of a computer?
    (a) Alpha-numeric character
    (b) Special digits
    (c) Binary digits
    (d) Real numbers

36. MICR stands for
    (a) Magnetic Ink Character Reader
    (b) Mark information code Reader
    (b) Magnetic information character Reader
    (d) Marker Ink cheque Reader

37. Which of the following devices cannot be shared in network?
    (a) CD-Drive   (b) Printer
    (c) Hard disk   (d) Mouse

38. Which memory has the shortest access time?
    (a) Virtual memory
    (b) Cache memory
    (c) External memory
    (d) Secondary memory

39. CAD stands for
    (a) Computer Aided Design
    (b) Computer Address Data
    (c) Computer Access Duration
    (d) Computer Application Digits

HOTS

1. Given below is an image of an area marked by A that allows you to jump to parent folders or subfolder in the path of the current folder. What is the name of this Window?

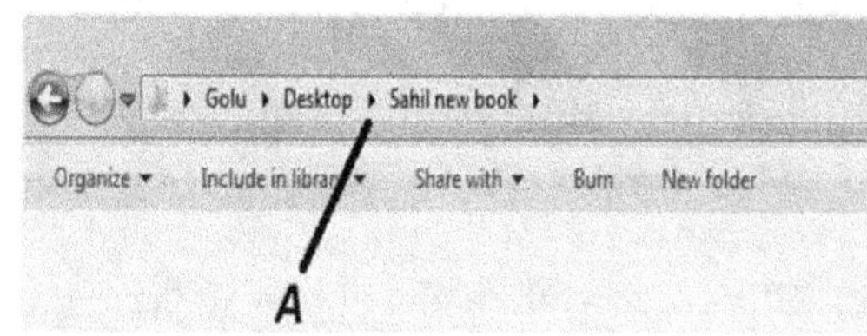

    (a) Breadcrumb
    (b) Jump trail
    (c) Navigation trail
    (d) Bread jump trail

2. Which of the following is not a difference between blu-ray disc and DVD?
    (a) The production cost of DVD is more than that of Blu-ray disc.
    (b) Read only memory type is not available in blu-ray whereas DVD supports read only memory.
    (c) Blu-ray disc uses violet-blue laser, where as DVD uses red laser.
    (d) A single layer blu-ray disc can store up to 25 GB data whereas a single layer DVD can store only 4, 7 GB of data.

3. What is the correct formula to calculate the transfer rate of a disk?
    (a) Data transfer in one revolution × rotational speed of disk.
    (b) No. of sectors per track × No. of bytes per track.
    (c) No. of sectors per track × rotational speed of disk.
    (d) No. of bytes per track × rotational speed of disk.

4. Which type of plotters uses jets of ink instead of ink pens?
    (a) A flatbed plotter
    (b) An inkjet plotter
    (c) A micro graphic plotter
    (d) A drum plotter

5. Arrange the following in ascending order of ease of access:
    1. Primary memory
    2. Secondary memory
    3. Cache memory
    (a) 3,2,1   (b) 2,1,3
    (c) 1,2,3   (d) 3,1,2

1. What are the main parts of a personal computer?

Ans.

Central Processing Unit (CPU): The computer's brain, the CPU is a computer's main chip. It calculates and processes information, and its speed is measured in Megahertz (MHz) and Gigahertz (GHz).

Hard Disk: The computer's main, long-term storage device is the hard disk.

Input devices: like keyboard and mouse and **output devices:** like the monitor are the main parts of a computer.

2. What are Monitors?

Ans.

Monitors are output devices that looks and works a lot like a TV screen. The monitor displays what we input as instructions by typing on the keyboard or clicking the mouse.

3. What are different components of Computer Performance?

Ans.

CPU Speed: Arguably the single most important factor that determines a computer's performance is the speed of its CPU.

RAM: Generally, the more RAM a computer has the better is its performance.

Multitasking: Microsoft Windows can run more than one program at a time. The more programs or tasks being done at a time, the longer it takes to complete each one, and hence a drop in computer performance.

4. What are different types of Language Processors?

Ans.

Language processors are divided into three types.

i. Assembler: An assembler converts a program written in an assembly language into its equivalent machine language.

ii. Compiler: A compiler converts a program or a source code written in a high-level language into the machine language before execution. It runs through the entire high-level language program in one go and reports all the errors it finds in the source code along with the line numbers. After all the errors are removed, the compiler gives the machine-level equivalent code called the object program or the object code. The saved object program can be executed a number of times without translating it again.

iii. Interpreter: An interpreter is a language processor that works by reading and executing the source code of a high-level language program line by line. If there is an error in any line, it reports it at the same time and program execution cannot resume until the error is rectified. The object code produced by the interpreter cannot be saved. So, every time the program is run, it needs to be interpreted again to obtain the object code.

5. Write short note on Open-source software.

Ans.

The Open-Source Initiative (OSI) is an organisation dedicated to promote open-source software.

Open-source software is distributed under a licensing arrangement. It allows the source code to be accessible to the users and organisations so that they may study and change it to achieve new levels of quality, growth and innovation. Open-source software may or may not be available free of cost.

On the other hand, proprietary software is a computer software on which there are restrictions on use, modification, copying or redistribution. These restrictions can be imposed by preventing access to the source code or by legal means such as through copyright and patents.

These days, a growing number of people and organisations have started using open-source software. The basic idea behind open-source software is to promote improvement in the quality of the software. When an underlying source code is available, people can improve and adapt it according to their needs and also help in fixing the errors. Developers believe that this collaborative work produces better software than the case in which only a very few programmers have the right to modify the source code.

Some examples of popular open-source software are:

i. Ubuntu (Operating System)

ii. Android (Operating System for smartphones and tablet computers)

iii. OpenOffice [Office Suite that includes a word processor (Writer), a spreadsheet (Calc), a presentation application (Impress), a drawing application (Draw), a formula editor (Math) and a database management application (Base)]

iv. Mozilla Firefox (Web browser)

v. Audacity (Sound editor)

vi. GIMP (Image editing software)

vii. VLC (Media player)

Evolution of Computers

2

Learning Objectives : In this chapter, students will learn about:
- ✓ History of Computers
- ✓ Different generations of computer

CHAPTER SUMMARY

Let us take a look at the journey of a computer from a mechanical abacus to present day ultra fast computers.

The First Computer

Around 3000 B.C. the Mesopotamians invented the earliest form of Bead & Wire counting machine known as Abacus. The Chinese improved the Abacus so that they could calculate fast. It is also called a Counting Frame.

Napier 'Logs' & 'Bones'

John Napier (1550–1617) developed the idea of Logarithms. He used logs to transform multiplication problem to addition problem. It is a manually operated calculating device.

The **Napier's Rods** consist of strips of wood or metal. **Napier's Bones** are three-dimensional, square in cross section, with four different **rods** engraved. A set of such **bones** can be enclosed in a carrying case.

Pascal's adding Machine

Blaise Pascal, a French Mathematician, invented a Machine in 1662 made up of gears which was used for adding numbers quickly. This machine was known as Adding Machine (also known as Pascaline) and was capable of addition and subtraction. It was a class of mechanical calculator used for bookkeeping.

Leibnitz Calculator

Gottfried Leibnitz a German Mathematician, improved the adding Machine and constructed a new machine in 1671 that was able to perform multiplication and division as well. This machine performed multiplication through repeated addition of numbers. Leibnitz's machine used stepped cylinder each with nine teeth of varying lengths instead of wheels as was used by Pascal. That is why it was also called the step reckoner.

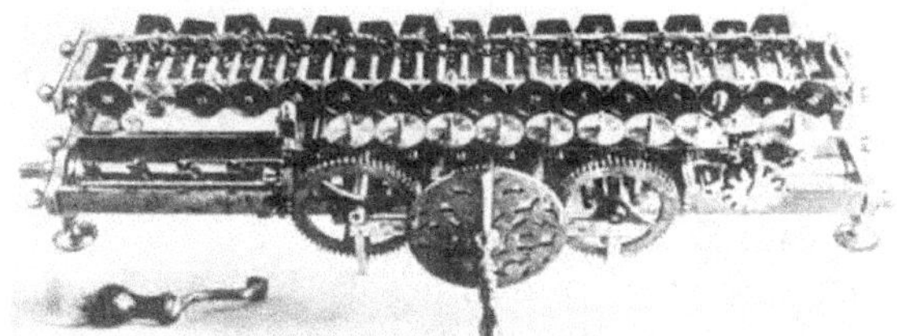

Jacquard's Loom

Joseph Jacquard manufactured punched cards at the end of American Revolution and used them to control looms in 1801. It was a mechanical loom that he invented. Thus the entire control weaving process was automatic. The entire operation was under a program's control.

Babbage's Difference Engine

Charles Babbage, a professor of mathematics, developed a machine called Difference engine in the year 1882. It was an automatic mechanical calculator designed to tabulate polynomial functions. This machine was expected to calculate logarithmic tables to high degree of precision. The difference engine was made to calculate various mathematical functions. The machine was capable of polynomial evolution by finite difference.

Babbage's Analytical Engine

In 1833, Charles Babbage started designing an analytical engine which was to become a real ancestor of modern day computer. The Analytical Engine was capable of performing all four arithmetic operation as well as comparison; it had a number of features starting from those which are in today's computer. He included the concept of central processor, memory, storage area and Input/output devices in his design. Owing to the lack of technology of the time, the Analytical engine was never built. Its design remained conceptual. His great inventions of Difference Engine and Analytical Engine earned Charles Babbage the title "Father of Modern Computers"-a fitting tribute to him.

Hollerith's Machine

In 1887, an American named Herman Hollerith (1869-1926) invented what was dreamt by Charles Babbage. He invented the first electro-mechanical Punched-card tabulator that used punched-cards for input, output and instructions. This machine was used by American department of census to compile their 1880 census data and were able to complete compilation in 3 years which earlier took roughly 10 years.

The first mouse was built in 1964 and was made of wood.

MARK-I

Professor Howard Aiken (1900-1973) in U.S constructed in 1943 an electromechanical computer named "MARK-I" which could multiply two 10 digit numbers in 5 second-a record at that time. MARK-I was the first machine which could perform according to pre-programed instructions automatically without any manual interface. This was the first operational general purpose computer.

Modern Computers

The First Generation Computers

The first generation computers used the thermionic valves (vacuum tubes) and machine language was used for giving instructions. The first generation computers used the concept of "Stored program". The computers of this generations were very large in size and their programming was a difficult task. Here are some examples:

ENIAC

This was the first electronic computer developed in 1946 by a tcam lead by Professor Eckert and Mauchly at the University of Pennsylvania in U.S.A. This computer was called Electronic Numerical Integrator And Calculator (ENIAC), which used high speed vacuum tube switching devices. It had a very small memory and it was used for calculating the trajectories of missiles. It took 200 microseconds for addition and about 2800 microseconds for multiplication.

EDVAC

The binary arithmetic was used in the construction of computer called the Electronic Discrete Variable Automatic Computer (EDVAC). Its development completed in 1950. With this, the operation become faster since the computer could rapidly access both the program and data.

EDSAC

The EDSAC, short for Electronic Delay Storage Automatic Computer was built by Professor M.V.Wilkes at Cambridge University in 1949 and used mercury delayed lines for storage. This allowed easy implementation of program loops.

UNIVAC-I

Commercial production of stored program electronic computer began in the early 1950's. One such computer was UNIVAC-I built by UNIVAC division of Remington Rand and delivered in 1951. This computer also used vacuum tubes. UNIVAC stands for Universal Automatic Computers.

Initial application of computers those days were in science and engineering but with the advent of UNIVAC-I, the prospects of commercial applications were perceived.

Though the first generation computers were welcomed by the government and universities as they greatly helped them in these tasks, however, the first generation computers suffered from great limitations like slow speed, restricted computing capacity, high power consumption, short mean time between failures, large size and limited programming capabilities.

The Second Generation Computers

The revolution in electronics too place with the invention of "Transistors" by Bardeen, Brattain and Shockley in 1946. Transistors were highly reliable as compared to Tubes. They occupied very less space and required only 1/10th of the power required by the tubes and they were 10 times cheaper than Tubes.

The increased reliability and availability of large memories paved the way for the development of HLLs (High Level Languages) such as FORTRAN, COBOL, ALGOL, SNOBOL, etc. With high speed CPUs and advent of magnetic tape and disk storage, operating systems came into use. Batch operating system rules the Second Generation Computers.

Here are some second generation computers:

IBM 1401

IBM 7094

It is a medium sized computer

RCA 501

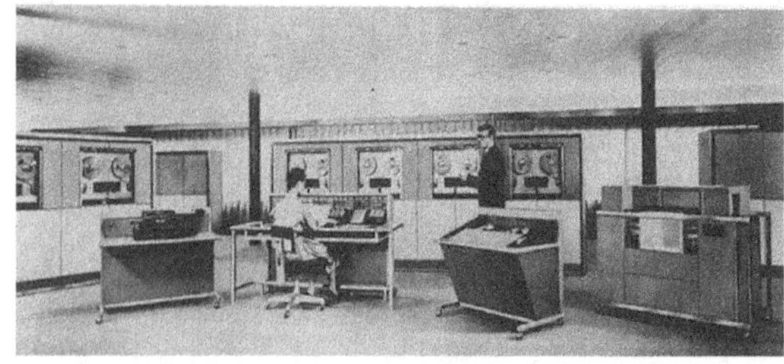

It is a medium sized computer, you can see magnetic tapes were used to store data.

UNIVAC 1108

It is a large-sized computer which occupies a large room, it was the fastest at that time, it uses a CRT screen for display and magnetic tape to store programs.

The 3rd Generation Computers

The third generation computers replaces transistors with integrated circuits popularly known as "Chips". The Integrated Circuit or IC was invented by *Jack Kilby* at Texas instruments in 1958.

An IC is a wafer of thin slice of extremely purified silicon crystals. A single IC has many transistors, resistors and capacitors along with the associated circuitry encapsulated in a small capsule with many leads.

The third generation computers using integrated circuits proved to be highly reliable, relatively inexpensive and faster. Less human labour was required at assembly stage. Examples of some mainframe computers developed during this generation are:- IBM 360 series, IBM 370/168, ICL 1900 series, ICL 2900, Honeywell Model 316, Honeywell 6000 series.

IBM 360

A Honeywell 6000 Series Computer

Some minicomputers during this phase are ICL-2903 manufactured by International Computers Limited. CDC 1700 manufactured by Control Data Corporationsand PDP-11/45 (Personal data processor 11/45).

Computers these days found place in other areas also like education, survey, small business, estimation, analysis etc.

The Fourth Generation Computers

The advent of microprocessor chip marked the beginning of fourth generation computers. Medium Scale Integrated circuits (MSI) yielded to large and Very Large Scale Integrated circuits (VLSI) packing about 50000 transistors in a chip. Semiconductor memories replaced magnetic core memories. The emergence of the microprocessor (CPU on a single chip) led to the emergence of an extremely powerful Personal Computer. Computer costs came down so rapidly that these found places at most offices and then homes. The faster accessing and processing speed and increased memory capacity helped in the development of much more powerful operating systems.

The second decade (around 1985) of fourth generation observed a great increase in the speed of microprocessor and size of main memory. The speed of microprocessor and speed of main memory and hard disk went up by a factor 4 every 3 years.

In 1995, the most popular CPU was Pentium, Power PC etc. Also RISC (Reduced Instruction Set Computer) microprocessor are preferred in powerful servers for numeric computing and file services. The hard disks were also available of the sizes up to 80 Gigabytes.

In this generation microcomputers of Apple and IBM developed, Portable computers came into existence.

World's First Portable Computer by IBM (The IBM 5100 – September 1975)

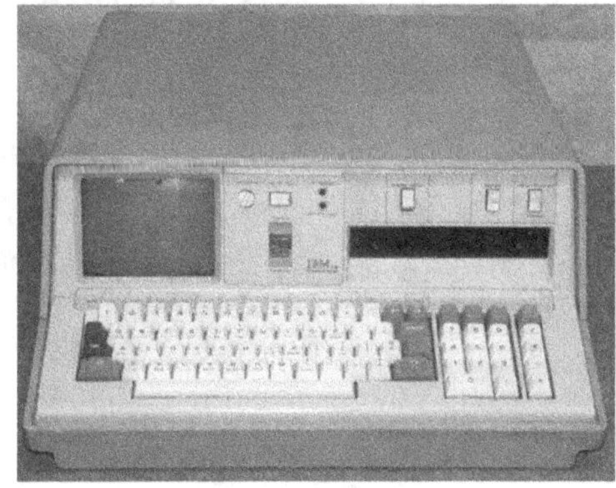

Toshiba T 1100

The Fifth Generation Computers

The fifth generation computing devices are based on Artificial Intelligence and are still in development, though there are features like voice recognition, face recognition, fingerprint recognition, gesture recognition etc. that are being used today. Applications like 6th sense technology are still in development.

The use of parallel processing and superconductor is helping to make artificial intelligence a reality. The goal of fifth generation computing is to develop devices that respond to natural language input and are capable of learning and self-organization.

The key developments of fifth generation computers are summed up as ULSI (Ultra Large Scale Integrations), scalable parallel computers, workstation clusters, Intranet, Internet, WWW, micro-kernels, portable software and hardware platforms, etc.

Computers will have to be able to classify information and search large database rapidly. Input devices become highly advanced.

Every gadget you see today is a 5th generation computer i.e, Your laptops, mobile phones, tablets, videogame consoles, smart watches, digital cameras and even some High-Tech pens. The fifth generation computers have huge memories which ranges in terabytes and even more. Secondary storage devices are becoming denser, earlier a compact disk (CD) was able to store about 100-200 MBs, now DVDs (Digital Versatile Disks) and Blu-Ray Disks of same size Stores data about 4 GB to 17 GB and some can store even 50 GB to 100 GB.

DELL XPS Convertible PC

MacBook Air

Video Game Consoles

- The Analytical Engine was capable of performing all four arithmetic operation as well as comparison; it had a number of features starting from those which are in today's computer.
- His great inventions of Difference Engine and Analytical Engine earned Charles Babbage the title "Father of Modern Computers"-a fitting tribute to him.
- MARK-I was the first machine which could perform according to pre-programed instructions automatically without any manual interface.
- An IC is a wafer of thin slice of extremely purified silicon crystals.

1. 4th and 5th generation of computers are powered by ______ chip.
   - (a) Mercury
   - (b) Silicon
   - (c) Thermal
   - (d) Wafer

2. First generation computers were
   - (a) Efficiently marketed to spread them for use in various businesses
   - (b) Computers used for mainly scientific calculations
   - (c) Having speeds in microseconds (millionth/sec)
   - (d) Running on sophisticated software

3. Which of following is not a feature of second generation computers?
   - (a) Transistors were used
   - (b) Core memory was developed
   - (c) Programming in mechanical language
   - (d) Easier to program than first generation computer

4. Data and information is temporarily stored in ________.
   - (a) Central processing unit
   - (b) Motherboard
   - (c) Data bus
   - (d) RAM

5. Which of these is not a major data processing function of a computer?
   - (a) Gathering data
   - (b) Processing data into information
   - (c) Analyzing data or information
   - (d) Storing the data or information

6. ________ operating system helped to put Microsoft on the computing map of world.
   - (a) Unix
   - (b) Basic
   - (c) DOS
   - (d) Fortan

7. ________ is the first name of two co-founder of Apple.Inc.
   - (a) Bill
   - (b) Steve
   - (c) Paul
   - (d) Heraldo

8. This computer language is made up of 0's and 1's and it is the basic computer code.
   - (a) Fortan
   - (b) Pascal
   - (c) Basic
   - (d) Binary

9. When representing letters, numbers and special characters in a binary language, we use combination of ________.
   - (a) Eight bytes
   - (b) Eight characters
   - (c) Eight nibbles
   - (d) Eight bits

10. The technologies used in commonly used PCs and the Apple Macintosh are based on different ________.
    - (a) Platforms
    - (b) Applications
    - (c) Frames
    - (d) Storage devices

11. Small, efficient, and economical PC-based servers have replaced ________ in several businesses.
    - (a) Micro computers
    - (b) Clients
    - (c) Laptops
    - (d) Mainframe

12. A marvel of technology, the ________ are the computers that perform complex scientific calculations.
    - (a) Servers
    - (b) Supercomputers
    - (c) Laptops
    - (d) PDA

13. Which of following is not a first generation computer?
    - (a) ENIAC
    - (b) UNIVAC-1
    - (c) EDVAC
    - (d) CDC

14. It was launched in 1950s. It was known to be the first commercially produced computer.
    - (a) Zues Z3
    - (b) UNIVAC-1
    - (c) ENIAC
    - (d) Harvard Mark I

15. It was used at the U.S Census Bureau in 1950. It was the first stored program computer in US that was successfully installed at a distant site after being moved from its site of manufacture.
    - (a) UNIVAC-1101
    - (b) Sinclair VX80
    - (c) EDVAC
    - (d) PDP 11

16. UNIVAC was used in 1952 to predict the outcome of a US presidential election. The election was contested between ______.
    - (a) Franklin D. versus Thomas H.
    - (b) Dwight D Eisenhower versus Adlai Stevenson
    - (c) Harry Truman versus Thomas H.
    - (d) All of these

17. Which of the following computer game was created by Steve Rusesll, Martin Graetz and Wayne Wiitanen?

(a) Galaga
(b) SpaceWar
(c) Pong
(d) Paperboy

18. The BASIC programming language was developed in 1964 by two professors of this college of _______.

(a) Stanford
(b) California
(c) Dartmouth
(d) Oxford

19. First ARPANET email is known to be sent in _______.

(a) 1965
(b) 1971
(c) 1982
(d) 1991

20. It is science. It tries to produce machines like computers and robots. They display intelligence similar to human beings. This is __________.

(a) Biotechnology
(b) Cross-over technology
(c) Simulation
(d) Artificial Intelligence

HOTS

1. _______ is a kind of mass storage device. It is used for archiving read-only data that needs on-line access, but where access time is not very critical.

(a) Disk Array
(b) Automated Tape Library
(c) CD-ROM Jukebox
(d) None of these

2. Select the incorrect match.

(a) Word's fastest super computer-Tianhe-2 (TH-2)
(b) Example of Hard disk-Floppy disk
(c) None-book-MacBook
(d) Search Engine-Lycos

3. _________ a 16-bit minicomputer, was the first polish minicomputer, created at Elwro by a team led by scientist Jacek Karpinski.

(a) MTTS 8800
(b) K-202
(c) PDP-8
(d) PDP-11

4. Match the following.

(i)	Memory Address Register	(a)	Holds address of next instruction to be executed.
(ii)	Memory Buffer Register	(b)	Holds address of active memory location.
(iii)	Program Control	(c)	Holds an instruction while it is being executed.
(iv)	Instruction	(d)	Holds information on its way to end from memory.

(a) (i)-(a), (ii)-(b), (iii)-(c), (iv)-(d)
(b) (i)-(a), (ii)-(c), (iii)-(d), (iv)-(b)
(c) (i)-(b), (ii)-(d), (iii)-(a), (iv)-(c)
(d) (i)-(b), (ii)-(d), (iii)-(c), (iv)-(a)

5. Identify it.

A. It is flash memory card.
B. It is developed by Toshiba.
C. It has contact pins that connect directly on the surface of the card.

(a) Compact flash
(b) SmartMedia Card
(c) Secure Digital Card
(d) Memory Stick

1. What is an adding machine?

Ans.

Blaise Pascal, a French Mathematician, invented a Machine in 1662 made up of gears which was used for adding numbers quickly. This machine was known as Adding Machine (also known as Pascaline) and was capable of addition and subtraction.

2. Write short note on the First Generation computers.

Ans.

The First Generation computers used the thermionic valves (vacuum tubes) and machine language was used for giving instructions. They used the concept of "Stored Program" The computers of this generations were very large in size and their programming was a difficult task.

3. What are the characteristics or technological developments on which the generations can be defined.

Ans.

The characteristics or technological developments which takes place in the computers and leads to the change in the computer generations are:-

- Size of the computers are reduced.
- Computers are cheaper.
- Computers are more powerful and has the ability to work efficiently.
- Computers are also the combination of hardware and software.

4. Write a short note on history of computers. Explain why Charles Babbage is known as the father of the modern-day computers?

Ans.

In the earlier ancient days, the device named as Abacus (A frame where 10 beads were attached to a wired strung) which was used for the calculation work. In the year 1642, a computer developed by Blaise Pascal could perform the limited calculation work. Leibniz also developed a computer, which could perform mathematical operations such as Addition, Subtraction Multiplications, division, and calculating the square roots. In such type of computers the instructions inserted could not be altered once entered. In the year 1822, Charles Babbage designed a unique machine which could perform calculations without human interruptions. Charles Babbage also designed machine as analytic engine. The analytical engine had a separate arithmetic department which could perform arithmetic operations and mechanism used to store the results and instructions. Such technology of the analytic engine provided the base to the modern computers and hence Charles Babbage was regarded as the Father of modern computers.

5. What is the full form of ENIAC. Who developed it?

Ans.

- It was the first electronic general-purpose computer where ENIAC stands for Electronic Numerical Integrator and Computer.
- This was developed by John Presper Eckert and John W. Mauchl in the year 1946.

MS Word

3

Learning Objectives : In this chapter, students will learn about:
- ✓ Basics of MS Word
- ✓ Working in MS Word
- ✓ Mail Merge

CHAPTER SUMMARY

First screen of ms-word display all the features provided by the application. When You will open Ms-word 2013 a window will display like below contains number of components.

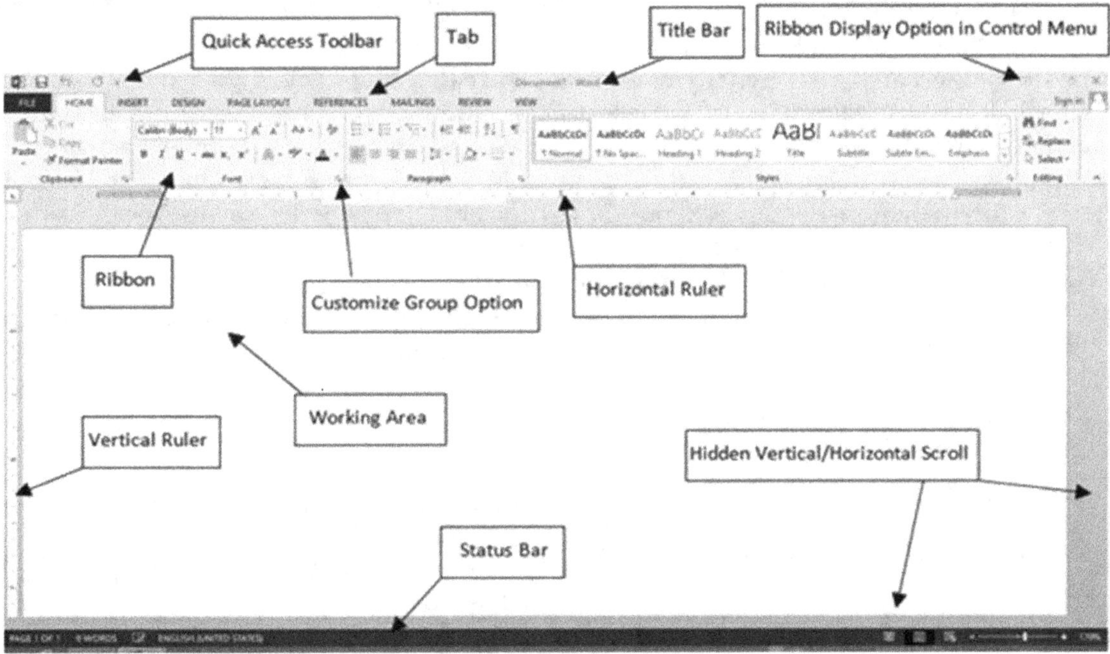

The File tab menu and backstage view contain commands for working with a program's files, such as Open, Save, Close, New, and Print.

To Create a New Document: Click the **File** tab, click the **New** tab, and click the **Create** button. Or, press **Ctrl + N**.

To Open a Document: Click the **File** tab and click the **Open** button, or press **Ctrl + O**.

To Save a Document: Click the **Save** button on the Quick Access Toolbar, or press **Ctrl + S**.

To Save a Document with a Different Name: Click the **File** tab, click the **Save As** button, and enter a new name for the document.

To Preview a Document: Click the **File** tab and click the **Print** tab, or press **Ctrl + P**.

To Print a Document: Click the **File** tab and click the **Print** tab, or press **Ctrl + P**. Click the print button.

To View Advanced Printing Options: Click the **File** tab and click the **Print** tab. Select from the options under Settings.

To Undo: Click the ↩ **Undo** button on the Quick Access Toolbar, or press **Ctrl + Z**.

To Move Text with the Mouse: Select the text you want to move, drag the text to a new location, and release the mouse button.

To Replace Text: Click the **Replace** button in the Editing group on the Home tab. Or, press **Ctrl + H**.

To Close a Document: Click the ✕ **Close** button, or press **Ctrl + W**.

To Correct a Spelling Error: Right-click the error and select a correction from the contextual menu. Or, press **F7** to run the Spell Checker.

To Use the Thesaurus: Right-click the word you want to look up and select **Synonyms** from the contextual menu. Select a word or select **Thesaurus** to search the Thesaurus.

To Minimize the Ribbon: Click the ⌃ **Minimize Ribbon** button on the Ribbon. Or, press **Ctrl + F1**. Or, double-click a tab. Or, right-click a tab and select **Minimize the Ribbon** from the contextual menu.

To Change Program Settings: Click the **File** tab and click the **Word Options** button.

To Get Help: Press **F1** to open the Help window. Type your question and press **Enter**.

Navigation Editing

To Open the Navigation Pane: Click the **Find** button in the Editing group on the Home tab. Or, press **Ctrl + F**.

To Search for a Word or Phrase: Click the **Search** box, type the word or phrase, and press **Enter**.

To Search for Graphics, Tables, Equations, or Comments: Click the 🔎 **Magnifying Glass** and select an option from the list. Click the **Search** box, enter the information you are searching for, and press **Enter**.

To View Search Results: Click the 🗐 **Browse the results from your current search** tab of the Navigation Pane.

To View a Document's Headings: Click the 🗐 **Browse the headings in your document** tab.

To View a Document's Pages: Click the 🗗 **Browse the pages in your document** tab.

Styles

To Apply a Style: Select the text to which you want to apply the style and select the style you want to use from the Styles Gallery in the Styles group on the Home tab.

To Apply a Document Theme: Click the **Themes** button in the Themes group on the Page Layout tab of the Ribbon and select a theme.

To View All available Styles: Click the **Dialog Box Launcher** in the Styles group on the Home tab.

To Change a Style Set: Click the **Change Styles** button in the Styles group on the Home tab and select **Style Set** from the menu. Select the Style Set you wish to use.

To Create a Style: Select the text that contains the formatting of the new style, right-click the text, and select **Styles** from the contextual menu. Select **Save Selection as a New Quick Style** from the contextual menu, enter a name for the style, and click **OK**.

To Check Your Styles: Select the text you wish to check. Click the **Dialog Box Launcher** in the Styles group on the Home tab of the Ribbon. Click the 🔍 **Style Inspector** button in the Styles task pane.

Formatting

To Format Text: Use the commands in the Font group on the Home tab, or click the **Dialog Box Launcher** in the Font group to open the Font dialog box.

To Copy Formatting with the Format Painter: Select the text with the formatting you want to copy and click the 🖌 **Format Painter** button in the Clipboard group on the Home tab. Then, select the text you want to apply the copied formatting to.

To Indent a Paragraph: Click the ⇥ **Increase Indent** button in the Paragraph group on the Home tab.

To Decrease an Indent: Click the ⅷ **Decrease Indent** button in the Paragraph group on the Home tab.

To Create a Bulleted or Numbered List: Select the paragraphs you want to bullet or number and click the ⅷ **Bullets** or ⅷ **Numbering** button in the Paragraph group on the Home tab.

To Change Page Orientation: Click the **Page Layout** tab on the Ribbon, click the **Orientation** button in the Page Setup group, and select an option from the list.

To Insert a Header or Footer: Click the **Insert** tab on the Ribbon and click the **Header** or **Footer** button in the Header & Footer group.

To Insert a Manual Page Break: Click the **Insert** tab on the Ribbon and click the **Page Break** button in the Pages group.

Editing

To Cut or Copy Text: Select the text you want to cut or copy and click the ✂ **Cut** or ▤ **Copy** button in the Clipboard group on the Home tab.

To Paste Text: Place the insertion point where you want to paste and click the **Paste** button in the Clipboard group on the Home tab.

To Preview an Item Before Pasting: Place the insertion point where you want to paste, click the **Paste** button list arrow in the Clipboard group on the Home tab, and select a preview option to view the item.

To Insert a Comment: Select the text where you want to insert a comment and click the **Review** tab on the Ribbon. Click the **New Comment** button in the Comments group. Type a comment, then click outside the comment text box.

To Delete a Comment: Select the comment, click the **Review** tab on the Ribbon, and click the **Delete Comment** button in the Comments group.

Drawing and Graphics

To Insert a Clip Art Graphic: Click the **Insert** tab on the Ribbon and click the **Clip Art** button in the Illustrations group. Type the name of what you are looking for in the "Search for" box and press **Enter**.

To Insert a Picture: Click the **Insert** tab on the Ribbon and click the **Picture** button in the Illustrations group. Find and select the picture you want to insert and click **Insert**.

To Insert a Screenshot: Click the **Insert** tab on the Ribbon and click the **Screenshot** button in the Illustrations group. Select an available window from the list, or select the **Screen Clipping** option to take a screen clip.

To Draw a Shape: Click the **Insert** tab on the Ribbon, click the **Shapes** button in the Shapes group, and select the shape you want to insert. Then, click where you want to draw the shape and drag until the shape reaches the desired size. Hold down the **Shift** key while you drag to draw a perfectly proportioned shape or straight line.

To Insert WordArt: Click the **Insert** tab on the Ribbon, click the **WordArt** button in the Text group, and select a design from the WordArt Gallery. Click the text box and enter your text. If necessary, click the text box and drag it to the desired position.

To Insert SmartArt: Click the **Insert** tab on the Ribbon, click the **SmartArt** button in the Illustrations group, select a layout, and click **OK**.

To Adjust Text Wrapping: Double-click the object, click the **Wrap Text** button in the Arrange group on the Format tab, and select an option from the list.

To Resize an Object: Click the object to select it, click and drag one of its sizing handles (○), and release the mouse button when the object reaches the desired size. Hold down the **Shift** key while dragging to maintain the object's proportions while resizing it.

To Format an Object: Double-click the object and use the commands located on the Format tab.

To Delete an Object: Select the object and press the **Delete** key.

Tables

To Insert a Table: Click the **Insert** tab on the Ribbon, click the **Table** button in the Tables group, and select **Insert Table** from the menu.

To Insert a Column or Row: Click the **Layout** tab under Table Tools on the Ribbon and use the commands located in the Rows & Columns group.

To Delete a Column or Row: Select the column or row you want to delete, click the **Layout** tab under Table Tools on the Ribbon, click the **Delete** button in the Rows & Columns group, and select an appropriate option from the menu.

To Adjust Column Width or Row Height: Select the column or row you want to adjust, click the **Layout** tab under Table Tools on the Ribbon, and use the commands located in the Cell Size group.

Hyperlinks in Word

If you want to include a **Web address** or **Email address** in your Word document, you can use **hyperlink** which once clicked will take the user to desired location.

Hyperlinks contain **two basic parts**: the **address** of the webpage, email address, or other location it is linking to; and the **display text (or image)**. For example, the address could be https://www.navneetmehra.com, and the display text could be **Navneet Mehra**.

To insert a hyperlink:

1. Select the text or image you want to make a hyperlink.
2. Right-click the selected text or image, then click **Hyperlink**.

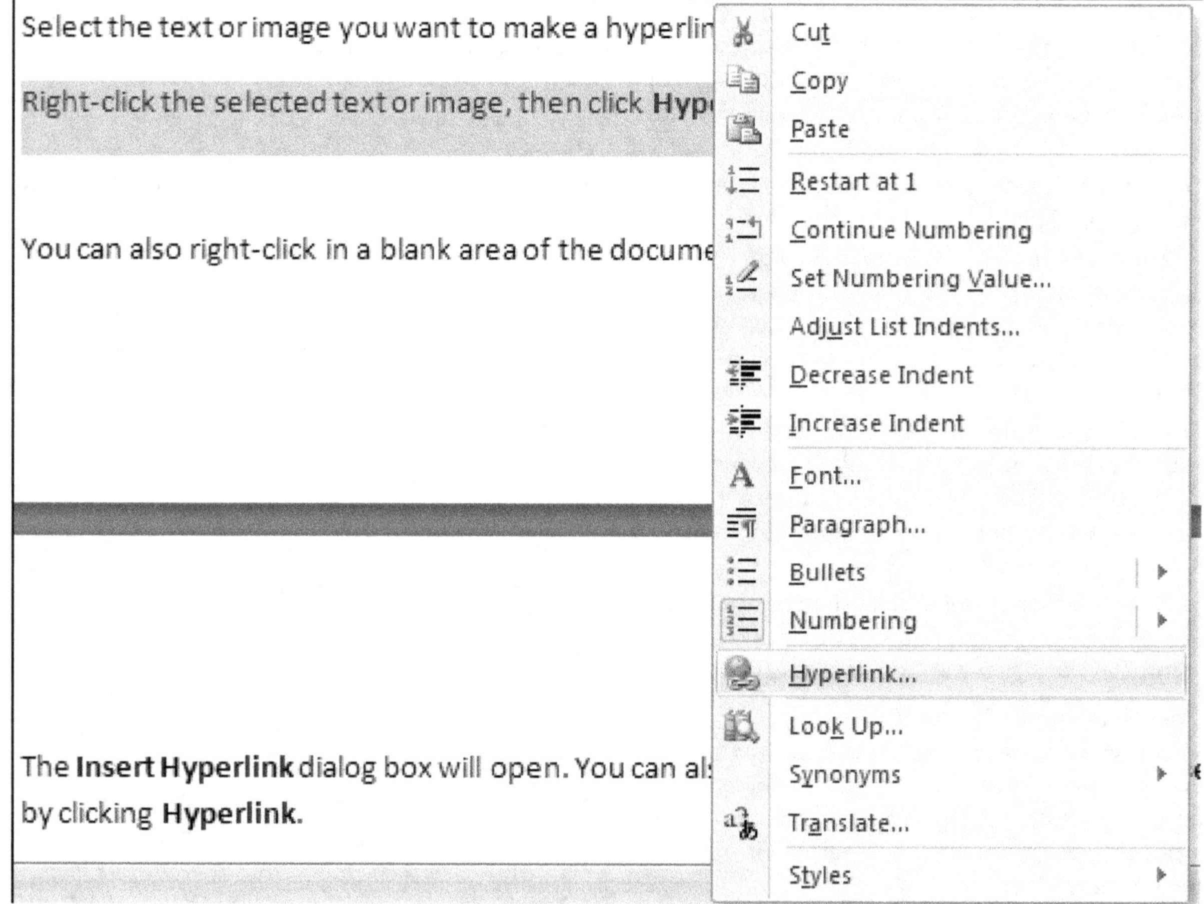

You can also right-click in a blank area of the document and click **Hyperlink**.

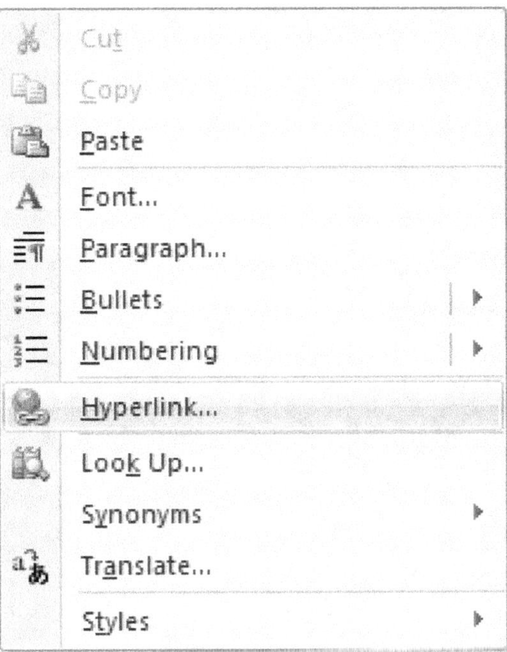

3. The **Insert Hyperlink** dialog box will open. This can also be opened from the **Insert tab** by clicking **Hyperlink**.

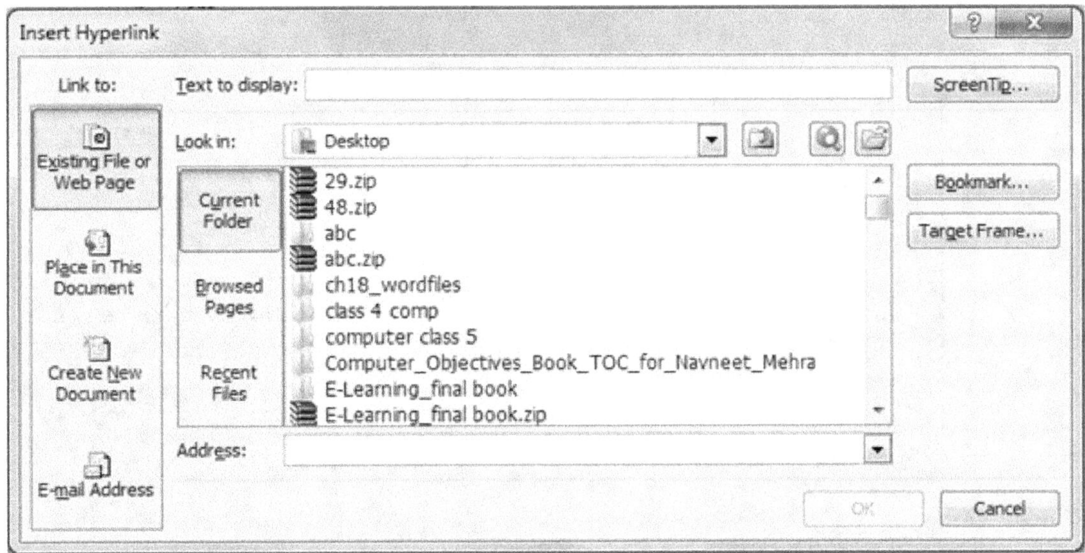

4. If you selected text, the words will appear in the **Text to display**: field at the top. You can change this text if you want.

5. Type the address you want to link to in the **Address**: field.

6. Click **OK**. The text or image you selected will now be a hyperlink.

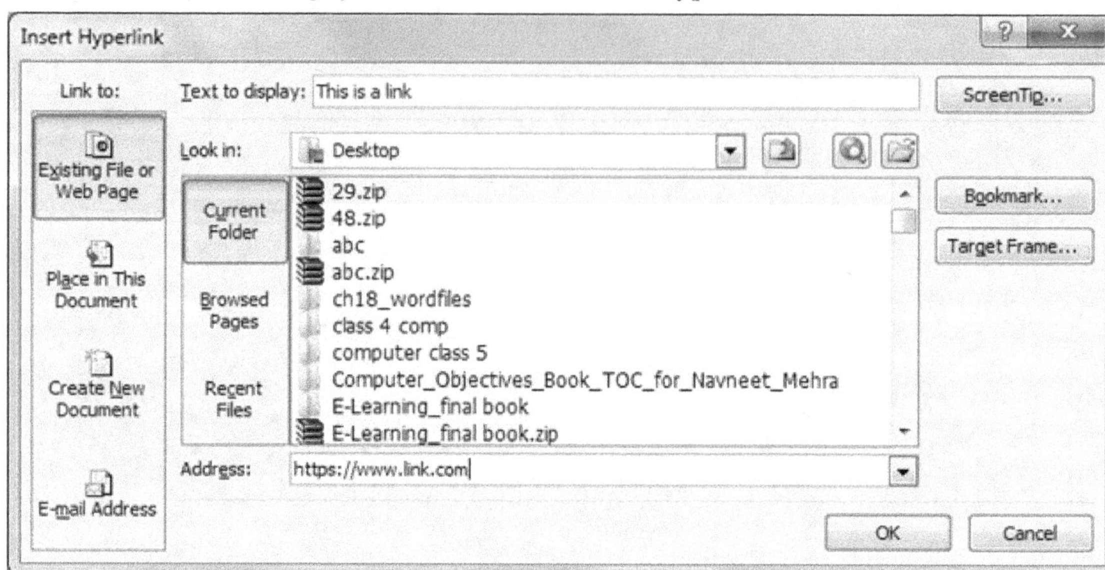

This is a link

You can also insert a hyperlink that links to **another portion of the same document** by selecting **Place in This Document** from the **Insert Hyperlink** dialog box.

To make an email address a hyperlink:
1. Right-click the selected text or image, then click **Hyperlink**.
2. The **Insert Hyperlink** dialog box will open.

3. On the left side of the dialog box, click **Email Address**.

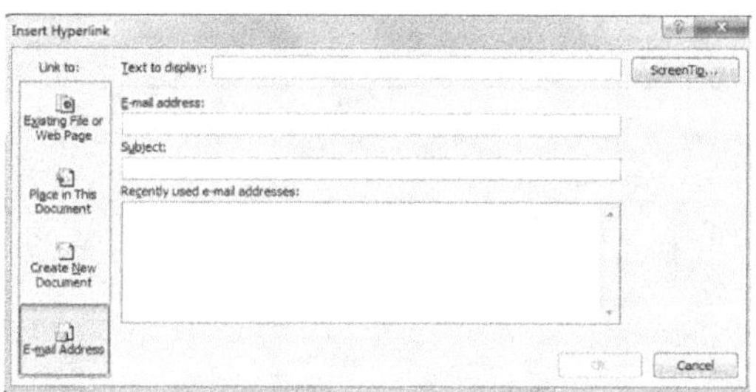

4. Type the email address you want to connect to in the **Email Address** box, then click **OK**.

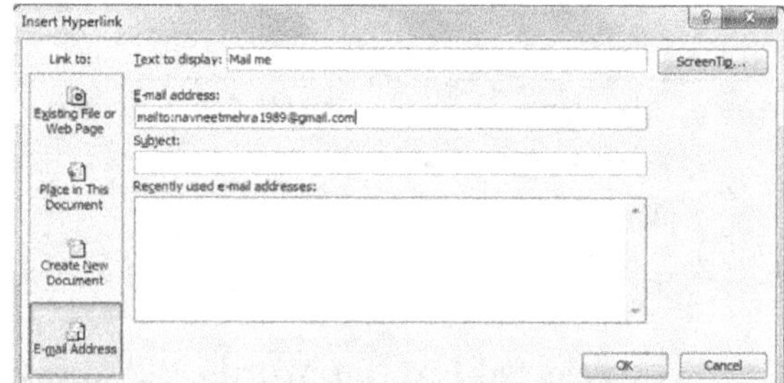

Word often recognizes email and web addresses as you type and will format them as hyperlinks automatically after you press the **Enter** key or the **spacebar**.

To click a hyperlink in Word, hold down the **Control** key and click the hyperlink.

To remove a hyperlink:
1. Right-click the hyperlink.
2. Click **Remove Hyperlink**.

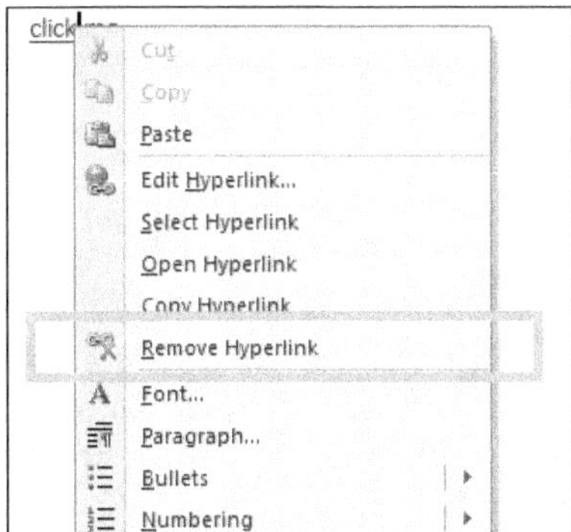

After you create a hyperlink, you should test it. If you have linked to a website, your web browser should automatically open and display the site. If it doesn't work, check the hyperlink address for misspellings.

Mail Merge

Mail Merge is a useful tool that will allow you to easily produce multiple letters, labels, envelopes, etc. using information stored in a database, or spreadsheet. When you are using a Mail Merge, you will need a recipient list, which is typically an Excel workbook.

To use Mail Merge:
1. Open an **existing** Word document, or create a **new** one.
2. Click the **Mailings** tab.
3. Click the **Start Mail Merge** command.
4. Select **Step by Step Mail Merge Wizard**.

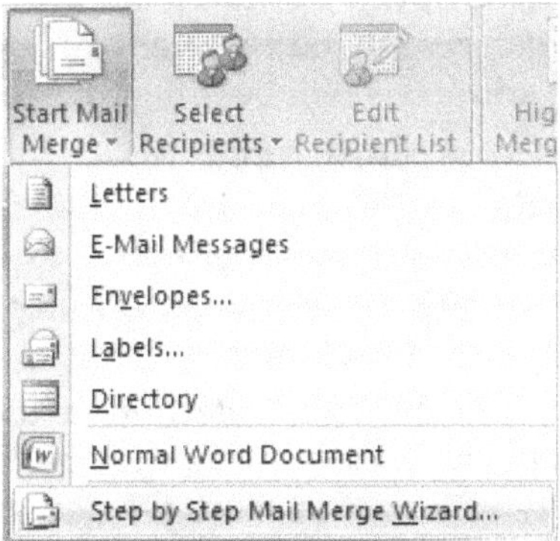

The Mail Merge task pane will appear which will guide you through all the steps to complete a merge.

Step 1:
1. Choose the type of document you want to create. In this example, select **Letters**.

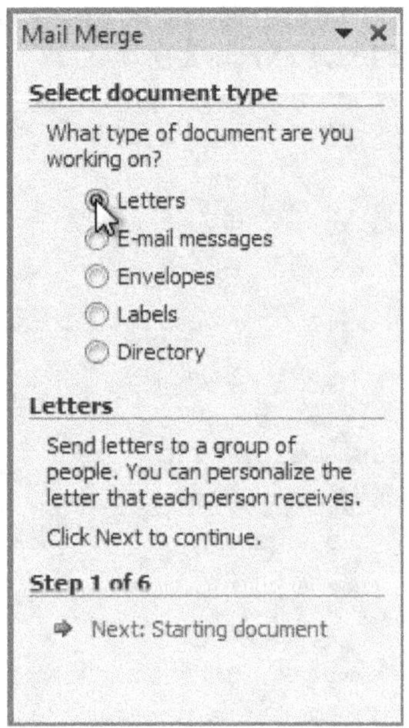

2. Click **Next: Starting document** to move to Step 2.

Step 2:
1. Select **Use the current document**.

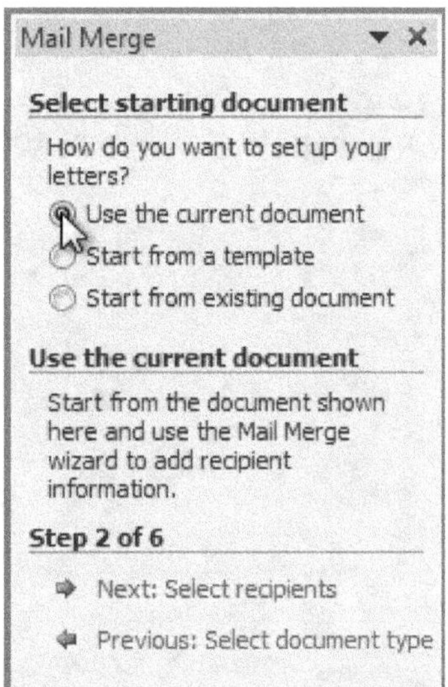

2. Click **Next: Select recipients** to move to Step 3.

Step 3:

Now you'll need an address list so Word can automatically place each address into the document. The list can be in an existing file, such as an **Excel workbook**, or you can **type a new address list** from within the Mail Merge Wizard.

1. From the **Mail Merge** task pane, select **Use an existing list**, then click **Browse**.

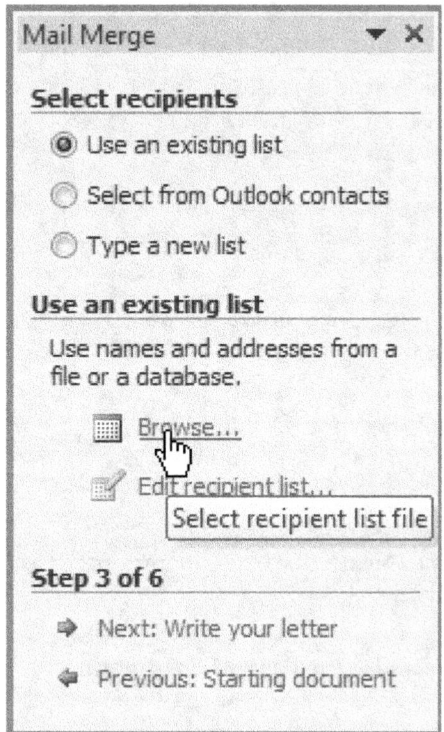

2. Locate your file in the dialog box (you may have to navigate to a different folder), then click **Open**.

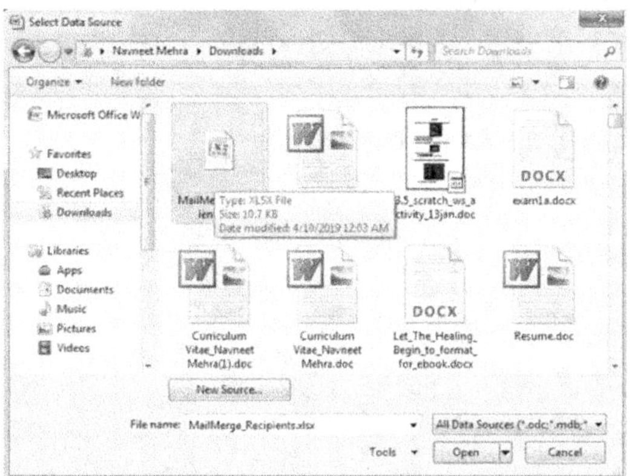

3. If the address list is in an Excel workbook, select the **worksheet** that contains the list, then click **OK**.

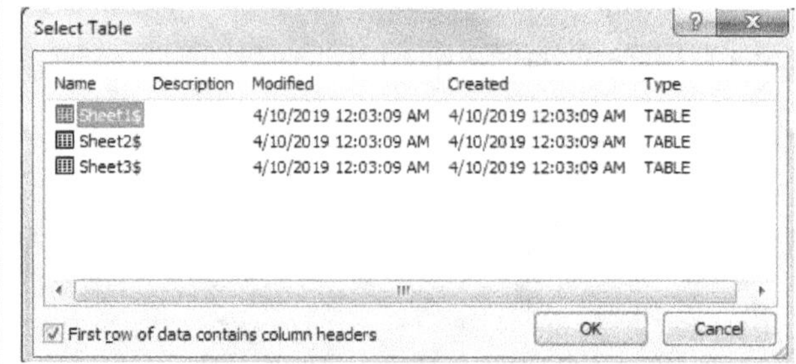

4. In the **Mail Merge Recipients** dialog box, you can **check** or **uncheck** each recipient to control which ones are used in the merge. When you're done, click **OK** to close the dialog box.

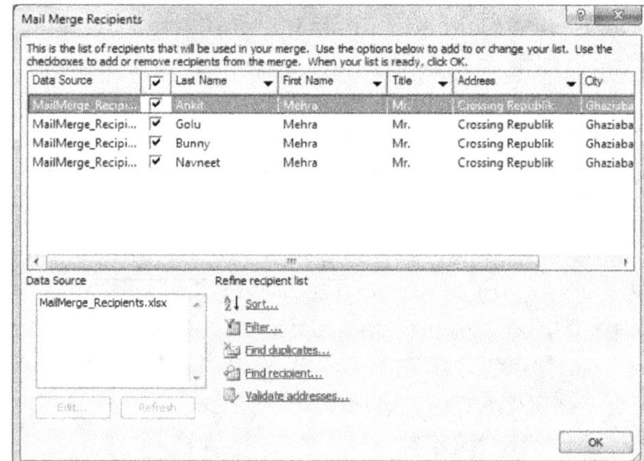

5. From the **Mail Merge** task pane, click **Next: Write your letter** to move to Step 4.

Step 4:

Now you're ready to write your letter. When it's printed, each copy of the letter will basically be the same, except the **recipient data**—like the **name** and **address**—will be different on each one.

To insert recipient data:

1. Place the insertion point in the document where you want the information to appear.

2. Select **Address block, Greeting line, Electronic postage**, or **More items** from the task pane.

3. Depending on your selection, a dialog box may appear with various options. Select the desired options, then click **OK**.

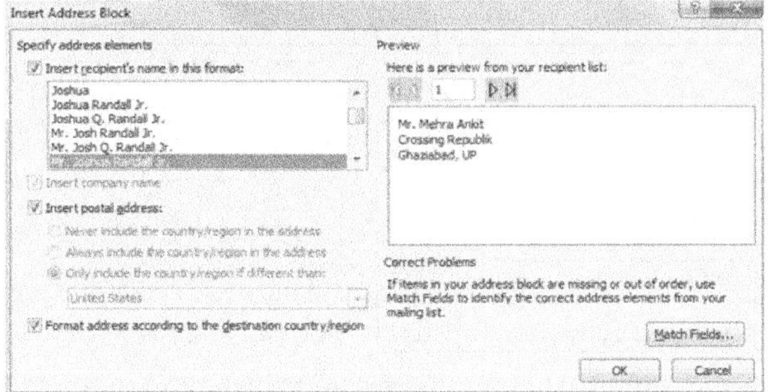

4. A placeholder appears in your document (for example: **«AddressBlock»**).
5. Repeat these steps each time you need to enter information from your data record.
6. From the **Mail Merge** task pane, click **Next: Preview your letters** to move to Step 5.

Step 5:

1. Preview the letters to make sure information from the recipient list appears correctly in the letter. You can use the left and right scroll arrows to view each document.
2. Click **Next: Complete the merge** to move to Step 6.

Step 6:

1. Click **Print** to print the letters.

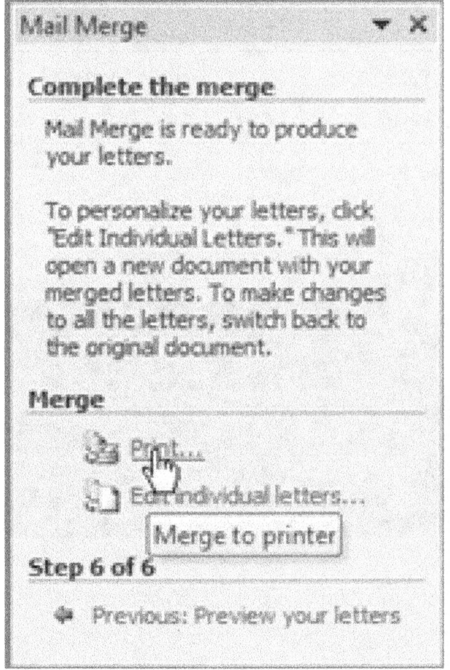

2. The **Merge to Printer** dialog box opens. Click **All**, then click **OK**.

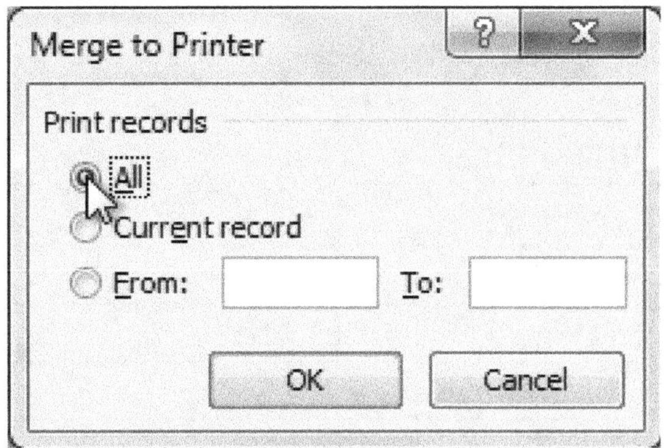

3. The **Print** dialog box will appear. Adjust the print settings if needed, then click **OK**.

Style Group

A style is a predefined combination of font style, color, and size of text that can be applied to selected text.

To select a style:

1. Select the text you want to format.

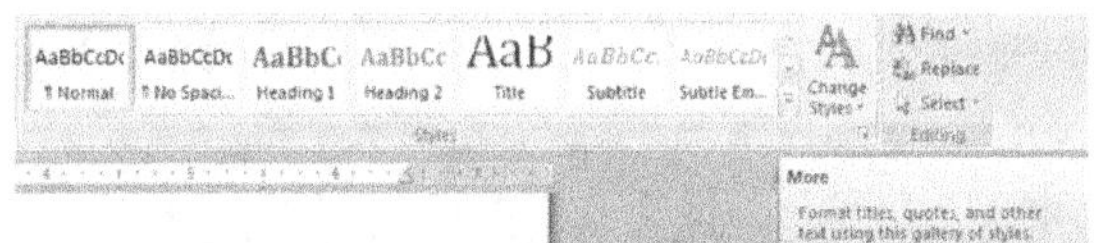

2. In the **Style** group on the **Home** tab, hover over each style to see a live preview in the document. Click the **More** drop-down arrow to see additional styles

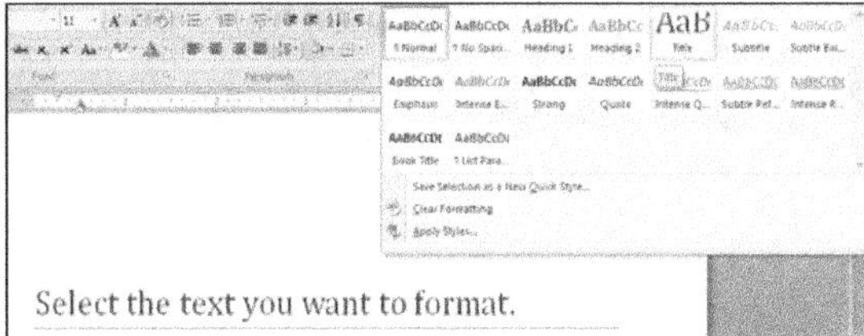

3. Select the style you want. The selected text appears formatted in the style.

Notes

1. The margins may vary according to piece of stationery chosen.
2. By default, Word displays the measure-ment of a document in (inches).

Shortcuts

Command	Shortcut
Open a Document	Ctrl + O
Create New	Ctrl + N
Save a Document	Ctrl + S
Print a Document	Ctrl + P
Close a Document	Ctrl + W
Help	F1
Navigation	**To Do**
Up One Screen	Page Up
Down One Screen	Page Down
Beginning of Line	Home
End of Line	End
Beginning of Document	Ctrl + Home
End of Document	Ctrl + End
Open the Go To dialog box	F5

Editing	To Do
Cut	Ctrl + X
Copy	Ctrl + C
Paste	Ctrl + V
Undo	Ctrl + Z
Redo or Repeat	Ctrl + Y
Formatting	**To Do**
Bold	Ctrl + B
Italics	Ctrl + I
Underline	Ctrl + U
Align Left	Ctrl + L
Center	Ctrl + E
Align Right	Ctrl + R
Justify	Ctrl + J
Text Selection	**To Do**
A Word	Double-click the word
A Sentence	Press and hold Ctrl and click anywhere in the sentence
A Line	Click in the selection bar next to the line
A Paragraph	Triple-click the paragraph
Everything	Ctrl + A

➡ Hyperlinks contain two basic parts: the address of the webpage, email address, or other location it is linking to; and the display text (or image).

➡ Mail Merge is a useful tool that will allow you to easily produce multiple letters, labels, envelopes, etc. using information stored in a database, or spreadsheet.

1. Split cell __________.
   (a) Splits all the cells of the table in to two equal halves
   (b) Requires the number of columns or rows to be created in the cell to be split
   (c) Requires the number of columns and rows and redraws a table
   (d) Combines two or more cell

2. The operation ▢ is used for ______.
   (a) Adding or changing border around a page
   (b) Choose a color background for page
   (c) Merge cells
   (d) Table properties

3. ______ is the maximum number of columns that can be inserted in a table in a MS Word document.
   (a) 35
   (b) 15
   (c) 63
   (d) 65

4. When you click Distribute Rows, it distributes the __________.
   (a) Height of the selected rows equally between them
   (b) Width of the selected rows equally between them
   (c) Header in the table
   (d) Width of the selected columns equally between them

5. In Table Tools, under Design tab, by shading you can __________.
   (a) Specify a color for page background
   (b) Specify a color for the background behind the selected text or paragraph
   (c) Highlight the text
   (d) Highlight the border of the selected cell in a table

6. You have been editing an existing letter in MS Word. You want to review the modifications to the letter since you last edited it, before you finally print it. Which feature of MS Word should you be using?
   (a) AutoSummarize
   (b) Compare and Merge documents
   (c) Track changes
   (d) Mail Merge Wizard

7. How do you increase the line spacing between two lines?
   (a) Home Tab → Insert → Line Spacing
   (b) Home Tab → Paragraph → Line and Paragraph Spacing
   (c) Insert Tab → Insert → Line Spacing
   (d) Insert Tab → Paragraph → Line Spacing

8. In newspaper column format, what is the minimum width of a column?
   (a) 0.25″   (b) 0.5″
   (c) 1.0″   (d) 1.5″

9. You can go to the Insert columns dialog box by ______.
   (a) Clicking Columns in the Insert card
   (b) Pressing Alt + O + C
   (c) Clicking Columns in page Setup of page Layout tab
   (d) Both (b) and (c)

10. The maximum size that you can specify for a font is ______ points.
    (a) 72   (b) 1638
    (c) 16038   (d) 68

11. Turabian and GB7714 are types of ________ styles.
    (a) Text   (b) Cross Reference
    (c) Footnote   (d) Citation

12. How can you change a page number style from 1, 2, 3 ______ to a, b, c ______?
    (a) Click page Layout → Header & Footer → Page Number → Format Page Numbers
    (b) Click Format → Header & Footer → Page Number → Format Page Numbers
    (c) Click Insert → Header & Footer → Page Number → Format Page Numbers
    (d) None of these

13. This button AB^1 is used to ______.
    (a) Insert a footnote
    (b) Format the selected text as uppercase
    (c) Format the selected text as superscript
    (d) Insert an endnote

14. Shortcut key to insert endnote text is ______.
    (a) Alt + Ctrl + E   (b) Alt + Ctrl + M
    (c) Alt + Ctrl + N   (d) Alt + Ctrl + D

15. You can choose settings for features like dictionary, proofing and language when you ______.
   (a) Click on the Tools Tab, click Options.
   (b) Click on the File Tab, click Word Options.
   (c) Right-click anywhere on the ribbon and choose Options.
   (d) Click on the View tab, click Properties.

16. Match the following.

Column - I	Column - II
(i) .docx	(a) A Word template with no macros or code.
(ii) .dotx	(b) A Word document that could contain macros or code.
(iii) .docm	(c) A standard Word document with no macros or code.
(iv) .dotm	(d) A Word template that could contain macros or code.

   (a) (i) – (c),(ii) – (a), (iii) – (d), (iv) – (b)
   (b) (i) – (c), (ii) – (a), (iii) – (b), (iv) – (d)
   (c) (i) – (a), (ii) – (c), (iii) – (b), (iv) – (d)
   (d) (i) – (b), (ii) – (d), (iii) – (c), (iv) – (a)

17. ______ automatically adjusts the amount of space between certain characters of a word typed in a font like Times New Roman, so that the entire word looks more evenly spaced.
   (a) Kerning   (b) Spacing
   (c) Scaling   (d) Positioning

18. Which MS Word feature has been used here?

   (a) WordArt   (b) Footnotes
   (c) Drop Cap   (d) Tab Stop

19. For Mail Merge in MS Word, ______ consists of names and addresses to be printed on labels and envelopes.
   (a) Data source
   (b) Main document
   (c) New document
   (d) Web site

20. The ___________ tab appears when we insert a picture in the word document.
   (a) Insert picture   (b) Format
   (c) Shapes   (d) Clip Art

HOTS

1. Shraddha is making a document in MS Word and now she wants to insert an image, and she also wants that whatever changes she makes to secure of image shall reflect in Word also. However, she does not want that if the original file is deleted, the image from word document also gets deleted. Which of the following options she should select?
   (a) Insert tab → illustrations group → Picture → click Insert in Insert Picture dialog box.
   (b) Insert tab → illustrations group → Picture → click Link to file in Insert picture dialog box.
   (c) Insert tab → illustrations group → Picture → click Insert and Link in Insert Picture dialog box.
   (d) Insert tab → illustrations group → Picture → Double click on the image.

2. What is the other way to select the entire document rather than pressing Ctrl + A in MS Word?
   (a) Triple click in the right margin when the pointer's shape is the arrow.
   (b) Triple click in the left margin when the pointer's shape is the arrow.
   (c) Triple click inside a paragraph.
   (d) Triple click anywhere in the document.

3. The Footnote Text style defines characters as ______________.
   (a) 12-point Times New Roman and paragraphs as single-spaced and right-aligned

(b) 10-point Times New Roman and para-graphs as double-spaced and left-aligned

(c) 12-point Times New Roman and para-graphs as double-spaced and right-aligned

(d) 10-point Times New Roman and para-graphs as single-spaced and left-aligned

4. The _____________ in the Resume Wizard dialog box indicates the wizard is ready to create the document.

(a) Start panel

(b) Address panel

(c) Add/Sort Heading panel

(d) Finish panel

5. The spike _______________.

(a) Allows you to combine text from several documents and then insert all the text into one document at one time

(b) Allows you to edit auto text entries

(c) Allows you to format auto text entries

(d) All of these

SUBJECTIVE QUESTIONS

1. How can you apply a Style in Word?

Ans.

Select the text to which you want to apply the style and select the style you want to use from the Styles Gallery in the Styles group on the Home tab.

2. How can you copy Formatting with the Format Painter?

Ans.

Select the text with the formatting you want to copy and click the **Format Painter** button in the Clipboard group on the Home tab. Then, select the text you want to apply the copied formatting to.

3. What steps are followed to draw a shape?

Ans.

Click the **Insert** tab on the Ribbon, click the **Shapes** button in the Shapes group, and select the shape you want to insert. Then, click where you want to draw the shape and drag until the shape reaches the desired size. Hold down the **Shift** key while you drag to draw a perfectly proportioned shape or a straight line.

4. What are the steps to create a mail merge in MS Word?

Ans.

To create a mail merge, we need to follow the below steps.

- We need to create a new data source and enter information
- Next, we need to create the main document
- Once it is done, we need to insert the fields into the main document
- At the end, we need to merge data source and the main document

Step 1 – We need to create a new data source and enter information

- To store the information like addresses and that has to be merged with the main document.
- To start with open a new Word document.
- Please create a table with the required information.
- Then save the document with the extension .doc.

First name	Last name	Add1	Add2	Add3
Bhaskar	Rambha	Banjara Hills	Road no. 3	Hyderabad
Ashok	Reddy	Kukatpally	Main Road	Hyderabad
Ravi	Kumar	Gandhi Nagar	RTC X Road	Hyderabad

Step 2 – Next we need to create the main document

■ Now from Tools menu, select Letters and Mailing and then Mail Merge.

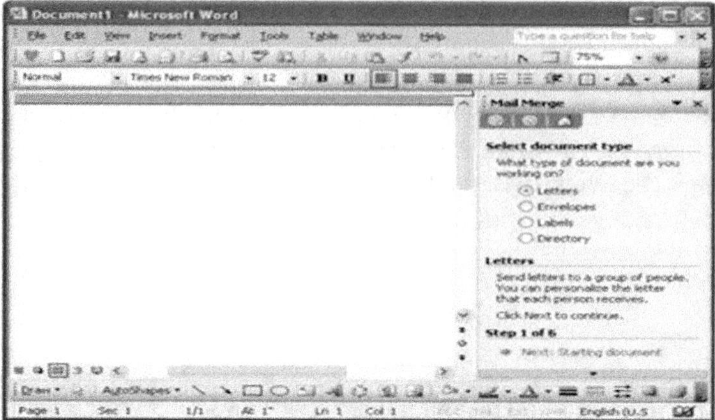

You will get 3 options to select from the following window:

■ Use the Current Document
■ Start from a template.
■ Start from Existing Document

Now you have to select: "Use the Current Document"

You can now type the body of the email, leaving sufficient space to place addresses later.

Now click on Write Your letter link (step 3) Then you will get following window.

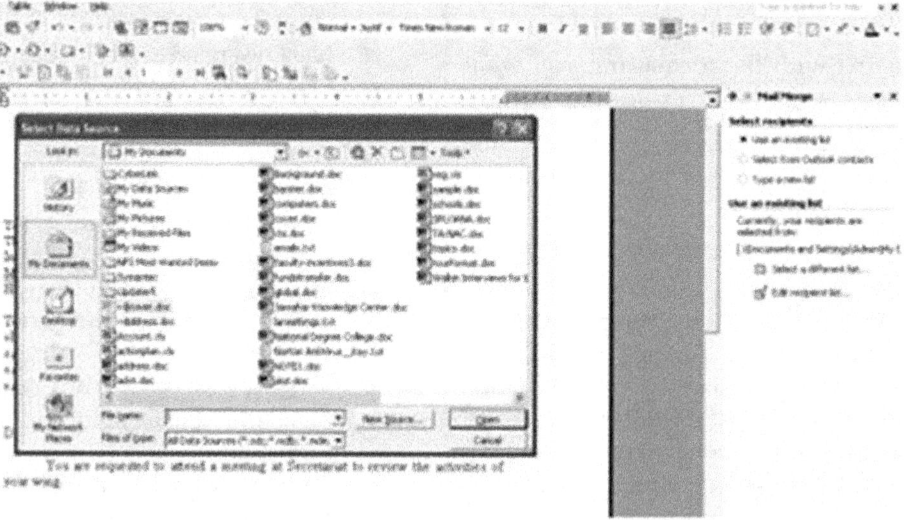

Now Select an Existing Data Source i.e. the file address.doc (initially we saved a word doc with tabular column) and Click on Open Button. Then you will get the following window.

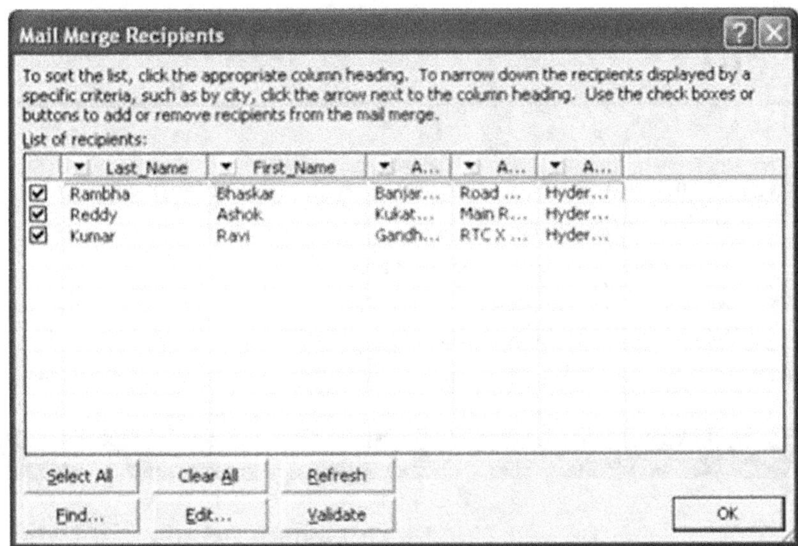

Now you have to add recipient information to your letter.

Click on More items and insert the fields wherever required. After inserting fields your document may look like this :

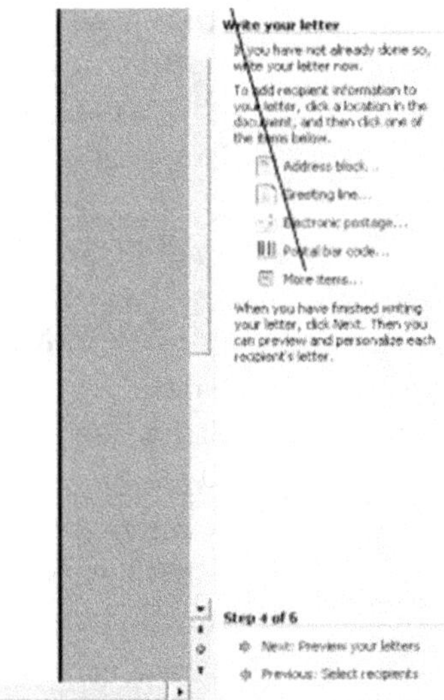

Once you set the preview you can complete the merge. Before printing a letter, you may print all letters or selectively. We can always check preview, before printing any document.

5. How you can insert an image from another file or folder in MS Word?

Ans.

Follow the steps given below to insert an image from another file or folder:
i.   Place the insertion point where you want the image to appear.
ii. Select the Insert tab on the Ribbon, then click the Pictures command under Illustrations Group.
iii. The Insert Picture dialog box will appear. Browse the picture in your computer.
iv. Select an Image and then click on Insert button.
v.   The image will appear in the document.

MS Excel 4

Learning Objectives : In this chapter, students will learn about:
- ✓ Basics of MS Excel
- ✓ Functions and formulas in MS Excel
- ✓ Working in MS Excel
- ✓ Macros and Charts in Excel

CHAPTER SUMMARY

Opening Screen

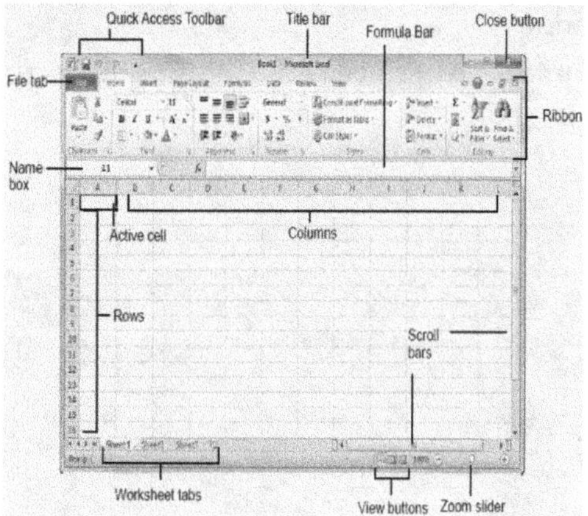

The Fundamentals

The **File** tab menu and Backstage view contain commands for working with a program's files, such as Open, Save, Close, New, and Print.

To Create a New Workbook: Click the **File** tab and select **New**, and click **Create**, or press **Ctrl + N.**

To Open a Workbook: Click the **File** tab and select **Open**, or press **Ctrl + O.**

To Save a Workbook: Click the **Save** button on the Quick Access Toolbar, or press **Ctrl + S.**

To Preview and Print a Workbook: Click the **File** tab and select **Print**, or press **Ctrl + P.**

To Undo: Click the ⤺ **Undo** button on the Quick Access Toolbar, or press **Ctrl + Z.**

To Redo or Repeat: Click the ⤻ **Redo** button on the Quick Access Toolbar, or press **Ctrl + Y.**

To Close a Workbook: Click the ✕ **Close** button, or press **Ctrl + W.**

To Get Help: Press **F1** to open the Help window. Type your question and press **Enter.**

Cell addresses: Cells are referenced by addresses made from their column letter and row number, such as cell A1, A2, B1, B2, etc. You can find the address of a cell by looking at the Name Box.

To Select a Cell: Click a cell or use the keyboard arrow keys to select it.

To Select a Cell Range: Click and drag to select a range of cells. Or, press and hold down the **Shift** key while using the **arrow keys** to move the mouse pointer to the last cell of the range.

To Select an Entire Worksheet: Click the **Select All** button where column and row headings meet. Or, press **Ctrl + A.**

To Minimize the Ribbon: Click the **Minimize Ribbon** button on the Ribbon. Or, press **Ctrl + F1.** Or, right click a **tab** and select **Minimize Ribbon** from the contextual menu.

To Change Program Settings: Click the **File** tab and select **Excel Options.**

To Use Zoom: Click and drag the zoom slider to the left or right. Or, click the **Zoom Out** and **Zoom In** buttons on the slider.

To Change Views: Click a **View** button in the status bar. Or, click the **View** tab and select a view.

Editing

To Edit a Cell's Contents: Select the cell and click the **Formula Bar,** or double-click the cell. Edit the cell contents and press **Enter.**

To Clear a Cell's Contents: Select the cell(s) and press the **Delete** key.

To Cut or Copy Data: Select cell(s) and click the **Cut** or **Copy** button in the Clipboard group on the Home tab.

To Paste Data: Place the insertion point where you want to paste and click the **Paste** button in the Clipboard group on the Home tab.

To Preview an Item Before Pasting: Place the insertion point where you want to paste, click the **Paste** button list arrow in the Clipboard group on the Home tab, and select a preview option to view the item.

To Paste Special: Select the destination cell(s), click the **Paste** button list arrow in the Clipboard group on the Home tab, and select **Paste Special.** Select an option and click **OK.**

To Copy Using Auto Fill: Point to the fill handle at the bottom-right corner of the selected cell(s), then drag to the destination cell(s).

To Complete a Series Using AutoFill: Select the cells that define the series. Click and drag the fill handle to complete the series.

To Move or Copy Cells Using Drag and Drop: Select the cell(s) you want to move or copy, position the pointer over any border of the selected cell(s), then drag to the destination cells. To copy, hold down **Ctrl** key while dragging.

To Insert a Column or Row: Right-click to the right of the column, or below the row you want to insert. Select **Insert** from the contextual menu, or click the **Insert** button in the Cells group on the Home tab.

To Delete a Column or Row: Select the row or column heading(s). Rightclick and select **Delete** from the contextual menu, or click the **Delete** button in the Cells group on the Home tab.

To Insert a Comment: Select the cell where you want to insert a comment and click the **Review** tab on the Ribbon. Click the **New Comment** button in the Comments group. Type a comment and click outside the comment box.

Formulas and Functions

To Total a Cell Range: Click the cell where you want to insert the total and click the **Sum** button in the Editing group on the Home tab. Verify the selected cell range and click the **Sum** button again.

To Enter a Formula: Select the cell where you want to insert the formula. Type = and enter the formula using values, cell references, operators, and functions. Press **Enter** when you are finished.

To Insert a Function: Select the cell where you want to enter the function and click the **Insert Function** button on the Formula Bar.

To Reference a Cell in a Formula: Type the cell reference (for example, B5) in the formula or click the cell you want to reference.

To Create an Absolute Cell Reference: Precede the cell references with a $ sign or press **F4** after selecting cell(s) to make it absolute.

To Use Several Operators or Cell Ranges: Enclose the part of a formula you want to calculate first in parentheses.

Charts

To Create a Chart: Select the cell range that contains the data you want to chart and click the **Insert** tab on the Ribbon. Click a chart type button in the Charts group and select the chart you want to use from the list.

To Insert a Sparkline: Select the cell range that contains the data you want to chart and click the **Insert** tab on the Ribbon. Select the sparkline you want to insert from the Sparkline group. Select the cell or cell range where you want to add the sparkline and click **OK.**

Formatting

To Format Text: Use the commands in the Font group on the Home tab, or click the **Dialog Box Launcher** in the Font group to open the Format Cells dialog box.

To Format Values: Use the commands in the Number group on the Home tab, or click the **Dialog Box Launcher** in the Number group to open the Format Cells dialog box.

To Copy Formatting with the Format Painter: Select the cell(s) with the formatting you want to copy and click the **Format Painter** button in the Clipboard group on the Home tab. Then, select the cell(s) you want to apply the copied formatting to.

To Apply a Cell Style: Select the cell(s) you want to apply a cell style to. Click the **Cell Styles** button in the Styles group of the Home tab on the Ribbon and select a style from the gallery.

To Format a Cell Range as a Table: Select the cells you want to apply table formatting to. Click the **Format as Table** button in the Styles group of the Home tab on the Ribbon and select a table format from the gallery.

To Apply a Document Theme: Click the **Page Layout** tab on the Ribbon, click the **Themes** button, and select a theme from the gallery.

To Apply Conditional Formatting: Select the cells to which you want to apply conditional formatting. Click the **Conditional Formatting** button in the Styles group of the Home tab. Select the formatting scheme you wish to use, then set the conditions in the dialog box.

To Adjust Column Width or Row Height: Drag the right border of the column header, or the bottom border of the row header. Double-click the border to AutoFit the column or row according to its contents.

Workbook Management

To Insert a New Worksheet: Click the **Insert Worksheet** tab next to the sheet tabs at the bottom of the program screen. Or, press **Shift + F11**.

To Delete a Worksheet: Select the sheet want to delete, click the **Delete** button in the Cells group on the Home tab, and select **Delete Sheet**. Or, right-click the sheet tab and select **Delete from the contextual menu.**

To Rename a Worksheet: Double-click the sheet tab, enter a new name for the worksheet, and press **Enter**.

To Change a Worksheet's Tab Color: Right-click the Sheet tab, select **Tab Color**, and choose the color you want to apply.

To Move or Copy a Worksheet: Click and drag a tab to move a worksheet. Hold down the **Ctrl** key while clicking and dragging to copy the worksheet.

To Split a Window: Drag either the vertical or horizontal split bar (located near the scroll bars) onto the worksheet.

To Freeze Panes: Place the cell pointer where you want to freeze the window, click the **View** tab on the Ribbon, click the **Freeze Panes** button in the Window group, and select an option from the list.

To Select a Print Area: Select the cell range you want to print, click the **Page Layout** tab on the Ribbon, click the **Print Area** button in the Page Setup group, and select **Set Print Area**.

To Adjust Page Margins, Orientation, Size, and Breaks: Click the **Page Layout** tab on the Ribbon and use the commands in the Page Setup group, or click the **Dialog Box Launcher** in the Page Setup group to open the Page Setup dialog box.

To Protect or Share a Workbook: Click the **Review** tab on the Ribbon and use the commands in the Changes group.

To Recover Autosaved Versions: Click the **File** tab on the Ribbon and select **Info**. Select an autosaved version from the Versions list. Or, click the **Manage Versions** button and select **Recover Draft Versions**.

Sorting Data

Sorting data in MS Excel rearranges the rows based on the contents of a particular column, for example, smallest to largest or alphabetically.

To Sort the data follow the steps mentioned below.

- Select the Column by which you want to sort data.
- Choose Sort & Filter option and select Sort option.

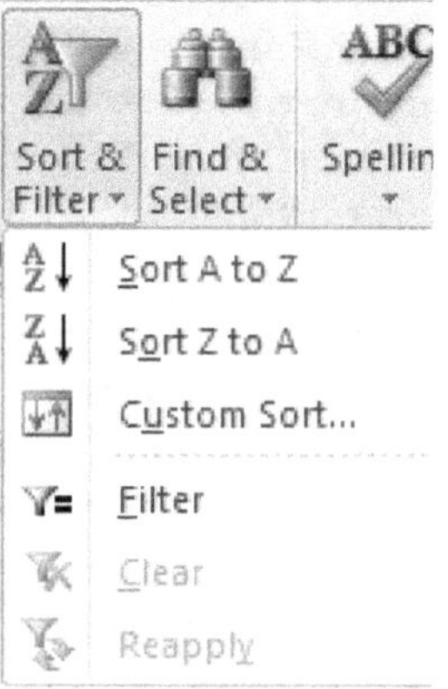

National Cyber Olympiad – 7

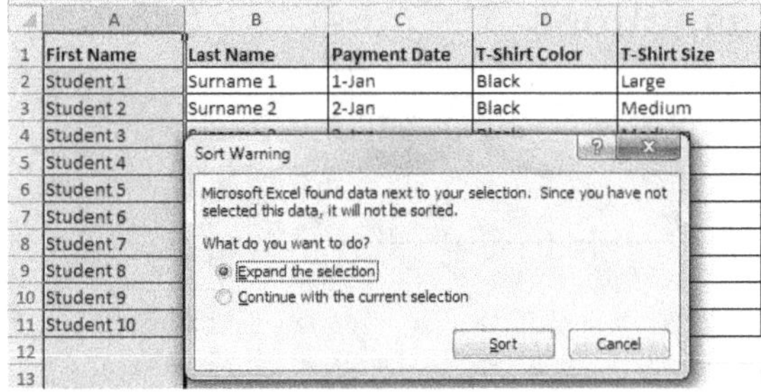

- If you want to sort data based on a selected column, Choose **Continue with the selection** or if you want sorting based on other columns, choose **Expand Selection**.
- You can Sort based on the below Conditions.
  - **Values** – Alphabetically or numerically.
  - **Cell Color** – Based on Color of Cell.
  - **Font Color** – Based on Font color.
  - **Cell Icon** – Based on Cell Icon.

Clicking Sort will sort the selection.

CAPTCHA means "Completely Automated Public Turing Test to tell Computers and Humans Apart".

Filtering Data

Filtering data in MS Excel refers to displaying only the rows that meet certain conditions. (The other rows gets hidden.)

Say, if you are interested in seeing data where T-Shirt color is Black, then you can set filter to do this. Follow the below mentioned steps to do this.

- Place a cursor on the Header Row.
- Choose **Filter** option from Sort & Filter option.

	A	B	C	D	E
1	First Name	Last Name	Payment Date	T-Shirt Color	T-Shirt Size
2	Student 1	Surname 1	1-Jan	Black	Large
3	Student 2	Surname 2	2-Jan	Black	Medium
4	Student 3	Surname 3	3-Jan	White	Medium
5	Student 4	Surname 4	4-Jan	Green	Medium
6	Student 5	Surname 5	5-Jan	Red	Medium
7	Student 6	Surname 6	6-Jan	White	Medium
8	Student 7	Surname 7	7-Jan	Green	Small
9	Student 8	Surname 8	8-Jan	Blue	X-Large
10	Student 9	Surname 9	9-Jan	Black	X-Large
11	Student 10	Surname 10	10-Jan	Black	Medium

- Click the drop-down arrow in the T-Shirt color header and remove the check mark from Select All, which unselects everything.

- Then select the check mark for Black which will filter the data and displays data where conditions meets.

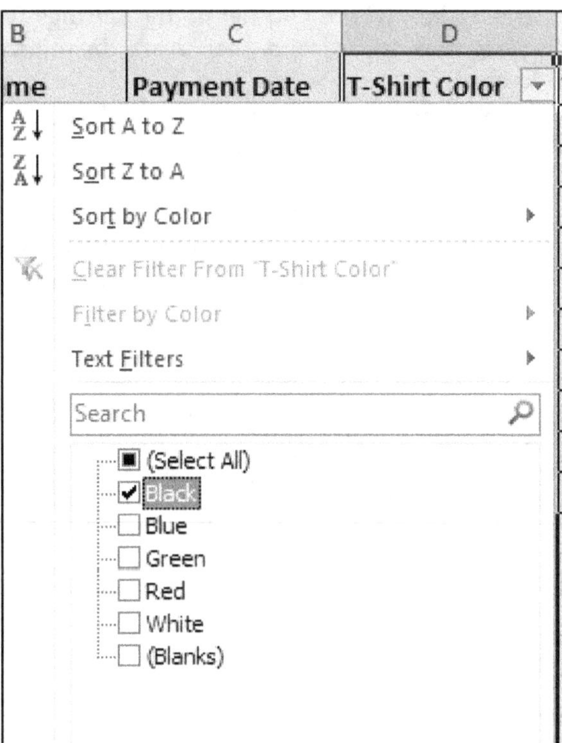

	A	B	C	D	E
1	First Name	Last Name	Payment Date	T-Shirt Color	T-Shirt Size
2	Student 1	Surname 1	1-Jan	Black	Large
3	Student 2	Surname 2	2-Jan	Black	Medium
10	Student 9	Surname 9	9-Jan	Black	X-Large
11	Student 10	Surname 10	10-Jan	Black	Medium

Macros

Macros enable you to automate almost any task that you can undertake in Excel. To view macros choose **View Tab » Macro dropdown**.

View tab contains a Macros command button to which a dropdown menu containing the following three options.

- **View Macros** – Opens the Macro dialog box where you can select a macro to run or edit.
- **Record Macro** – Opens the Record Macro dialog box where you define the settings for your new macro and then start the macro recorder.
- **Use Relative References** – Uses relative cell addresses when recording a macro, making the macro more versatile by enabling you to run it in areas of a worksheet other than the ones originally used in the macro's recording.

Now let's create a simple macro that will automate the task of making cell content Bold and apply cell color.

- Choose View Tab » Macro dropdown.
- Click on Record Macro as below.
- Now Macro recording will start.
- Do the steps of action, which you want to perform repeatedly. Macro will record those steps.
- You can stop the macro recording once done with all steps.

Insert tabs

The Insert tab allows you to add other elements such as charts, cliparts and images, among others, to your workbook.

Tables

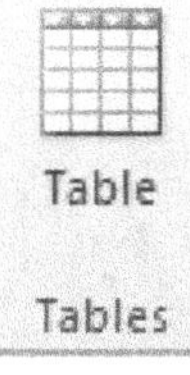

Table - Displays the "Create Table" dialog box. When you define your data as a table it makes it easier to sort, filter and apply formatting.

Illustrations

Pictures - Displays the "Insert Picture" dialog box.

Clip Art - Toggles the display of the Clip Art task pane to let you insert drawings, movies, sounds, photos etc.

Shapes - The drop-down contains the commands: Recently Used Shapes, Lines, Rectangles, Basic Shapes, Block Arrows, Equation Shapes, Flowchart, Stars and Banners and Callouts.

Charts

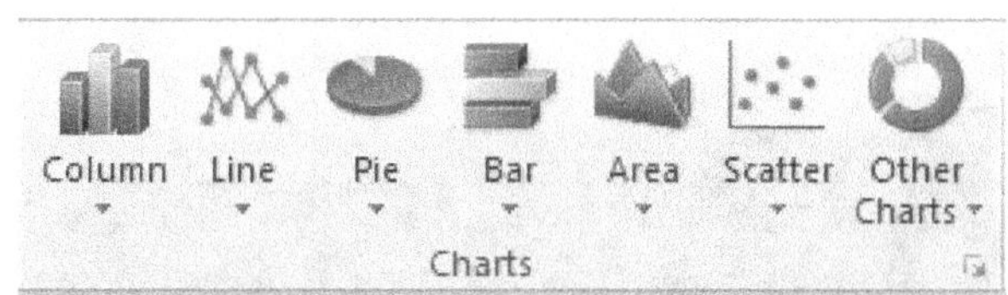

Column and Bar - The drop-down contains the commands: 2-D Column, 3-D Column, 2-D Bar, 3-D Bar and More Column Charts.

Line and Area - The drop-down contains the commands: 2-D Line, 3-D Line, 2-D Area, 3-D Area and More Line Charts.

Pie - The drop-down contains the commands: 2-D Pie, 3-D Pie, Doughnut and More Pie Charts.

Scatter - The drop-down contains the commands: Scatter, Bubble and More Scatter Charts.

Other Charts - Provides access to other chart types. The drop-down contains the commands: Stock, Surface, Doughnut, Bubble, Radar and All Chart Types.

Sparklines

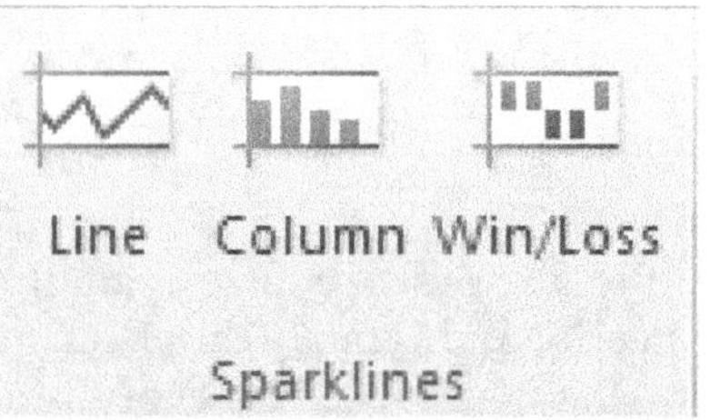

Line - Displays the "Create Sparklines" dialog box which lets you insert a line chart within a single cell.

Column - Displays the "Create Sparklines" dialog box which lets you insert a column chart within a single cell.

Win/Loss - Displays the "Create Sparklines" dialog box which lets you insert a win/loss chart within a single cell.

Links

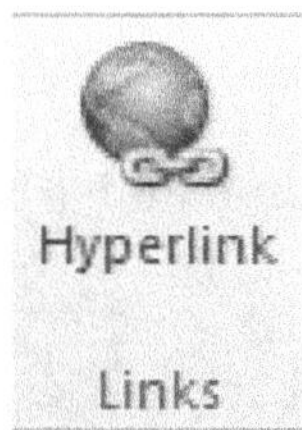

Hyperlink - Displays the "Insert Hyperlink" dialog box.

Text

Text Box - Inserts a textbox that can be positioned anywhere on the page.

Header & Footer - Switches to Page Layout view and automatically puts your cursor in the header box.

WordArt - Gives you a choice of Word Art styles to insert. The drop-down contains a gallery of different styles.

Symbols

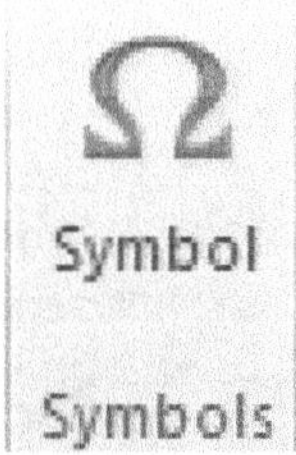

Symbol - Displays the "Symbol" dialog box.

Page Layout Tab
Themes

- **Themes** - Changes the overall look and feel of your workbook including colours, fonts and effects.
- **Colors** - Displays a list of all the available colours and lets you change the colour component of the active theme.
- **Fonts** - Displays a list of all the available fonts and lets you change the font component of the active theme.
- **Effects** - Displays a list of all the available effects and lets you change the effect component of the active theme.

Page Setup

You can quickly display the "Page Setup" dialog box, Page tab, by clicking on the launcher in the bottom right corner of this group.

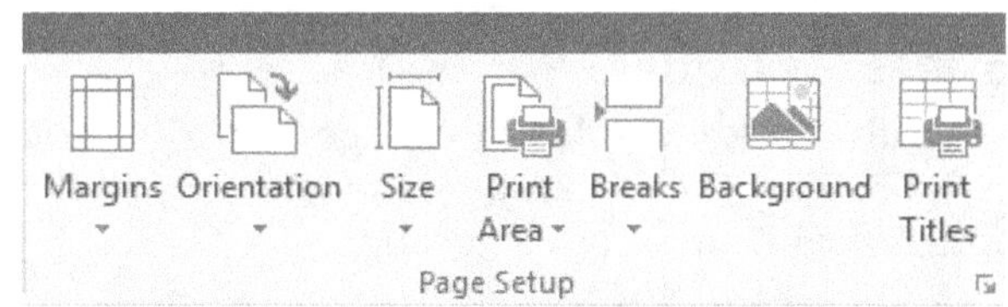

- **Margins** - Lets you choose from one of your built-in margin settings or lets you customise your own.
- **Orientation** - Lets you switch between Portrait and Landscape.
- **Size** - Lets you select from all the different available paper sizes.
- **Print Area** - This drop-down contains the commands: Set Print Area and Clear Print Area.
- **Breaks** - This drop-down contains the commands: Insert Page Break, Remove Page Break and Reset All Page Breaks.

- **Background** - Displays the "Sheet Background" dialog box to let you add a background image to the back of a worksheet.
- **Print Titles** - Displays the "Page Setup" dialog box, Sheet tab. This allows you to enter rows or columns to repeat.

Scale to Fit

You can quickly display the "Page Setup" dialog box, Page tab, by clicking on the launcher in the bottom right corner of this group.

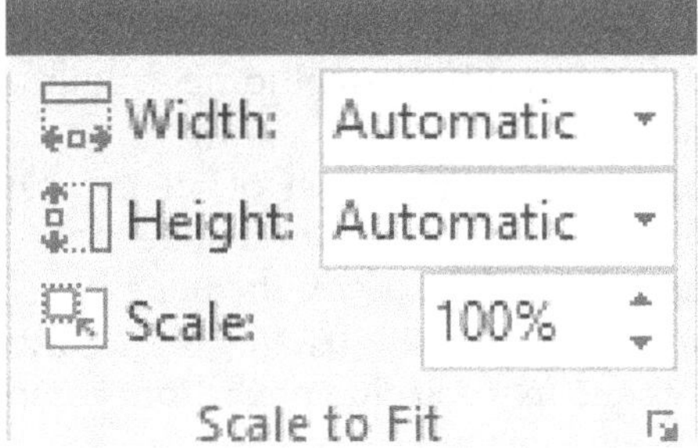

- **Width** - Choice of 1 to 9 pages. The combo box contains Automatic, 1 to 9 pages and More Pages.
- **Height** - Choice of 1 to 9 pages. The combo box contains Automatic, 1 to 9 pages and More Pages.
- **Scale** - Changes the page scale in increments of 5%.

Sheet Options

You can quickly display the "Page Setup" dialog box, Sheet tab, by clicking on the launcher in the bottom right corner of this group.

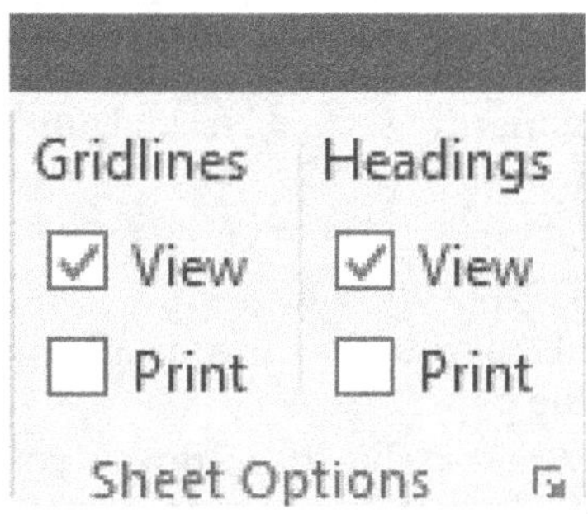

- **Gridlines View** - Toggles the display of gridlines on the active worksheet.
- **Gridlines Print** - Toggles whether the gridlines are printed.
- **Headings View** - Toggles the displays of row and column headers on the active worksheet.
- **Headings Print** - Toggles whether the row and column headers are printed.

Arrange

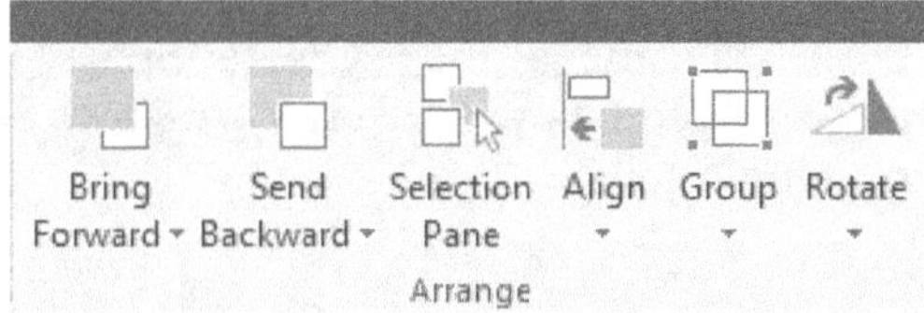

- **Bring Forward** - The button brings the selected object forward one level. The drop-down contains the commands: Bring to Front and Bring Forward.
- **Send Backward** - The button brings the selected object back one level. The drop-down contains the commands: Send to Back and Send Backward.
- **Selection Pane** - Displays the Selection Task Pane.
- **Align** - This drop-down contains the commands: Align Left, Align Center, Align Right, Align Top, Align Middle, Align Bottom, Distribute Horizontally, Distribute Vertically, Snap to Grid, Snap to Shape, View Gridlines.
- **Group** - This drop-down contains the commands: Group, Regroup and Ungroup.
- **Rotate** - Rotate or flip the selected object. Drop-Down. This drop-down contains the commands: Rotate Right 90, Rotate Left 90, Flip Vertical, Flip Horizontal and More Rotation Options.

Notes

- When there are an odd number of values, median is simply the middle number. When there is even number of values, the median is the mean of two middle numbers.
- In Excel a formula is mathematical equation used to calculate a value and must begin with an equal (=) sign. A Function is a predefined formula that performs calculations by using specific values in a particular order. Excel has hundred of functions that can be used to perform simple or complex calculations, e.g. Average, Median, Mode, Min, Max, Count, etc.

- You do not need to type (A2: A10) every time, alternately you can click-drag your mouse to high light these cells and hit enter. This make using Excel so much faster.
- **MEAN** is most common type of average and usually refer to the arithmetic mean.
- The **MEDIAN** is the number in the middle, when the numbers are listed in order.
- The **MODE** is the number that occurs most frequently.
- The **RANGE** is the difference between the lowest and highest values in a list.
- Formula is a mathematical equation used to calculate a value and must begin with an equal (=) sign.
- A function is a predefined formula that performs calculations by using specific value in a particular order.
- Formula is a mathematical equation used to calculate a value and must begin with an equal (=) sign.
- Have you ever thought that if instead of writing the figure you write the cell numbers, i.e. (B2*(B3/100)*B4), would you get the same result? Yes, If you write the formula using the cell numbers in the cell B5, you get the same result. But your calculations become live. If you change any figure like principal, Rate, Time, (i.e., 600, 6, 3) the result simple interest shall also change instantly.
- You can use Excel to calculate all the calculations like Maximum, Minimum, Range, Mean, Mode, Median, Interest, Profit, Area, Loss, Perimeter, etc.
- There are various Functions available in Excel, which you can used to speed up your calculations.
- If the function that you need for some calculation is not available in Excel, you can create your own.
- All formula in excel start with equal to sign, i.e. '='.
- A pie chart is a circular chart divided into sectors.
- The pie chart is divided into several different sections. You can use legends to analyse each colour section.

Keyboard Shortcuts

Command	Shortcut
Open a Workbook	Ctrl + O
Create New	Ctrl + N
Save	Ctrl + S
Preview and Print	Ctrl + P
Close a Workbook	Ctrl + W
Help	F1
Run Spelling Check	F7
Calculate worksheets	F9
Create an absolute, normal, or mixed reference	F4
Navigation	
Move Between Cells	→, ↑, ↓, ←
Right One Cell	Tab
Left One Cell	Shift + Tab
Down One Cell	Enter
Up One Cell	Shift + Enter
Down One Screen	Page Down
Up One Screen	Page Up
To Cell A1	Ctrl + Home
To Last Cell	Ctrl + End
Go To Dialog Box	F5
Editing	
Cut	Ctrl + X
Copy	Ctrl + C
Paste	Ctrl + V
Undo	Ctrl + Z
Redo	Ctrl + Y
Find	Ctrl + F
Replace	Ctrl + H
Select All	Ctrl + A
Edit active cell	F2
Clear cell contents	Delete

Formatting	
Bold	Ctrl + B
Italics	Ctrl + I
Underline	Ctrl + U
Open Format Cells Dialog Box	Ctrl + Shift + F

Select entire row	Shift + Space
Select entire column	Ctrl + Space
Hide selected rows	Ctrl + 9
Hide selected columns	Ctrl + 0

➡ Cells are referenced by addresses made from their column letter and row number, such as cell A1, A2, B1, B2, etc.

➡ Macros enable you to automate almost any task that you can undertake in Excel.

1. A row column arrangement of data, and the formulas to manipulate it is called a ______.
   - (a) Spreadsheet
   - (b) Table sheet
   - (c) Grid sheet
   - (d) Role sheet

2. Where is the address of the active cell displayed in an active worksheet?
   - (a) Row heading
   - (b) Status Bar
   - (c) Name Box
   - (d) Formula Box

3. Current date and time in a cell can be entered using the formula ______.
   - (a) = TODAY( )
   - (b) = NOW ()
   - (c) = TIME ()
   - (d) = CURRENTTIME ()

4. $\sum$ is ______.
   - (a) The Auto Correct button
   - (b) The Auto Format button
   - (c) The Auto Sum button
   - (d) The conditional format button

5. The error value # NULL! appears in a cell because ______.
   - (a) The formula is trying to multiply a value
   - (b) The formula refers to a cell that is not valid
   - (c) The formula uses an intersection of two ranges that do not intersect
   - (d) The formula is trying to divide by Zero

6. When applying conditional formatting to a cell, you can compare the conditions against ______.
   - (a) Cell value
   - (b) Applied formula
   - (c) Both (a) and (b)
   - (d) None of these

7. Paper spreadsheets can have all advantages of electronic spreadsheets except ______.
   - (a) Rows and Columns
   - (b) Headings
   - (c) Speed and Accuracy
   - (d) None of these

8. Which of the following is NOT present is insert tab?
   - (a) [icon]
   - (b) [icon]
   - (c) Ω
   - (d) [icon]

9. In MS Excel, hyperlinks can be ______.
   - (a) Special shapes like stars and banners
   - (b) Drawing objects like rectangles, ovals
   - (c) Text and pictures
   - (d) All of these

10. Which of the following is a valid cell range?
    - (a) A1
    - (b) A1-C4
    - (c) A1:C4
    - (d) C4:A1

11. With the formula bar active, you can see ______.
    - (a) The Insert Function button
    - (b) The Cancel button
    - (c) The Enter button
    - (d) All of these

12. The function of the given icon is ______.
    - (a) To add a new row
    - (b) To create subtotals
    - (c) To insert a new function
    - (d) To create a sum function

13. Which of these is not an MS Excel valid function?
    - (a) COUNTIF
    - (b) SUMIF
    - (c) COUNTA
    - (d) COUNTUP

14. Identify the given icon.
    - (a) Orientation
    - (b) Text Direction
    - (c) Decrease Indent
    - (d) Wrap Text

15. What is the most appropriate formula you can put in the cell B2 to calculate a 9% tax, if value in A2 is 73745.98?
    (a) =A2*0.09
    (b) =A2*0.09%
    (c) =A2*1. 09
    (d) =A2+(A2*0.09)

16. If the current cell shows the results of a formula, what key should be pressed so that the actual formula is displayed in the cell?
    (a) F1
    (b) F2
    (c) F3
    (d) F4

17. A '$' sign in a cell reference like in A1 means that ______.
    (a) The cell reference is relative
    (b) The cell is formatted to dollars.
    (c) The cell reference is absolute.
    (d) The cell reference is invalid.

18. Why should you select this button?

    (a) To get external data form an existing source.
    (b) To get external data from text.
    (c) To get external data from other sources.
    (d) To get external data from the web.

19. The first step while creating a formula for a cell is __________.
    (a) Select the cell you want to place the formula into.
    (b) Type the equals sign (=) to tell Excel that you're about to enter a formula.
    (c) Enter the formula using any input values and the appropriate mathematical operators that make up your formula.
    (d) Choose the new command from the file menu.

20. The formula 'NETWORKDAYS' is used to return the ______.
    (a) Network of days
    (b) Number of whole workdays between two dates
    (c) Number of months in a year
    (d) Number of days a person worked in Excel

21. The Format cells dialog box contains which of the following categories?
    (a) Font
    (b) Border
    (c) Fill
    (d) All of these

22. To do what if analysis, which of the following tools should you use?
    (a) Data Table
    (b) Goal Seek
    (c) Scenario Manager
    (d) All of these

23. What type of chart is this?

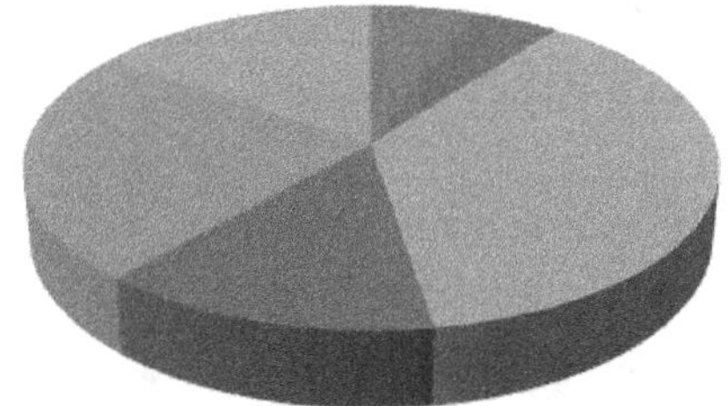

    (a) Doughnut
    (b) Radar
    (c) Bar
    (d) Pie

24. Auto Fill feature ______.
    (a) Extends a sequential series of data
    (b) Adds the cell values
    (c) Applies a border around the selected cells
    (d) Continues a pattern into one or more adjacent cells

25. To select the entire row containing the current cell, press ______.
    (a) Shift + Space
    (b) Space
    (c) Ctrl + Space
    (d) Alt + Space

1. In MS Excel 2010, what would be the result of the formula given below?

   =SUM(CHOOSE(2, A1:A10, B1:B10, C1:C10)

   (a) It will show the second largest sum.

   (b) It will add the value in the range B1:B10

   (c) It will add the value in the first two ranges.

   (d) It will add the value in the range C1:C10.

2. The keyboard shortcut to scroll the screen so that active cell is visible in MS Excel is ______.

   (a) Ctrl + Backspace (b) Ctrl + O

   (c) Alt + Backspace   (d) Ctrl + Spacebar

3. Which of the following is correct description of Auto Complete feature of MS Excel?

   (a) It will force MS Excel to display value in multiple lines within the cell.

   (b) It automatically fills the entry based on other entries that you already made in column, when you type the first few letters of a text.

   (c) It inserts a series of values or text items in a range of cells.

   (d) None of these

4. Which of the following methods is not used to enter data in the cell?

   (a) Press Esc

   (b) Press Tab

   (c) Press Enter

   (d) Use any arrow key

5. How will you merge a range of cells?

   (a) Ctrl + Shift + M

   (b) Ctrl + M

   (c) Select the cells you want to merge and right click and select format cell

   (d) Select the cells you want to merge, and select Merge cells options.

1. How do you enter a Formula in Excel?

Ans.

   Select the cell where you want to insert the formula. Type = and enter the formula using values, cell references, operators, and functions. Press Enter when you are finished.

2. How do you create a Chart in Excel?

Ans.

   Select the cell range that contains the data you want to chart and click the Insert tab on the Ribbon. Click a chart type button in the Charts group and select the chart you want to use from the list.

3. How can you apply Conditional Formatting?

Ans.

   Select the cells to which you want to apply conditional formatting. Click the Conditional Formatting button in the Styles group of the Home tab. Select the formatting scheme you wish to use, then set the conditions in the dialog box.

4. How you can insert date and time in a cell of worksheet?

Ans.

   The following are the steps to insert date and time format in a cell of a worksheet:

   - Click on the cell in which the date and time is to be inserted.
   - Click on the Formulas
   - Choose Date & Time from the ribbon to open the function drop down list.
   - Click on NOW in the list to bring up the function's dialog box.
   - Click Ok
   - The current date and time will appear in the cell.

- When you click on the cell, the complete function = NOW ( ) appears in the formula bar above the worksheet.
- If you want the cell to show only the current date or time, change the cell's format to show either date or time only.

5. What are Charts in Excel? Explain some of the common ones.

Ans.

A chart is a tool you can use in Excel to communicate your data graphically. Charts allow your audience to see the meaning behind the numbers in the spreadsheet more easily, and to make visual comparisons and trends much easier.

There are many different types of charts available in MS-Excel some of them are discussed below:

Column Chart

The column chart is used to compare values among one or more series of data points. In this chart, the vertical axis (y-axis) always displays numeric values and the horizontal axis (x-axis) displays time or other categories.

Line Chart

The line chart mainly displays trends over time. In this chart the x-axis displays time or other category and y-axis displays numerical values.

Pie Chart

A pie chart can display only one series of data. It displays the contribution of each value to the total.

Bar Chart

The bar chart is just like a column chart but it can display and compare a large number : series better than the column chart.

Area Chart

Area chart is just like the line chart but the difference is that the area below the plot line is solid. It highlights differences between many sets of data over a period of time.

Learning Objectives : In this chapter, students will learn about:
- ✓ Fundamentals of MS PowerPoint
- ✓ Slide master and theme

CHAPTER SUMMARY

Opening Screen

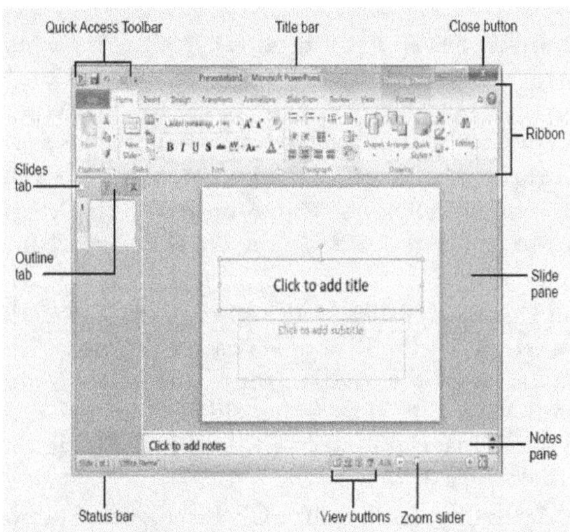

Fundamentals

The File tab menu and Backstage view contain commands for working with a program's files, including New, Open, Save, Print and Close.

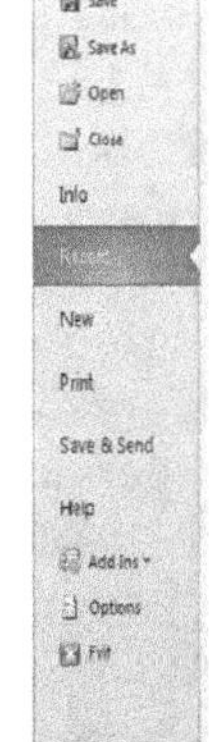

To Create a New Presentation: Click the **File** tab, click **New**, and click **Create**. Or, press **Ctrl + N**.

To Open a Presentation: Click the **File** tab and click **Open**, or press **Ctrl + O**.

To Save a Presentation: Click the **Save** button on the Quick Access Toolbar, or press **Ctrl + S**.

To Save a Presentation with a Different Name: Click the **File** tab, click **Save As**, enter a new name for the presentation, and click **Save**.

To Preview and Print a Presentation: Click the **File** tab and click **Print**, or press **Ctrl + P**.

To Close a Presentation: Click the **File** tab and click **Close**, or press **Ctrl + W**.

To Get Help: Press **F1** to open the Help window. Type your question and press **Enter**.

To Exit PowerPoint: Click the **File** tab and click **Exit**.

To Insert a New Slide: Click the **Home** tab and click **New Slide** in the Slides group, or press **Ctrl + M**.

To Change the Slide Layout: Click the **Home** tab, click the **Layout** button in the Slides group, and select a layout.

To Return a Slide to its Default Settings: Click the **Home** tab and click the **Reset** button in the Slides group.

To Apply Theme to a Document: Click the **Design** tab on the Ribbon, click the ＝ **More** button in the Themes group, and select a theme from the gallery.

To Change the Slide Background: Click the **Design** tab on the Ribbon, click the **Background Styles** button in the Background group, and select a background.

To View the Slide Master: Click the **View** tab on the Ribbon, click the **Slide Master** button in the Master Views group, and click the **Slide Master** or the appropriate **Layout Master** in the Outline pane.

To Insert a Header or Footer: Click the **Insert** tab on the Ribbon and click the **Header & Footer** button in the Text group. Select the option(s) that you want and click **Apply** or **Apply to All**.

To Add a Section: Click the **Home** tab on the Ribbon, click the **Section** button in the Slides group, and click **Add Section**.

Formatting

To Cut or Copy Text: Select the text you want to cut or copy and click the **Cut** or **Copy** button in the Clipboard group on the Home tab.

To Paste Text: Place the insertion point where you want to paste and click the **Paste** button in the Clipboard group on the Home tab.

To Format Selected Text: Use the commands in the Font group on the Home tab, or click the **Dialog Box Launcher** in the Font group to open the Font dialog box.

To Copy Formatting with the Format Painter: Select the text with the formatting you want to copy and click the **Format Painter** button in the Clipboard group on the Home tab. Then, select the text you want to apply the copied formatting to.

To Change Paragraph Alignment: Select the paragraph(s) and click the appropriate alignment button (**Align Left**, **Center**, **Align Right**, or **Justify**) in the Paragraph group on the Home tab.

To Create a Bulleted or Numbered List: Select the paragraphs you want to bullet or number and click the **Bullets** or **Numbering** button in the Paragraph group on the Home tab.

To Change Paragraph Line Spacing: Select the paragraph(s), click the **Line Spacing** button in the Paragraph group on the Home tab, and select an option from the list.

To Correct a Spelling Error: Right-click the error and select a correction from the contextual menu. Or, press **F7** to run the Spell Checker.

Transitions and Animation Effects

To Add a Slide Transition: Navigate to the slide you want to add a transition to. Click the **Transitions** tab on the Ribbon, click the **More** button in the Transition to This Slide group, and select a transition effect.

To Add an Animation Effect to an Object: Select the object that you want to animate, click the **Animations** tab on the Ribbon. Click the **More** button in the Animation group, and select an animation effect.

To Copy Animation Effects from One Object to Another: Select the object with the animation effect you want to copy, click the **Animations** tab on the Ribbon, and click the **Animation Painter** button in the Advanced Animation group. Then, click the object you want to apply the copied animation effect to.

Images, Multimedia, and Objects

To Insert a Picture: Click the **Insert** tab on the Ribbon and click the **Picture** button in the Illustrations group. Find the picture you want to insert and click **Insert**.

To Insert a Clip Art Graphic: Click the **Insert** tab on the Ribbon and click the **Clip Art** button in the Images group. Type the name of what you're looking for in the "Search for" box and click **Go**.

To Insert a Video file: Click the **Insert** tab on the Ribbon and click the **Video** button in the Media group. Find the video you want to insert and click **Insert**.

To Insert a Video from the Web: Click the **Insert** tab on the Ribbon, click the **Video** button list arrow in the Media group, and select **Video from Web Site**. Paste the video's **Embed** code into the Insert Video from Web Site dialog box and click **Insert**.

To Insert an Audio clip: Click the **Insert** tab on the Ribbon, click the **Audio** button list arrow in the Media group, and select **Audio from File**. Find the audio clip that you want to insert and click **Insert**.

To Draw a Shape: Click the **Insert** tab on the Ribbon, click the **Shapes** button in the Shapes group, and select the shape you want to insert. Then, click where you want to draw the shape and drag until the shape reaches the desired size. Hold down the **Shift** key while you drag to draw a perfectly proportioned shape or straight line.

To Insert SmartArt: Click the **Insert** tab on the Ribbon and click the **SmartArt** button in the Illustrations group. Select the SmartArt you want to insert and click **OK**.

To Format an Object: Double-click the object and use the commands located on the Format tab.

To Move an Object: Click the object and drag it to a new location. Release the mouse button when you're finished.

To Resize an Object: Click the object to select it, click and drag one of its sizing handles (⬚○⬚), and release the mouse button when the object reaches the desired size. Hold down the **Shift** key while dragging to maintain the object's proportions while resizing it.

To Delete an Object: Select the object and press the **Delete** key.

The Outline Pane

The **Slides** tab contains a thumbnail image of every slide in the presentation; click a thumbnail to jump to that slide. You can also rearrange, add, or delete slides here.

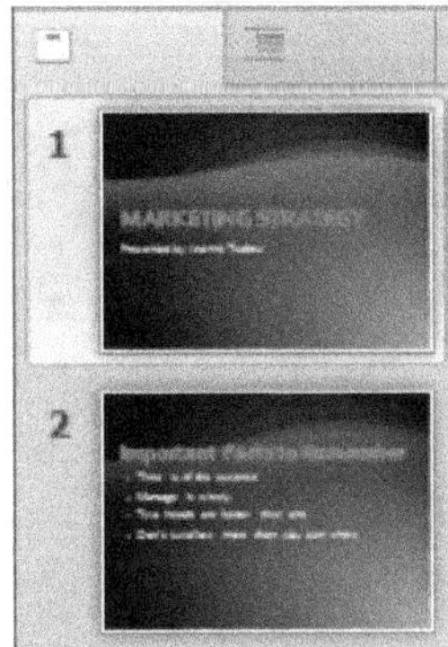

The **Outline** tab focuses on the content of the presentation. Use this tab when you want to adjust the textual structure or add large amounts of text.

Views

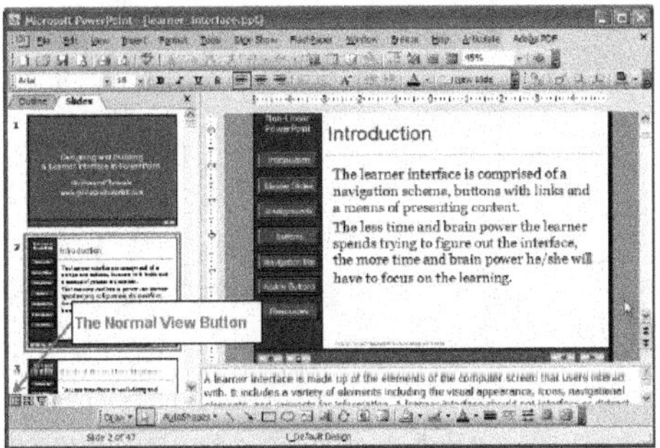

Normal View: This is the default view in PowerPoint. Normal view includes the Outline pane, Slide pane, and Notes pane.

Slide Sorter View: It displays all the slides in the presentation as thumbnails (tiny images). Use Slide Sorter view when you want to rearrange the order of slides or add transition effects between slides.

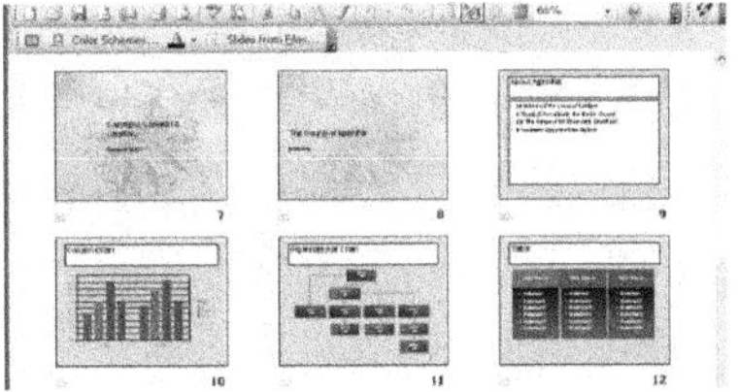

Reading View: Similar to Slide Show view, it displays the presentation in a window with simple controls, making it easy to review.

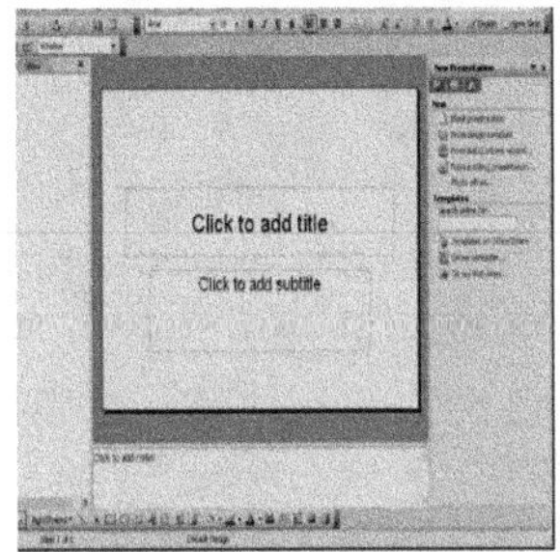

Slide Show view: It displays the presentation as an electronic slide show. Whenever you deliver a presentation in front of an audience, Slide Show view is definitely the view you want to use.

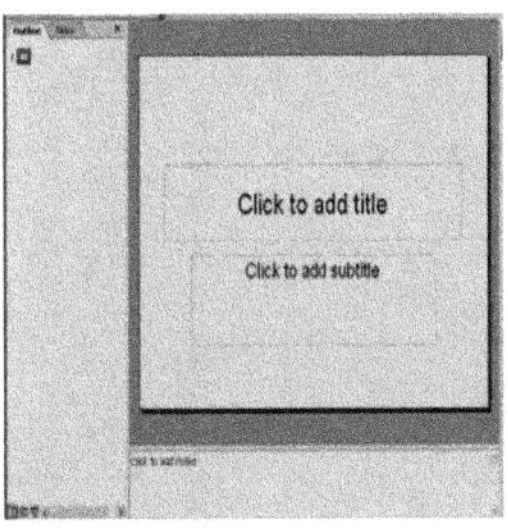

Slide Show Delivery

To Present a Slide Show: Click the **Slide Show** button on the status bar, or press **F5**.

To Use the Laser Pointer: In Slide Show view, press and hold down the **Ctrl** key while clicking and holding the **left mouse button**.

To Use the Pen: In Slide Show view, press **Ctrl + P** and then draw on the screen. Press **Ctrl + A** to switch back to the arrow pointer. Press **E** to erase your doodles.

To Advance to the Next Slide: Press **Spacebar**. Or, click the **left mouse button**.

To Go Back to the Previous Slide: Press **Backspace** or **Page Up**.

To Add Slide Timings: Click the **Slide Show** tab on the Ribbon and click the **Rehearse Timings** button in the Set Up group. Navigate through the presentation, pausing on each slide for the amount of time you wish to display it during your show. Click **Yes** to save your timings.

To End a Slide Show: Press **Esc**.

Working with Slides Master and Themes

Slide master is simple way of applying changes to the entire slide. Every presentation has at least one slide master, but you can have more than one. Given below are the steps to customize your slide master.

Step 1 – Go to the Master Views group under the View ribbon.

Step 2 – Click on **Slide Master** to open the **Slide Master** Ribbon.

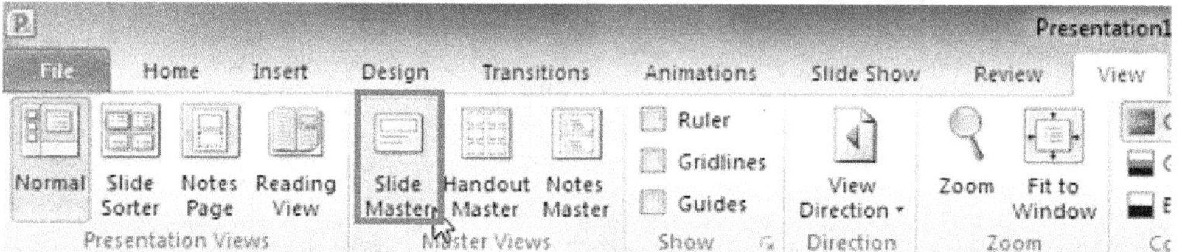

The top most slide in the left sidebar is the **Master** slide. All the slides within this master template will follow the settings you add on this master slide.

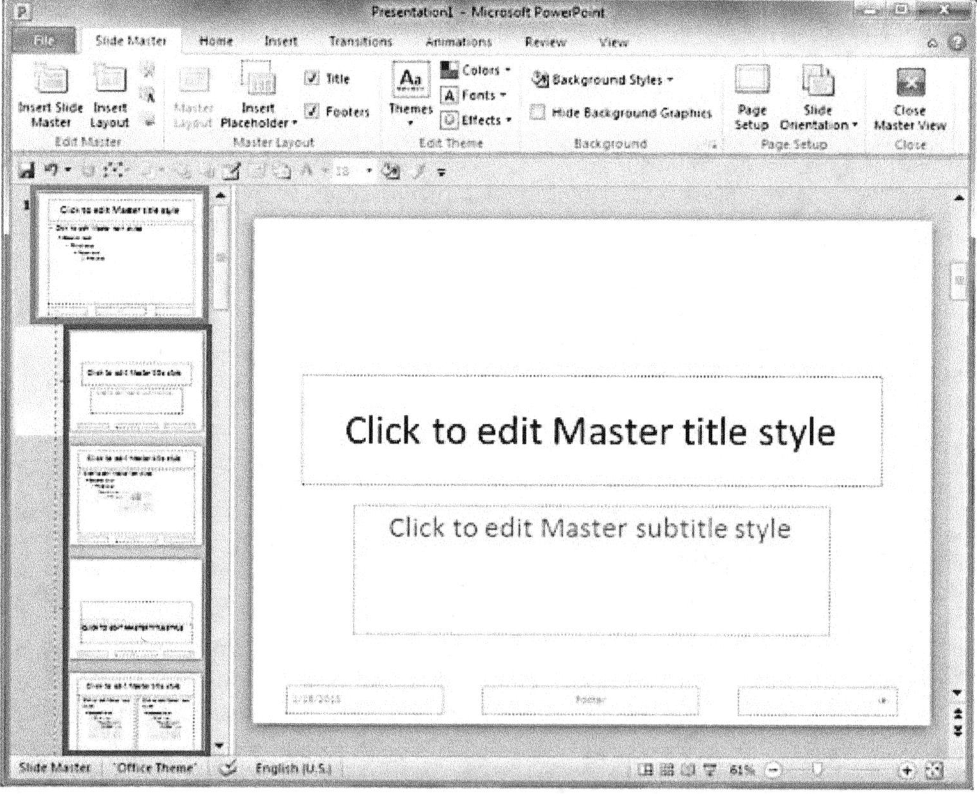

Step 3 – You can make changes to the master slide in terms of the theme, design, font properties, position and size of the title and other content using the remaining ribbons which are still accessible.

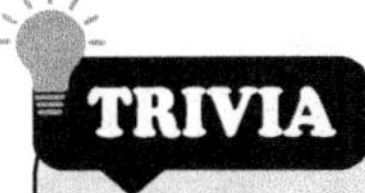

The three most commonly used passwords in the world are 123456, password and 12345.

Applying a Theme

1. Click on the **Design** tab at the top of the screen.
2. Within the **Themes** section of the ribbon, several built-in templates are available for use. To select a theme, simply click on it. You can also preview a theme by hovering your mouse over each theme for one to two seconds.

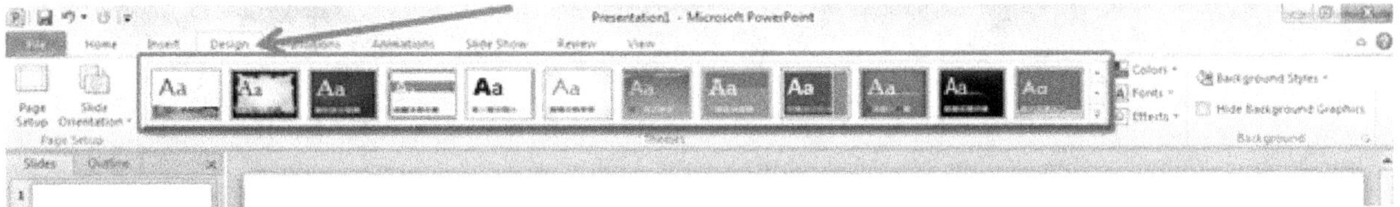

Keyboard Shortcuts

Command	Shortcut
Open a Presentation	**Ctrl + O**
Create New	**Ctrl + N**
Save a Presentation	**Ctrl + S**
Print a Presentation	**Ctrl + P**
Close a Presentation	**Ctrl + W**
Insert a New Slide	**Ctrl + M**
Help	**F1**
Editing	
Cut	**Ctrl + X**
Copy	**Ctrl + C**
Paste	**Ctrl + V**
Undo	**Ctrl + Z**
Redo or Repeat	**Ctrl + Y**
Find	**Ctrl + F**
Replace	**Ctrl + H**
Select All	**Ctrl + A**

Formatting	
Bold	**Ctrl + B**
Italics	**Ctrl + I**
Align Left	**Ctrl + L**
Center	**Ctrl + E**
Justify	**Ctrl + J**
Navigation	
The Next Slide	**Spacebar**
The Previous Slide	**Backspace**
Slide Show Delivery	
Begin Slide Show	**F5**
Resume Slide Show	**Shift + F5**
End Slide Show	**Esc**
Jump to Slide	*Slide* **# + Enter**
Toggle Screen Black	**B**
Toggle Screen White	**W**
Pause Show	**S**
Show/Hide Pointer	**A**
Change Arrow to Pen	**Ctrl + P**
Change Pen to Arrow	**Ctrl + A**
Erase Doodles	**E**

➡ The Slides tab contains a thumbnail image of every slide in the presentation.
➡ The Outline tab focuses on the content of the presentation.
➡ Slide master is simple way of applying changes to the entire slide.

1. The File tab menu and _______ view contain commands for working with a program's files including New, Open, Save etc.
   (a) Normal View   (b) Backstage View
   (c) Slide View   (d) None of these

2. _______ is not present in Design tab.
   (a) Page Setup
   (b) Background Styles
   (c) Slide Orientation
   (d) Rehearse Timings

3. To automatically place your school logo at the same position on every slide, you should insert the school logo on the _______.
   (a) Handout master   (b) Notes master
   (c) Slide master   (d) All of these

4. Use the _______ tab, to insert an image to your presentation.
   (a) Home   (b) Design
   (c) Insert   (d) All of these

5. In slide show view, the movement that you see when one slide changes to another is called a _______.
   (a) Transition   (b) Animation
   (c) Fade   (d) View

6. To correct a spelling error found in spell check, _______ on the misspelled word.
   (a) Double click   (b) Hover over
   (c) Right click   (d) None of these

7. _______ is generally the first slide of the presentation. It is used to introduce a topic and set the tone for the presentation.
   (a) Table slide   (b) Graph slide
   (c) Bullet slide   (d) Title slide

8. Select the _______ view at the bottom of the PowerPoint window to present your presentation.
   (a) [icon]   (b) [icon]
   (c) [icon]   (d) [icon]

9. The print pane in the Backstage view can _______.
   (a) Adjust the page orientation
   (b) View the print preview
   (c) Print your presentation
   (d) All of these

10. _______ is not a transition effect.
    (a) Blinks diagonal   (b) Dissolve
    (c) Fade   (d) Blinds

11. Given below are a few actions. Which of the following can you assign to a slide object or an action button?
    (a) Run a macro   (b) Play a sound
    (c) Hyperlink   (d) All of these

12. You can change a bullet's _______.
    (a) Color   (b) Size
    (c) Shape   (d) All of these

13. When you hide a slide, the hidden slide _______.
    (a) Is not displayed in the slide show
    (b) Is deleted
    (c) Content is hidden, and a blank slide is displayed in lieu
    (d) Contents are deleted

14. A multi-hierarchical list is also called a _______.
    (a) Multilevel list   (b) Animated list
    (c) Distributed list (d) Tracked list

15. When the Draw Table feature is selected, the mouse pointer appears as a _______.
    (a) Solid plus sign   (b) Solid arrow
    (c) I-beam   (d) Pencil

16. The brightness and contrast of an image can be adjusted using the _______ command.
    (a) Color
    (b) Compress Pictures
    (c) Corrections
    (d) Crop

17. To add shadow to a shape, use the _______ tool.
    (a) Shape Fill   (b) Shape Outline
    (c) Shape Effects   (d) Send Backwards

18. To display a context on a slide, _______.
    (a) Click the shortcut button on the Home Tab
    (b) Right click on the current slide
    (c) Click an object on the current slide
    (d) All of these

19. When text in a placeholder does not fit in one slide, you can split Text Between Two slides by using the ___________ that appears when the slide is filled.
   (a) Auto Fit Options Button
   (b) Split Slide Option Button
   (c) Distribute Text Option Button
   (d) Format slide Option Button

20. ______ is not a type of an animation effect.
   (a) Entrance   (b) Equation
   (c) Emphasis   (d) Exit

21. If you have two copies of your presentation with some changes in both, you can combine the copy with original presentation, and then accept or discard changes into the presentation. Which of the following features of PowerPoint will allow you to do this?
   (a) Track changes
   (b) Document inspector
   (c) Compare
   (d) Custom Animation

22. ___________ gives a printed copy of your presentation.
   (a) Outline
   (b) Speaker notes
   (c) Audience handouts
   (d) All of these

23. You can use the ___________ option to add voice-over narration to your PowerPoint presentation.
   (a) Create Video
   (b) Rehearse Timings
   (c) Broadcast Presentation
   (d) Record Side Show

24. When you are working on a slide in Normal view, where is the slide number indicated?
   (a) On the right side of the status bar
   (b) On the left side of the status bar
   (c) At the centre of the status bar
   (d) In the Screen Tip box

25. Placeholders cannot be ______.
   (a) Stretched to fit across multiple slides
   (b) Moved, resized and rearranged
   (c) Rearranged with the layout feature
   (d) Reset after changes have been made

HOTS

1. In MS PowerPoint, when the insertion point is flashing in a box, what should be pressed to select the text box itself?
   (a) Alt   (b) Esc
   (c) Ctrl   (d) Alt + Ctrl

2. While making a presentation in MS-Power Point, Sheetal has set different slide timing on individual slides. Now she wants to check the timing of slide, which view is the best for the purpose?

   (a) 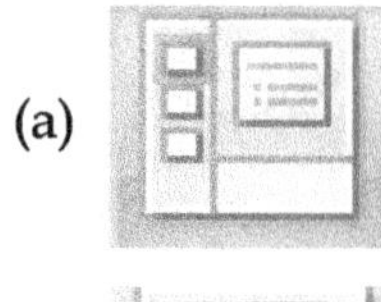   (b) 

   (c)    (d) 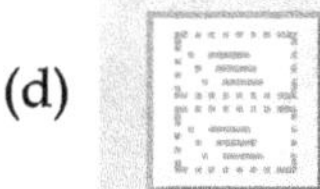

3. In normal view, how can you quickly change to handout master view?
   (a) Click the outline tab and select handout master view
   (b) Press the shift key and click the handout master view button
   (c) On the view menu, click slide sorter, and click handouts.
   (d) Ctrl + F11

4. How can you quickly reinstate a deleted footer placeholder in master view?
   (a) Re-apply the slide layout
   (b) Create a new slide master
   (c) Re-apply the footer placeholder
   (d) Reinsert the slide

5. Which of the following allows you to select more than one slide in a presentation?
   (a) Ctrl + Click each slide
   (b) Shift + Click each slide
   (c) Alt + Click each slide
   (d) Shift + drag each slide

1. How can you view the Slide Master?

Ans.

Click the **View** tab on the Ribbon, click the **Slide Master** button in the Master View group, and click the **Slide Master** or the appropriate **Layout Master** in the Outline pane.

2. What are the steps to add transitions and animation effects?

Ans.

To Add a Slide Transition: Navigate to the slide you want to add a transition to. Click the **Transitions** tab on the Ribbon, click the ▽ **More** button in the Transition to This Slide group, and select a transition effect.

To Add an Animation Effect to an Object: Select the object that you want to animate, click the **Animations** tab on the Ribbon. Click the ▽ **More** button in the Animation group, and select an animation effect.

3. Write the steps for customizing and Broadcasting Slide Shows.

Ans.

Following are the steps for customizing the slide show:

- With respect to class 7 computer lessons, a slideshow is nothing but the created presentation can be displayed on a full screen making it more presentable.
- These slide shows are created with animated effects to text and graphics.
- There are a variety of animations and effects that can be applied to text or graphics.

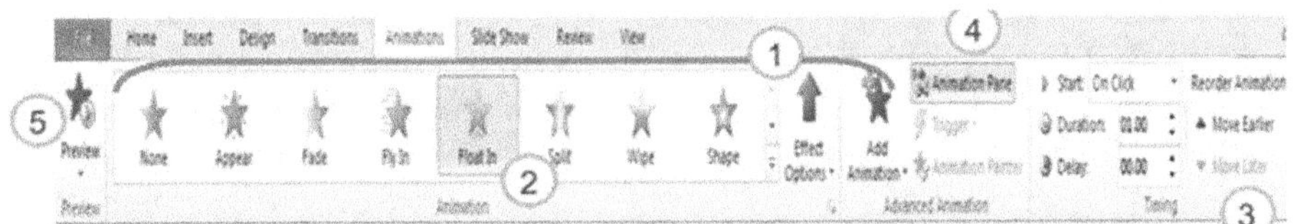

i. The Effect Options – has additional animation options in the Animation group. It adds value to the animation options to animate text and graphics upon Entrance, Exit and as an Emphasis.

ii. When the pointer is moved over any animation, it will be highlighted in a golden colour and a preview of the animation will appear. We can check the preview and then the same to all the slides.

iii. The Timing group allows you to set the exact time to play the selected animations. It can set automatically after a few seconds or minutes. It can also be set with the click of a mouse.

iv. The Animation Pane displays all of the animations you have applied to each slide.

v. Finally, preview command helps you to preview the current slide.

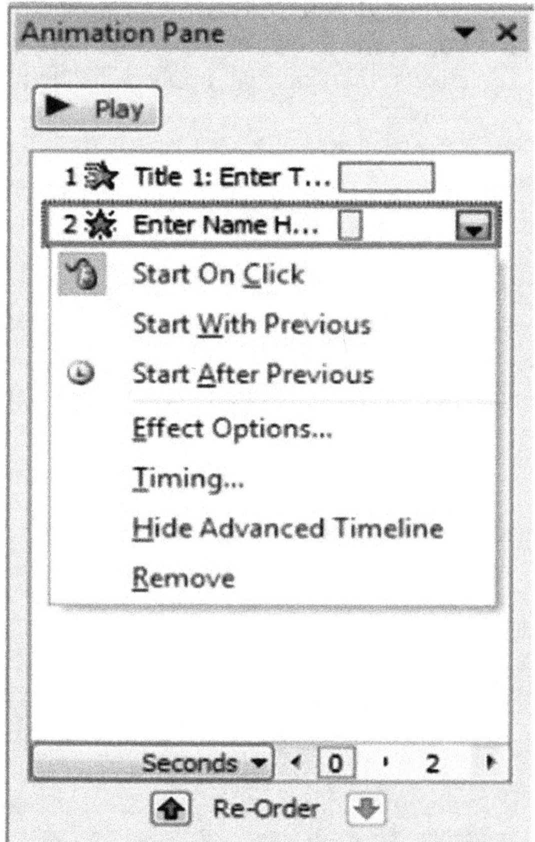

4. How can you use different Views from the PowerPoint Window?

Ans.

There are view buttons in the bottom-right corner of the PowerPoint window. From here, you can change the view to Normal, Slide Sorter, Reading or Slide Show by just clicking on them.

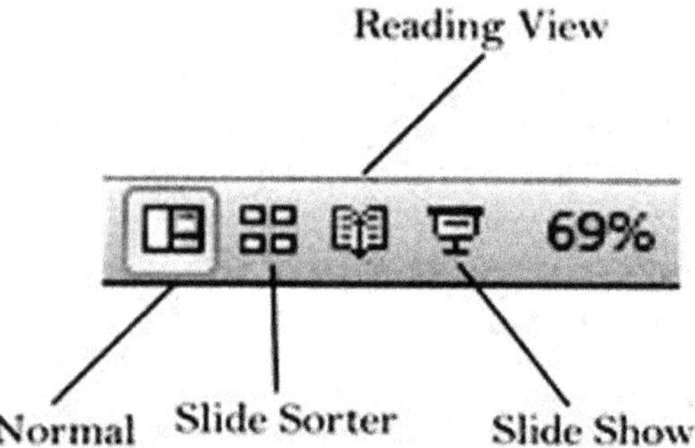

- **Normal View:** Normal is the default view where you can create and edit your slides in center slide pane and all of the slides will appear on the slides tab in the left task pane.
- **Slide Sorter:** Slide sorter is a view of your slides in thumbnail form. The slides are presented horizontally, which allow you to see more slides at the same time.
- **Reading View:** When you click on this view, it fills the PowerPoint window with a preview of your presentation.
- **Slide Show view:** Play your slide show in the PowerPoint window to see animation and transitions without switching to the full-screen slide show.

5. How you can Insert Music or Sound in a Slide?

Ans.

PowerPoint allows you to add sound to your presentation in several ways. You can do this by using a sound file on your computer, choose from hundreds of sounds available through the audio on my PC, or play tracks from an audio CD. PowerPoint also allows you to use sound from 'Online Audio' options so you can play the sounds that you want.

To insert a sound file from your computer:
- Select the slide where you want to add sound.
- Select the **Insert** tab.
- Click the drop-down arrow on the **Audio** command in the **Media** group.

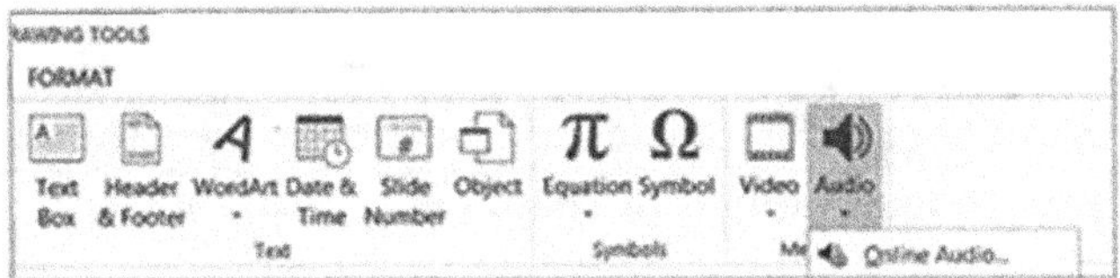

- Select Audio on My PC from the menu. The Insert Sound dialog box will appear.

- Locate the sound file on your computer.
- Select the file.
- Click Insert.

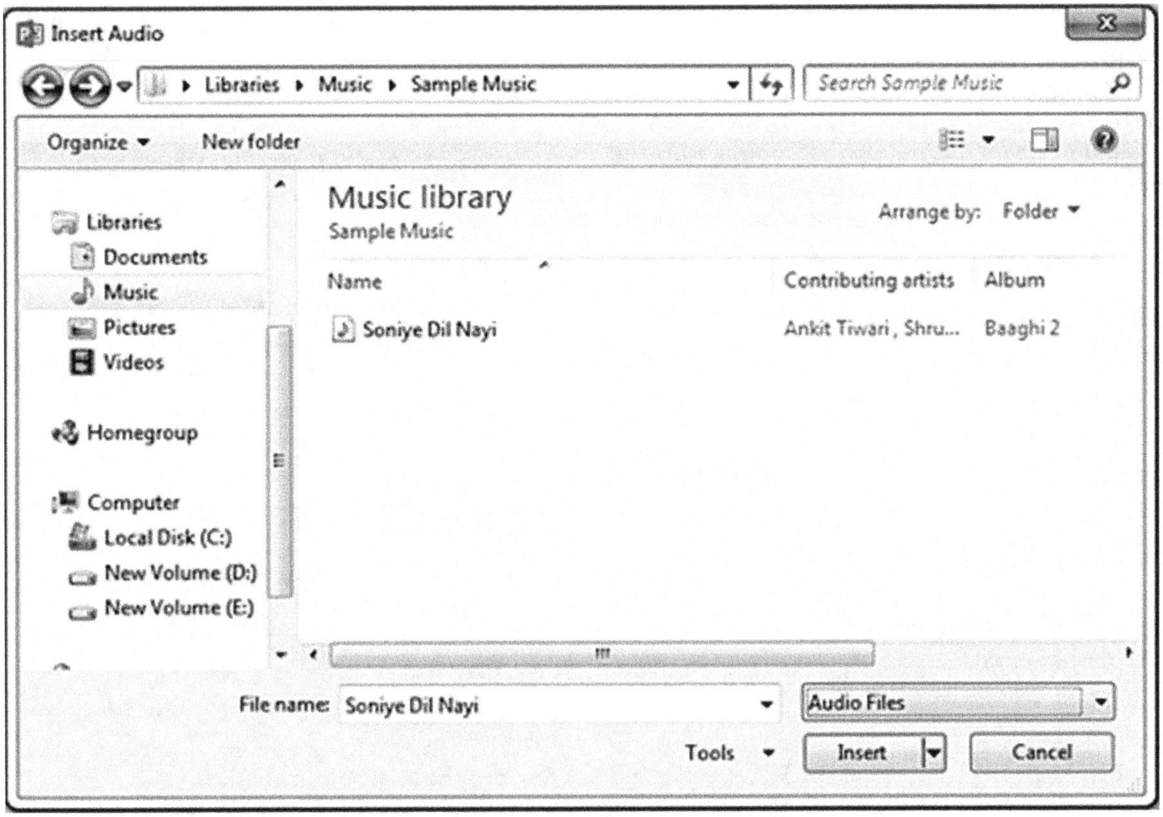

Select Automatically or When Clicked. Automatically will start the sound automatically as soon as the slide appears in slide show view, while when Clicked will start the sound when you click.

Programming in QBASIC 6

Learning Objectives : In this chapter, students will learn about:
- ✓ Basics of QBasic

CHAPTER SUMMARY

QuickBASIC is an easy-to-learn programming language (and therefore ideal for beginners), based on DOS operating system, but also executable on Windows.

QBASIC is the slimmed-down version of QuickBASIC. Compared to **QuickBASIC**, QBASIC is limited as it lacks a compiler. Therefore QBASIC cannot be used to produce executables (.exe files). The source code (usually files with .bas extension) can only be executed immediately by the built-in QBASIC interpreter. Furthermore, QuickBASIC has a more extensive command set than QBASIC.

Syntax Example

Example: Hello, World - Shortest version:

    ? "Hello, World"

Example: Hello, World - Extended version:

    CLS
    PRINT "Hello, World"
    END

Example: 99 bottles of soft drink:

    LET BOTTLES = 99: LET BOTTLES$ = "99":
    LET BOTTLE$ = "bottles"
    FOR A = 1 TO 99
    PRINT BOTTLES$; BOTTLE$; "of soft drink
    on the wall,"; BOTTLES$; BOTTLE$; "of soft
    drink."
    LET BOTTLES = BOTTLES - 1
    IF BOTTLES > 0 THEN LET BOTTLES$ =
    LTRIM$(STR$(BOTTLES)): LET PRONOUN$
    = "one"
    IF BOTTLES = 0 THEN LET BOTTLES$ = "no
    more": LET PRONOUN$ = "it"
    IF BOTTLES <> 1 THEN LET BOTTLE$ =
    "bottles"
    IF BOTTLES = 1 THEN LET BOTTLE$ =
    "bottle"
    PRINT "Take"; PRONOUN$; "down and pass
    it around,"; BOTTLES$; BOTTLE$; "of soft
    drink on the wall."
    PRINT: NEXT A
    PRINT "No more bottles of soft drink on the
    wall, no more bottles of soft drink."
    PRINT "Go to the store and buy some more,
    99 bottles of soft drink on the wall."

> **TRIVIA**
>
> Bill Gate's house was designed on a Mac computer.

Key Points

Microsoft's Visual Basic was the successor of QuickBASIC.

Here are the key points about it:

1. A project is saved with extension (.vbp).
2. A form is saved with extension (.frm).
3. Every control on the toolbox has properties used to change or modify that control's behavior and appearance on the form. These are displayed in properties Window.

4. Before you can create a Visual Basic Program, you must first create a Visual Basic Project (.vbp) and decide where you want to store it. A Visual Basic project can consist of multiple files and forms that represent different parts of your entire Visual Basic Program. To keep your project organized, Visual Basic creates a new folder and creates all the files/forms that make up your Visual Basic program into it.

5. The dotted pattern on the form is called Grid. When you move items, they only ('snap') form one point to another. This is a useful feature to align and lay the elements nicely over the form.

6. When you open code window, it shows the ' name of the object' for which the code is being written and 'the event' to which the code for this object will respond. In the above window, the code is for CMD-SHOW button and shall execute when user clicks this button. In the drop down list boxes, all the objects used in the form and all possible events associated with that object are listed.

7. As you type, Visual Basic text editor checks each and every word and code phrase. Words that appear/become blue are called keywords or reserved words. Similarly, when you apostrophe (') before some code, it becomes green (from apostrophe (') to end that line only). These are known as comments and are used to make code more understandable. Comments are not executed and have no effect on the program.

8. BASIC code consists of programming commands that tell the computer, step by step, what to do.

9. The most common elements of a user interface are:
   ■ Windows (also called Forms)
   ■ Controls.

10. Generally, the first screen that you open VB is the New Project screen. If this is not the case you can open the New Project screen using File > New Project or Ctrl + N.

11. Captain property is used to change the captain of the control e.g. Form, Label, Command Button, etc.

12. Front property is used to change the style and size for the controls like label, command button, etc.

13. Now () Return the current date and time together.

14. Hour () Returns an integer specifying a whole number 0 and 23 represent the hour of the day.

15. Minute () Returns an integer specifying a whole number between 0 and 59 represent the minute of the day.

16. Second () Returns an integer specifying a whole number between 0 and 59 represent the second of the minute.

17. 'BackColor' property is used to change the background colour of the form.

18. "ForeColor" property is used to change the foreground colour of label.

19. You can select multiple labels by clicking with mouse holding the Ctrl key.

20. .exe is the extension for the executable application in VB.

21. Image control is used to place an image on the form.

22. Stretch property of image control make an image fit to the size of the control if set to true.

➡ QBASIC is the slimmed-down version of QuickBASIC.
➡ QuickBASIC has a more extensive command set than QBASIC.
➡ Microsoft's Visual Basic was the successor of QuickBASIC.

1. What is the group instructions directing a computer called?
   (a) Storage
   (b) Memory
   (c) Logic
   (d) Program

2. What is the full form of BASIC?
   (a) Beginners All Purpose Symbolic Instruction Code
   (a) Basic All program Symbolic Integrated Computer
   (c) Basic All proper Symbolic Insert Code
   (d) Basic All print Syntax Instruction Code

3. Which of the following is the file name of QBASIC program?
   (a) QBasic.exe
   (b) QBASIC.doc
   (c) QBasic.ppt
   (d) QBASIC.xis

4. BASIC was developed in the year _________.
   (a) 1964
   (b) 1966
   (c) 1968
   (d) 1962

5. What is the shortcut key to run a QBASIC program?
   (a) Alt + F9
   (b) Alt + F5
   (c) Shift + F5
   (d) Shift + F9

6. If the QBASIC window fills the entire screen, you can press ________ to make it smaller?
   (a) Alt + Enter
   (b) Alt + Esc
   (c) Alt + Fa
   (d) Alt + F5

7. In BASIC language, what are the values which do not change during the execution of program?
   (a) Variables
   (b) Constants
   (c) Operators
   (d) Error

8. How are the string constants represented?
   (a) They are enclosed in a double quotation mark
   (b) They are enclosed in a single quotation mark
   (c) They are enclosed in square brackets
   (d) They are enclosed in parentheses

9. Which of the following is an INVALID representation of constants in QBASIC language?
   (a) "Hello"
   (b) "16/10/2005"
   (c) 0.742
   (d) "Q"BASIC"

10. In QBASIC language, what are the quantities which change values during the execution of a program?
    (a) Variables
    (b) Constants
    (c) Errors
    (d) Operators

11. String variables must end with a ______ sign?
    (a) S
    (b) +
    (c) –
    (d) @

12. Which of the following is an INVALID numeric variable?
    (a) T24
    (b) A
    (c) M2
    (d) 2B43

13. Which of the following is a string variable?
    (a) PS
    (b) M2
    (c) OB
    (d) TITLE

14. Which of the following are relational operators?
    (a) *
    (b) ^
    (c) AND
    (d) <>

15. What are instructions in QBASIC called?
    (a) Operators
    (b) Programs
    (c) Statement
    (d) String

16. What is the input command for string values?
    (a) INPUT P
    (b) INPUT P$
    (c) INPUT $P
    (d) INPUT "P"

17. Which command is used to clear the screen of QBASIC windows?
    (a) REM
    (b) NOT
    (c) CLR
    (d) CLS

18. What will the given command do?
    LET C = A + B
    (a) The string variable C receives the value of A + B
    (b) The numerical valuable C is assigned the value of A + B
    (c) The string variable C is assigned the expression A + B
    (d) An error message is displayed

19. What is the output of the given program?
    10 INPUT "Enter your favorite subject" 20 END
    (a) Computer
    (b) Favorite
    (c) Subject =
    (d) Enter your favorite subject

20. Which statement is used for writing comments in the QBASIC program?

    (a) LET   (b) REM
    (c) INPUT   (d) PRINT

21. In the given QBASIC statement, which is the variable?

    LET Q$ = "QBASIC"

    (a) Q   (b) 10
    (c) LET   (d) "Q BASIC'

22. What will the output of the given QBASIC program?

    LET P$ = "BRAIN"
    LET Q$ = "MAPPING"
    LET R$ = P$ + Q$
    PRINT R$

    (a) BRAIN MAPPING
    (b) MAPPING BRAIN
    (c) BRAINMAPPING
    (d) None of these

23. Identify the number of row which has an arrow.

    10 REM A program to find the even and odd numbers
    20 CLS
    30 INPUT "Enter number", a
    40 IF A%2 = 0 THEN
    50 PRINT A; "is even number"
    60 ELSE
    70 PRINT A; "is odd numbers'
    80 END

    (a) 40   (b) 30
    (c) 80   (d) 10

24. Which of the following operators are used in conditional statement?

    (a) Relational operators
    (b) Logical operators
    (c) Arithmetic operators
    (d) Bitwise operators

25. Ankit wrote the given program in QBASIC. But while executing it, an error occurred. Identify the error.

    10 LET A$ = "INDIA"
    20 LET B$ = A$ + "1"
    30 PRINT B$$

    (a) Line 20 has a string to assign numeric
    (b) Line 30 has too many $ signs
    (c) Line 10 has directly given string to a variable
    (d) There is no error in the program

26. Which of the following is a valid numeric constant?

    (a) 0/A   (b) 46.25
    (c) Basic   (d) "56478"

27. Which of the following BASIC commands is used to enter values while the program is being executed?

    (a) LET   (b) PRINT
    (c) INPUT   (d) GOTO

28. What is the output of the following program?

    age = 10
    DO
    PRINT age
    Age = age + 1
    LOOP WHILE age < 10

    (a) 9   (b) 11
    (c) 10   (d) 12

29. In high resolution mode, the screen is divided into _____ horizontal and ____ vertical pixels.

    (a) 320, 200   (b) 200, 320
    (c) 640, 200   (d) 640, 400

30. When you use a ______ in a PRINT statement, the items are printed without any spaces between them

    (a) SEMI COLON (:)   (b) TAB
    (c) SPACE   (d) COMMA (,)

31. In high resolution mode, what are the coordinates for the bottom right corner of the screen?

    (a) (639, 199)   (b) (639, 0)
    (c) (0, 639)   (d) (199, 639)

32. In this mode, a QBASIC statement is executed as soon as you press the Enter key. It is the __________.

    (a) Program Mode
    (b) Status Mode
    (c) Intermediate Mode
    (d) Immediate Mode

33. What will be the output of the following program?

```
DECLARE FUNCTION AREA(L,B)
LET L=10
4e3LET B=5 to LET B=5
PRINT "The area=";AREA(L,B)
END
FUNCTION AREA(L,B)
A=L*B
AREA=A
END FUNCTION
```

(a) The area = 35   (b) The area = 50
(c) The area = 15   (d) The area = 55

34. Which is the loop that is executed when the condition is false?
(a) FOR…NEXT
(b) DO WHILE…LOOP
(c) DO…LOOP WHILE
(d) DO UNTIL…LOOP

35. What is the default value of STEP in FOR… NEXT?
(a) –1   (b) 0
(c) 1   (d) 2

36. What will be the output if the following code is executed?

```
FOR N = 10 TO 5 STEP - 2
PRINT N;
NEXT I
```

(a) 10 8 6 4   (b) 10 8 6
(c) Error   (d) 10 8

37. For placing a comment in a program, we use _______.

(a) REM   (b) 'd'(apostrophe)
(c) Both (a) and (b)   (d) LET

38. Which statement is used to set the resolution of the display screen?
(a) CANVAS   (b) RESOLUTION
(c) LOCATE   (d) SCREEN

39. A GOTO statement _______.
(a) Instructs the computer to GOTO a specific line number
(b) Can be used to skip some statement
(c) Can be used to repeat some statements
(d) All of these

40. Which of the following is NOT a valid Screen mode?
(a) SCREEN 1   (b) SCREEN 5
(c) SCREEN 9   (d) SCREEN 13

41. What will be the output of the following code?

```
CLS
COLOR 14, 2
```

(a) Foreground color is set to yellow and Background color is set to green.
(b) Foreground color is set to green and Background color is set to yellow.
(c) Foreground color is set to green and Background color is set to default.
(d) Foreground color is set to blue and Background color is set to green.

42. This command fills in one pixel of the screen with a specified color. The coordinates of the pixel is only defined.
(a) GOSUB   (b) PSET
(c) SCREEN   (d) LINE

43. Which of the given line of codes will cause the computer to produce the following result?
If the value of a string variable is YES, transfer control to the line labeled ONE'
(a) IF A – "YES" THEN GOSUB ONE
(b) IF A$ = "YES" THEN GOSUB ONE
(c) GOSUB ONE IF A$ = "YES"
(d) IF A = "YES" TRANSFER ONE

44. What is the output of the following QBASIC code?

```
NAME$ = "BUNNY BINNY"
PRINT LEN (NAME$)
```

(a) 10   (b) 11
(c) 12   (d) 13

45. Which of the following is the correct command to make a box filled with yellow color in QBASIC?
(a) SCREEN 13
    LINE (60,10) – (60,10), 9, BF
(b) SCREEN 13
    LINE (10, 60) – (100,100), 13, B
(c) SCREEN 13
    LINE (10,60) – (100, 100), 14 BF
(d) SCREEN 13
    LINE (60,10) – (10, 60), 4 BF

1. What will be output of the given QBASIC code?

Code A	Code B
FOR 1 = 1 TO 5	FOR 1 = 1 TO 5
STEP 2	STEP 1
PRINT 1	PRINT 1
NEXT 1	I = I + 1 NEXT 1

   (a) Both will print
   1
   2
   3

   (b)

Code A	Code B
1	1
3	2
5	3
	4
	5

   (c)

Code A	Code B
1	1
3	2
5	4

   (d)

Code A	Code B
1	1
2	3
3	5
4	
5	

2. What is the correct QBASIC code to set the whole background to be red and foreground color to be yellow?
   (a) COLOR 6, 14
       PRINT "This text is yellow over Red"
   (b) COLOR 14, 4
       CLS
       PRINT "This text is yellow over Red"
   (c) COLOR 4, 14
       PRINT "This text is yellow over Red"
   (d) COLOR 4,14
       CLS
       PRINT "This text is yellow over Red"

3. It consists of sequence of characters which must be enclosed by quotation mark. It is known as _______?
   (a) Numeric Variable
   (b) Numeric Constant
   (c) String Variable
   (d) String Constant

4. Which of the following is not a reserved word or contain a space?
   (a) Numbers   (b) Strings
   (c) Constants   (d) Variable

5. These are formed from the character of the Qbasic character set. They are known as?
   (a) Reserved Word   (b) Variable
   (c) Constants   (d) Numbers

1. How does QBASIC differ from QuickBasic?

Ans.

   QBasic is the slimmed-down version of QuickBasic. Compared to **QuickBasic**, QBASIC is limited as it lacks a compiler. Therefore QBASIC cannot be used to produce executables (.exe files). The source code (usually files with .bas extension) can only be executed immediately by the built-in QBASIC interpreter. Furthermore, QuickBasic has a more extensive command set than QBASIC.

2. Write a program to input any number from 0 to 9 and check whether it is single digit number or not using SELECT CASE statement.

Ans.

```
CLS
INPUT"ENTER THE NUMBER";N
SELECT CASE N
CASE 0
PRINT "It is single"
CASE 1
```

PRINT "It is single"
CASE 2
PRINT "It is single"
CASE 3
PRINT "It is single"
CASE 4
PRINT "It is single"
CASE 5
PRINT "It is single"
CASE 6
PRINT "It is single"
CASE 7
PRINT "It is single"
CASE 8
PRINT "It is single"
CASE 9
PRINT "It is single"
CASE ELSE
PRINT "It is not single"
END SELECT
END

3. Write a program to enter any two numbers their Sum, Product and the Difference.

Ans.

```
CLS
Input " Enter any number" ;A
Input " Enter any number" ;B
Let Sum = A+B
Let Difference= A-B
Let Product = A*B
Print" the sum =" ;Sum
Print" the Difference =" ;Difference
Print" the Product =" ; Product
End
```

4. Write a program to input student's name, marks obtained in four different subjects, find the total and average marks.

Ans.

```
Cls
Input" Enter the name " ;N$
Input" Enter the marks in English" ;E
Input" Enter the marks in Maths" ;M
Input" Enter the marks in Science" ;S
Input" Enter the marks in Nepali" ;N
Let S=E+M+S+N
Let A=S/4
Print " The name of the student is" ;N$
Print " The total marks is" ;S
Print " The Average marks" ;A
End
```

5. Write a program to find 10%,20% and 30% of the input number.

Ans.

```
Cls
Input" Enter any number" ;N
Let T=10/100*N
Let Twe=20/100*N
Let Thi=30/100*N
Print " 10%of input number=" ;T
Print " 20%of input number=" ;Twe
Print " 30%of input number=" ;Thi
End
```

Internet and Viruses

Learning Objectives : In this chapter, students will learn about:
- ✓ Internet Explorer
- ✓ Internet safety

CHAPTER SUMMARY

Microsoft Edge is a web browser developed by Microsoft. Edge was introduced as a new browser with the release of Windows 10. It offers a simple and minimalist interface, making it that much easier to browse the Internet.

In previous versions of Windows, the default web browser was Internet Explorer. Starting with Windows 10, Edge has replaced IE as the new default browser.

Differences between Edge and Internet Explorer

If you've used a version of Windows 8.1 or earlier, you're probably used to browsing with Internet Explorer. Even though Edge is fairly similar to IE, you may need to adjust to some of these key differences between the two:

- Edge has taken the History, Downloads, and Favorites features and compressed them into one menu called the Hub.
- When you open Edge or a new tab, there's no address bar at the top of the window. Instead, the address bar will be in the center of the screen with the words Where to next? above it. This is still a standard address bar, capable of navigating to websites and performing searches, but it's just in a different location.
- In IE, the navigation buttons will show you a drop-down menu of your recently visited websites. Edge does not have this feature.
- Overall, Edge has a much simpler and more stripped-down interface than IE, making it a faster and more streamlined browser.

To open Edge

From the desktop, locate and select the Edge icon on the taskbar. You can also access it from the Start button.

To navigate to a website

In Edge, you can use the address bar to navigate to other websites and conduct web searches.

To navigate to a website, type a web address into the address bar, then press Enter.

To conduct a web search, type a search term into the address bar. A list of possible search terms will appear. Press Enter to search or select a suggestion.

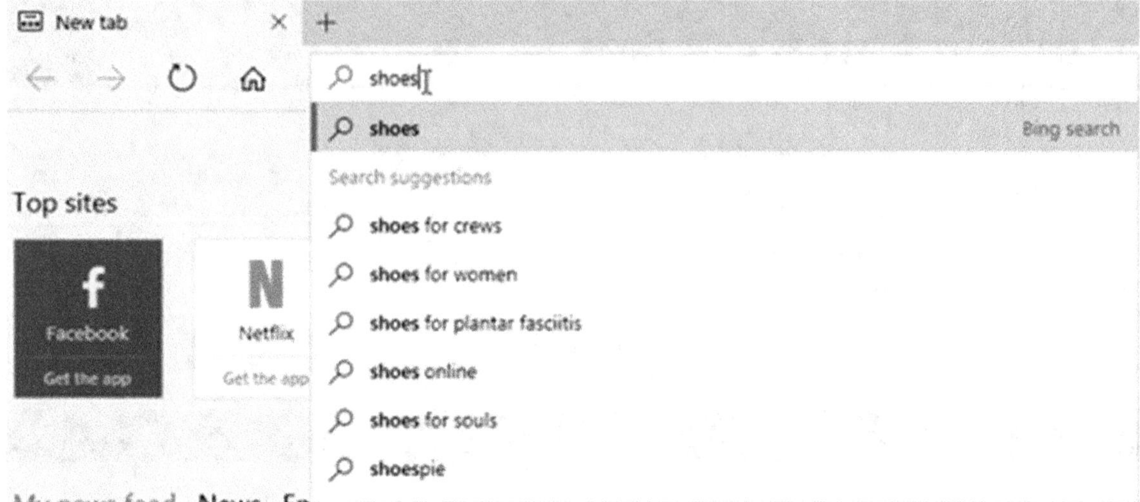

Navigating in Edge

Edge uses three main buttons for navigation: the Back, Forward, and Refresh buttons.

- The Back and Forward buttons allow you to move through pages you have recently viewed.
- The Refresh button will reload the current page. If a website stops working, try using the Refresh button. If a webpage doesn't load correctly, it will temporarily become the Stop button, which you can click to stop a webpage from loading.

Windows and tabs

Like all browsers, Edge allows you to open new windows to view different pages. In addition, Edge allows you to open multiple websites in the same window using tabs. Tabs are usually more convenient than opening several windows at the same time.

To open a new window: Click the More button, then select New window. You can also press Ctrl+N on your keyboard. The new window will appear.

To open a new tab: Click the New tab button next to the current open tab. You can also press Ctrl+T on your keyboard. The new tab will appear. Type an address, then press Enter to navigate to a new page. The page will appear in the new tab.

To switch between tabs: Click any tab that is not currently selected. The tab will be selected.

To close a tab: To close a tab, click the **X** located on the right side of that tab. You can also press Ctrl+W on your keyboard to close the current tab.

To open a link in a new tab: Tabs can also make it easier to browse the web. If you find a link to a website, you can open that link in a new tab. This allows you to open the site without losing your place on the original page.

Right-click the link you want to open, then select Open in new tab from the drop-down menu. The website will open in a new tab. Click the tab to view the website.

Browsing history

Like all browsers, Edge keeps a record of the websites you visit, which is known as your browsing history. Edge allows you to search your history to find a previously viewed page and delete your history for the sake of privacy.

To view your browsing history:

- Click the Hub button.
- Select the History tab.

In the History section, you can view your recent browsing history. The history includes every site you've viewed in the past. The list is sorted by date, so the most recent history appears at the top of the page. If you want to return to a website, simply click the link.

Downloading files

Edge can display many different types of documents, media, and other files, including PDF and MP3 files. But there may be times when you'll want to access a file outside of the browser. To do this, you'll need to download the file directly to your computer.

For example, let's say you need to complete and print a form you find online. You could download it to your computer, then open it with the appropriate program (such as Microsoft Word) to edit it.

To download a file

If you click a link to a file, it may download automatically. However, depending on the file type, it may just open within the browser. To prevent a file from opening in Edge, you can use Save Target As to download it to your computer. Right-click the file you want to download, then select Save target as. A dialog box will appear. Select the location where you want to save the file, enter a file name, and click Save. The file will begin downloading, and the download progress will appear at the bottom of the browser. When the download is complete, click Open to open the file.

For various reasons, many websites do not allow you to download content. For example, YouTube does not offer a way to download its videos.

To access your downloads

Edge makes it easy to view and manage all of your downloads. Click the Hub button, then select the Downloads button. The Downloads tab will appear with a list of all of your downloaded files. From here, you can open previously downloaded files and clear your list of downloads.

Malicious Web Scripts and Spywares

Malicious Web scripts are computer programs written to obtain proprietary information without permission. Preventing malicious Web scripts from attaching themselves to browsers has become increasingly difficult because of the following reasons:

- Many browsers are configured to provide increased functionality at the expense of security.
- A growing number of Web sites require users to enable certain features or install more software.

- Many users do not know how to configure Web browsers securely.
- Many users are unaware of how to determine if their computers have been compromised.
- A growing amount of proprietary information is finding its way into unauthorized hands.

Spyware is a general term describing software that performs a number of unwanted functions. It often infiltrates computers during software installation and is capable of:

- Changing a computer's settings.
- Causing a system to slow down or crash.
- Switching a Web browser's home page.
- Adding browser components that a user does not want or need.
- Causing large numbers of pop-up advertisements to appear.

What can you do to avoid these threats?

- Download software exclusively from reputable companies.
- Only visit legitimate Web sites.
- Rely on true experts, including IT professionals, to configure and maintain your network systems.

Following these steps can go a long way toward preventing malicious Web scripts and spyware from affecting the performance of a computer or network.

Samsung is 38 years and 1 month older than Apple.

Internet Safety
Internet Safety Tips for Teens

Many teenagers use the Internet to keep in touch with friends, find homework support and read the latest news. In addition to the millions of sites to visit and things to do, the Internet also gives teens many ways to get into trouble, or to be taken advantage of financially or physically. Teenagers should protect themselves online by:

- Never giving out key information such as full name, home address, phone number, passwords, and names of family members or credit card numbers.

- Using a nickname in chat rooms that is different from their real name.
- Telling a parent, or another adult, if a chat room conversation becomes uncomfortable.

Internet Safety Tips for Younger Children

For elementary school-age children, the Internet offers a wide range of learning opportunities, but it can also put their safety at risk. Youngsters can protect themselves online by getting parents' permission before:

- Giving out personal information, such as address, phone number and parents' work numbers.
- Sending a picture or other items.
- Installing software, or downloading programs or files from the internet.

Parents should learn how to monitor their children's online activity, including checking the history files to see which Web sites have been visited. They may also choose to install software that filters out inappropriate Web sites, monitors activity, blocks access to various kinds of sites, or blocks Internet access during specific times.

Preparation Saves Time and Money

A computer virus is a software program designed to replicate itself and spread to other computers. Viruses can spread through USB drives, CD-ROMs, email attachments and the Internet. Signs that a computer is infected with a virus include:

- Slower-than-normal operation
- Crashing and re-starting every few minutes
- Malfunctioning of applications
- Inability to print correctly
- Distorted menus and dialog boxes.

Actions to prevent viruses include:

- Open attachments from known parties only.
- Install only commercial operating software from CD-ROMs or DVDs purchased from legitimate software vendors.
- Download software from reputable Web sites only.
- Install good anti-virus software.

If a computer becomes infected with a virus, taking the following steps can remove it:

- Install and update anti-virus software.
- Perform a thorough computer scan.
- Download, install and run a "malicious software removal" program. (**NOTE:** Virus removal software only eliminates existing viruses and does not prevent other viruses from infecting a system.)

Anatomy of a Worm

A worm is a software program that replicates itself over network computers. Unlike a virus, which may be programmed only to infect multiple files on one computer, worms are spread through email, instant messaging, file-sharing and the Internet to infect multiple computers. Worms come in "good" and "bad" varieties. "Good" worms may be used to download software patches to fix vulnerabilities in a system. "Good" worms, however, can increase network traffic considerably, slowing down a computer's operation. The best protection against harmful computer worms is:

- Using software produced only by reputable companies.
- Updating Anti-Virus and Anti-Spyware software regularly.
- Opening email messages from known parties only.

Spoofed and Forged Email

Spoofing consists of falsifying an identity or data to gain unauthorized access to a computer. Spoofing is easy because Simple Mail Transfer Protocol (SMTP), which enables the transfer of email from one server to another and lacks authentication. Tactics that spoofers and forgers use include:

- Sending email from a "system administrator" asking users to change their passwords and threatening to suspend their accounts if they do not comply.
- Posing as a person of authority and asking users to send them a copy of a password file or other sensitive information.

To prevent spoofing or forging, users should:

- Allow email to enter at a single point only.

- Configure mail delivery systems to prevent direct connection to SMTP ports.

Use cryptographic signatures to exchange authenticated email messages.

Stop Mobile Viruses

A mobile virus is a malicious computer program that targets mobile phones or wireless-enabled personal digital assistants (PDAs). As the number and complexity of wireless phone and PDA networks increase, it has become more difficult to secure networks against viruses. To prevent mobile viruses, users should:

- Be careful when accepting Bluetooth files.
- Deactivate Bluetooth functions if a device becomes infected.
- Delete messages from unknown senders.
- Avoid installing programs of uncertain origin.
- Download ring tones and games from official Web sites only.
- Delete the infected application and reinstall it.

Prevent RAT Infestation

Remote Access Trojans (RATs) are malicious software programs that control a computer through an Internet connection. A RAT can expose a user to scams and can enable a criminal to view and change a computer's files without the user's knowledge. RATs are often hidden in files that are downloaded from the Internet. They also appear in email or Instant Messages disguised as attachments. To keep RATs from infiltrating a computer, users should:

- Share their primary email addresses only with people they know.
- Use trusted software from reputable companies.
- Use a firewall.
- Keep operating, anti-virus and anti-spyware software updated.

- Malicious Web scripts are computer programs written to obtain proprietary information without permission.
- Spyware is a general term describing software that performs a number of unwanted functions.
- Viruses can spread through USB drives, CD-ROMs, email attachments and the Internet.
- Spoofing consists of falsifying an identity or data to gain unauthorized access to a computer.
- Remote Access Trojans (RATs) are malicious software programs that control a computer through an Internet connection.

1. Find the odd one out.
   (a) www.blogger.com
   (b) www.tumblr.com
   (c) www.blogspot.com
   (d) www.google.com

2. Identify this internet tool.
   It is used for locating information on the internet. It matches search terms with indexed pages.
   (a) Database
   (b) Deep Web
   (c) URL
   (d) Search Engine

3. You cannot browse websites on the internet using ______.
   (a) Broadband
   (b) Dial-up
   (c) 3G/4G
   (d) FTP

4. Which of the following is the use of the internet?
   (a) Software sharing
   (b) Organization promotion
   (c) On-line shopping
   (d) All of these

5. ______ is a program that is used to access various internet resources.
   (a) Address
   (b) Browser
   (c) Provider
   (d) Protocol

6. ______ is authoring/maintaining/adding/updating articles to an existing blog.
   (a) Weblog
   (b) Blogging
   (c) Links
   (d) Forum

7. Internet ______ are like 24-hour coffee shops with people eager to communicate anytime they want.
   (a) Online libraries
   (b) Chat room
   (c) Electronic post offices
   (d) Blogs

8. ______ is a program that may interrupt the normal operation of a computer.
   (a) Routine
   (b) Disabler
   (c) Virus
   (d) Destroyer

9. ______ is/are phase of a virus.
   (a) Infection
   (b) Attack
   (c) Both (a) and (b)
   (d) None of these

10. Which of the following statements is true for a Boot Virus?
    (a) It infects boot/master boot records on a hard disk.
    (b) It is the most active while a computer is booting
    (c) Disk killer is a well known boot virus
    (d) All of these

11. Which of the following statements is true for a program Files virus?
    (a) It infects executable/program files like .exe and .com
    (b) It is loaded in memory as soon as the program executes.
    (c) Sunday virus is a type of Program file virus.
    (d) All of these

12. To identify, prevent, quarantine and remove viruses, you need a ______ software.
    (a) Clean virus
    (b) Antivirus
    (c) Remove virus
    (d) None of these

13. To prevent virus from infecting your computer, you should ______.
    (a) Equip your PC with a licensed antivirus program
    (b) Scan flash drives and floppy disks before copying data from them
    (c) Not install pirated software from unknown sources on your computer
    (d) All of these

14. Identify the following.
    It is software program.
    It monitors a user's computing habits.
    It records user's personal information.
    It sends the recorded information to third parties without the user's knowledge.
    (a) Spyware
    (b) Adware
    (c) Malware
    (d) None of these

15. What is the process of sending message from one person to another person via computer called?
(a) Email   (b) SMS
(c) Advertisement   (d) Marketing

16. What does ISP stand for?
(a) Internet Service Provider
(b) Information Service Provider
(c) Internet Service Program
(d) Information Service Program

17. E-mail has become one of the fastest messaging services. What does e-mail stand for?
(a) Electrical Mail   (b) Electronic Mail
(c) Energetic Mail   (d) Emergency Mail

18. Which of the following is the first page of website?
(a) Home page
(b) Web page
(c) Relative page
(d) Previous page

19. What is the full form of DNS?
(a) Data Numbering Service
(b) Device Networking System
(c) Domain Naming System
(d) Data Naming Service

20. Match the following.

Abbreviation	Stands for	
1.	.com	P.	Education
2.	.edu	Q.	India
3.	.in	R.	Australia
4.	.au	S.	Commercial

(a) 1P, 2Q, 3R, 4S   (b) 1Q, 2R, 3S,4P
(c) 1R, 2S, 3P, 4Q   (d) 1S, 2P, 3Q, 4R

21. What range of numbers does an IP address contain?
(a) 1 to 100   (b) 1 to 1000
(c) 0 to 255   (d) 1 to 500

22. Every page on the internet has a unique address. What is the address called?
(a) Website   (b) Webpage
(c) HTTP://   (d) URL

23. Which of the following domain names is used for non-profit institutional websites?
(a) Gov   (b) Org
(c) Com   (d) Net

24. Which of the following is/are the advantage(s) of E-mail?
(a) E-mail is quicker than ordinary postage.
(b) The message may consist of only few lines of text or several lines.
(b) We can receive the message at any time.
(d) All of these

25. Which two characters does an email address contain?
(a) @ and underscore   (b) @ and dot
(c) @ and dash   (d) @and plus

26. In the URL http://www.unifiedcouncil.com, which part is the protocol name?
(a) .com   (b) www
(c) http   (d) unified

27. When you chat with people or send an e-mail, why should you not to type a message in ALL CAPITAL LETTERS?
(a) It means that we are shouting or being rude.
(b) It will be uneasy for us to type.
(c) It will not get displayed in the computer of the recipient.
(d) It is impossible to type in capital letters.

28. What does CC in e-mail stand for?
(a) Correct Copy
(b) Carbon Copy
(c) Copy to Copy
(d) Combined Copy

29. While sending an e-mail, what does BCC stand for?
(a) Blank Correct Copy
(b) Best Combine Copy
(c) Blank Copy to Copy
(d) Blind Carbon Copy

30. In exam@unifiedcouncil.com, what does "@" symbol stand for?
(a) Rounded 'a'   (b) At the rate of
(c) Hash   (d) Ampersand

31. Which of the following is not a search engine?

(a) G-mail   (b) Yahoo

(c) AltaVista   (d) Google

32. Which of these is an e-mail service provider?

(a) www.yahoo.com

(b) www.naukri.com

(c) www.irctc.com

(d) www.spontine.com

33. In order to send e-mail to another class on the school's local area network, one must first know the _________ of the class.

(a) Teacher

(b) E-mail password

(c) Computer type

(d) E-mail address

34. Golu is setting up his new e-mail account. He needs to create a new password to ensure privacy and security. Which of the following should one do?

(a) Pick a password used by another person

(b) Use personal information for the new password

(c) Pick random letters for the new password

(d) Use a combination of words and numbers for the new password

35. Which of the following options signs you out of your e-mail account?

(a) Sign in   (b) Sign out

(c) Forward   (d) New

36. How many numbers are separated by dots does a numeric web address contain?

(a) Three   (b) Two

(c) Four   (d) One

37. What is the purpose of CC?

(a) It allows the sender to send the message to several people at a time.

(b) It allows the sender to attach different types of files.

(c) It allows the sender to receive many messages at a time.

(d) It restricts the sender to send only one message at a time.

38. In a website address, what does .mil stand for?

(a) Multinational site

(b) Military site

(c) Educational site

(d) Commercial site

39. Which one of the following domain name is used for networking organization website?

(a) .int   (b) .net

(c) .com   (d) .org

40. To: navneet@xyz.com

BCC: shraddha@abc.com, bunny@abc.com

Which of the following statements is true?

(a) Navneet does not know that the e-mail was also sent to Shraddha and Bunny.

(b) Shraddha knows that the e-mail was sent to Navneet and Bunny.

(c) Bunny knows that the same e-mail was sent to Navneet and Shraddha.

(d) Everyone knows that the e-mail was sent to 3 people.

41. Google allows up to _______ size of files to be exchanged through e-mail.

(a) 10 MB   (b) 25 MB

(c) 30 GB   (d) 40 GB

42. Which feature of an e-mail has identical message sent to many people, especially advertisements?

(a) Inbox   (b) Draft

(c) Spam   (d) Chat

43. What is the feature that allows a person to communicate with real time in Gmail?

(a) Chat   (b) Spam

(c) Reply   (d) Compose

44. Where do you save the e-mail addresses of your friends who are in regular touch with you?

(a) Contacts   (b) Phonebook

(c) Address book   (d) File

45. What are the benefits of e-mail?

(a) Speed

(b) Cost effectiveness

(c) Record keeping

(d) All of these

46. In the e-mail, navneet@del2.vsnl.net.in. What does del2 refer to?
    (a) User name   (b) Server
    (c) Network   (d) India

47. Which of the following is used to separate the username and fully qualified domain name?
    (a) +   (b) *
    (c) #   (d) @

48. What kind of data can you send via e-mail?
    (a) Audio   (b) Video
    (c) Pictures   (d) All of these

49. In which of the following sites can you set up an e-mail address?
    (a) www.google.com
    (b) www.gov.nic.in
    (c) www.outlook.com
    (d) www.isro.com

50. What is the URL country code for France?
    (a) .fe   (b) .fr
    (c) .fc   (d) .fn

HOTS

1. Jyoti has installed some programs from Windows Live at the end of the download and install process, the Window Live installer is asking for Windows Live ID. In which of the following cases she doesn't already have a Windows Live ID?
    (a) If she uses Hotmail
    (b) If she uses Xbox Live
    (c) If she uses Gmail
    (d) If she uses Windows Live Messenger

2. Before downloading which package can be downloaded through internet for testing purpose?
    (a) Shareware
    (b) Pirated Software
    (c) Backup Copy
    (d) Beta Software

3. Based on the packet's address, the device that has been designed to forward packets to specific ports is?
    (a) Speciality Hub
    (b) Filtering Hub
    (c) Switching Hub
    (d) Port Hub

4. __________ topology is not of a broadcast type?
    (a) Bus   (b) Ring
    (c) Mesh   (d) Star

5. IP is defined in-
    (a) RFC 790   (b) RFC 791
    (c) RFC 792   (d) RFC 793

SUBJECTIVE QUESTIONS

1. How you can view and Open Favorites?

Ans.

Click the View favorites, feeds, and history button, or press Alt + C. If necessary, click the Favorites tab. Select a favorite to open it in the current tab. Click the arrow button to the right of a favorite to open it in a new tab.

2. How will we know if our computer is virus affected?

Ans.

If any of the following issue is experienced, then probably your system is affected by a virus.

- Your system will be slow.
- It will take time to load programs on your computer.
- The documents stored in the system get corrupted or deleted.

- The files get renamed with different names with some extension.
- There will be frequent unusual error messages on the screen.

3. What are the ways can computer virus spread?

Ans.

A virus can spread through any of the following ways:

- By opening an infected email link or an attachment from an unknown source.
- By downloading infected programs from the internet.
- It can also be transmitted through external storage such as an infected floppy disk, pen drives and CDs.

4. What are some common services Provided by Internet?

Ans.

Following are some common services provided by the Internet.

- **Email:** Using Email you can send any information, greeting or any type of file, such as a picture to any location of the world.
- **Ticket booking:** Using Internet you can book your railway ticket, air ticket or movie ticket. You do not need to go anywhere, just connect your computer with the Internet and book whatever you want.

- **Banking:** Using Internet you can check the status of your bank account. You can also transfer money from one account to other account.
- **Searching:** It is one of the most important features through which we are able to grasp knowledge of anything through any of the search engine. GOOGLE is one of the common search engine through which we can get any information regarding any topic, organization, and many other things can be learned through this.
- **Chatting:** Using Internet, you can chat with your friends in live environment. There are various chatting tools available in market, such as Google Talk.
- **E-learning:** E-learning is a new revolution in learning world. Using Internet you can learn any subject anywhere anytime.

5. What is the use of a Ethernet Networking Card or Network Interface Card (NIC)?

Ans.

The NIC (Network Interface Card) is also called Ethernet Networking card. It is a circuit are equipped with microchips that is physically installed within an active network node, such as a computer, a server or a printer. It enables to connect your computer with network.

Networking 8

CHAPTER SUMMARY

A network is any collection of independent computers that communicate with one another over a shared network medium. A computer network is a collection of two or more connected computers. When these computers are joined in a network, people can share files and peripherals such as modems, printers or CD-ROM drives.

Every network includes:

- At least two computers Server or Client workstation.
- Networking Interface Card's (NIC)
- A connection medium, usually a wire or cable, although wireless communication between networked computers and peripherals is also possible.
- Network Operating system software, such as Microsoft Windows NT, Novell NetWare, Unix and Linux.

Need of Computer Network

The following are the purposes filled by a computer network:

- **File sharing:** Networking of computers helps the users to share data files.
- **Hardware sharing:** Users can share devices such as printers, scanners, CD-ROM drives, hard drives etc.
- **Application sharing:** Applications can be shared over the network, and this allows to implement client/server applications via network.

- **User communication:** Networks allow users to communicate using e-mail, video conferencing, newsgroups etc.
- **Network gaming:** A lot of network games are available, which allow multi-users to play from different locations.

Types of Networks

LANs (Local Area Networks)

A network is any collection of independent computers that communicate with one another over a shared network medium. *LANs are networks usually confined to a geographic area,* such as a single building or a college campus.

WANs (Wide Area Networks)

Wide area networking combines multiple LANs that are geographically separate. This is accomplished by connecting the different LANs using services such as dedicated leased phone lines, dial-up phone lines (both synchronous and asynchronous), satellite links, and data packet carrier services.

Intranet

An intranet is a private network utilizing Internet-type tools, but available only within that organization. For large organizations, an intranet provides an easy access mode to corporate information for employees.

MANs (Metropolitan area Networks)

This refers to a network of computers within a City.

Other Types of Area Networks

While LAN, MAN and WAN are by far the most popular network types mentioned, you may also commonly see references to these others:

- *Metropolitan Area Network:* A network spanning a physical area larger than a LAN but smaller than a WAN, such as a city. A MAN is typically owned and operated by a single entity such as a government body or large corporation.
- *Campus Area Network:* A network spanning multiple LANs but smaller than a MAN. It is commonly used in a university or local business campus.
- *Storage Area Network:* A Storage Area Network connects multiple servers and storage devices on a single network. This network typically uses Fibre Channel connections. It also allows sharing the storage infrastructure, without implying data sharing. It is also known as Server Area Network.
- *System Area Network:* In System Area Networks, computers are connected to each other by using a reliable, very-low latency, high speed 1 Giga Bits Per Second (Gbps). It also uses Fiber Channel connection that uses special System Area Network adapters. It links high-performance computers using high-speed connections in a cluster configuration. It is also known as Cluster Area Network.
- *Small Area Network:* Like the familiar Local Area Network (LAN) used to connect computers within an office or building, a *Small Area Network* is used to connect Integrated Circuit (IC) components on a printed circuit board, or within a box or system. Due to its low cost, flexibility, and space saving characteristics, Small Area Networks provide device control, media security, and health monitoring connectivity in electronic products ranging from cell phones, to PCs, to large computer server system.
- *Personal Area Network:* A personal area network (PAN) is a computer network used for data transmission among devices such as computers, telephones and personal digital assistants. PANs can be used for communication among the personal devices themselves, or for connecting to a higher level network and the Internet.
- *Desk Area Network:* DAN is an architecture for a multimedia workstation that is based around an ATM interconnect. The architecture is designed to interconnect workstations, multimedia devices and bridges to other networks.
- *Controller Area Network:* CAN is a serial communications bus specifically designed for in-vehicle networks but also used in industrial automation and medical equipments. CAN supports distributed real time control with high level of security.
- *Public Network:* Public Network are those networks which are installed and run by the telecom authorities and are made available to any organisation or individual who subscribe it.
- *Public Switched Telephone Network (PSTN):* The features of the PSTN are its low speed, the analog nature of transmission, a restricted bandwidth and its widespread availability. PSTN is designed for telephone, modems, FAX.
- *Public Switched Data Network (PSDN):* The main features of PSDN are their high level of reliability and the high quality of the connection provided. PSDN is very popular for connecting public and private mail system to implement electronic mail services with other companies.
- *Private Network:* Private network is used by particular individual or organisation. Private network may follow standards guideline or may not follow these guidelines. It depends upon the organisation or individuals for which it has been developed e.g Intranet.
- *Virtual Private Network (VPN):* VPN uses a technique known as tunnelling to transfer data securely on the Internet to a remote access server on your workplace network. Using a VPN helps you save money by using the public Internet instead of making long-distance phone calls to connect securely with your private network.

TRIVIA

86% of people try to plug in their USB devices upside down.

Network Interface Cards

Network interface cards, commonly referred to as NICs, and are used to connect a PC to a network.

IP Addressing

An IP (Internet Protocol) address is a unique identifier for a node or host connection on an IP network. An IP address is a 32 bit binary number usually represented as 4 decimal values, each representing 8 bits, in the range 0 to 255 (known as octets) separated by decimal points. This is known as "dotted decimal" notation.

Example: 123.167.222.500

Topology

Topology refers to the geometric arrangement of a computer system. Common topologies include bus, star, and ring.

Bus Topology

Bus networks use a common backbone (a single cable) to connect all devices. The cable functions as a shared communication medium that devices attach to with help of connectors. A device which wants to communicate with another device on the network sends a broadcast message to the cable so that all other devices see, but only the intended recipient will actually accept and processes the message.

Ring Topology

In a ring network, every device has exactly two neighbors for communication purpose. All messages travel through a ring in the same direction (either "clockwise" or "counterclockwise"). A failure in any cable or device breaks the loop and can take the entire network down. To implement a ring network, FDDI, SONET, or Token Ring technology is used.

Star Topology

A star network features a central connection point known as a "hub node" that may be a network hub, switch or router. Devices typically connect to the hub with Unshielded Twisted Pair (UTP) Ethernet.

Compared to the bus topology, a star network generally requires more cable, but a failure in any star network cable will only take down one computer's network access and not the entire LAN. (If the hub fails, however, the entire network also fails.)

- A network is any collection of independent computers that communicate with one another over a shared network medium.
- LANs are networks usually confined to a geographic area, such as a single building or a college campus.
- An intranet is a private network utilizing Internet-type tools, but available only within that organization.
- A Storage Area Network connects multiple servers and storage devices on a single network.
- A personal area network (PAN) is a computer network used for data transmission among devices such as computers, telephones and personal digital assistants.
- VPN uses a technique known as tunnelling to transfer data securely on the Internet to a remote access server on your workplace network.
- Topology refers to the geometric arrangement of a computer system.
- Compared to the bus topology, a star network generally requires more cable, but a failure in any star network cable will only take down one computer's network access and not the entire LAN.

1. Which of the following is not a type of Computer Network?
   (a) Local Area Network (LAN)
   (b) Personal Area Network (PAN)
   (c) Remote Area Network (RAN)
   (d) Metropolitan Area Network (MAN)

2. What is the full Form of NIC?
   (a) New Internet Connection
   (b) Network Interface Card
   (c) Network Interface Connection
   (d) Net Interface Card

3. Star Topology is based on a central device that can be __________?
   (a) Hub
   (b) Switch
   (c) Only (a)
   (d) Both (a) and (b)

4. Which topology requires a central controller or hub?
   (a) Star
   (b) Bus
   (c) Ring
   (d) None of these

5. Which topology requires a multipoint connection?
   (a) Star
   (b) Bus
   (c) Ring
   (d) None of these

6. This was the first network.
   (a) CSNET
   (b) NSFNET
   (c) ANSNET
   (d) ARPANET

7. __________ refers to the physical or logical arrangement of a network.
   (a) Data flow
   (b) Mode of operation
   (c) Topology
   (d) None of these

8. Devices can be arranged in a _____ topology.
   (a) star
   (b) ring
   (c) bus
   (d) all of these

9. A _______ is a data communication system within a building, or campus, or between nearby buildings.
   (a) MAN
   (b) LAN
   (c) WAN
   (d) none of these

10. A _______ is a data communication system spanning states, countries, or the whole world.
    (a) MAN
    (b) LAN
    (c) WAN
    (d) none of these

11. _______ is a collection of many separate networks.
    (a) WAN
    (b) Internet
    (c) LAN
    (d) None of these

12. A _______ is a set of rules that governs data communication.
    (a) Forum
    (b) Protocol
    (c) Standard
    (d) None of these

13. The device, which converts digital signal into analog, and the vice versa, is known as:
    (a) Modem
    (b) Modulator
    (c) Generator
    (d) Analogue

14. Which is the most popular and commonly used LAN (Local Area Network) protocol?
    (a) Ethernet
    (b) Internet
    (c) Relay
    (d) LANR

15. WAP stands for
    (a) Wired Application Protocol
    (b) Wireless Analog Protocol
    (c) Wireless Application Protocol
    (d) Wired Analog Protocol

16. Interconnection of various computer systems located atdifferent places is known as:
    (a) Connectors
    (b) Network
    (c) Internet
    (d) None of these

17. LAN stands for
    (a) Logical Area Network
    (b) Low Area Network
    (c) Loaded Area Network
    (d) Local Area Network

18. Which of these is not a type of network?
    (a) LAN
    (b) BAN
    (c) SAN
    (d) MAN

19. Which network is also known as Server Area Network?
    (a) Storage Area Network
    (b) Client Area Network
    (c) Workstation Area Network
    (d) Distributed Area Network

20. Which of the following technique is used by VPN?
    (a) Tunneling
    (b) Multiplexing
    (c) Cascading
    (d) Switching

1. Which of these is a standard interface for serial data transmission?
   (a) ASCII   (b) RS232C
   (c) 2   (d) Centronics

2. Which type of topology is best suited for large businesses which must carefully control and coordinate the operation of distributed branch outlets?
   (a) Ring   (b) Local area
   (c) Hierarchical   (d) Star

3. Which of the following transmission directions listed is not a legitimate channel?
   (a) Simplex
   (b) Half Duplex
   (c) Full Duplex
   (d) Double Duplex

4. "Parity bits" are used for which of the following purposes?
   (a) Encryption of data
   (b) To transmit faster
   (c) To detect errors
   (d) To identify the user

5. What kind of transmission medium is most appropriate to carry data in a computer network that is exposed to electrical interferences?
   (a) Unshielded twisted pair
   (b) Optical fiber
   (c) Coaxial cable
   (d) Microwave

1. List some key advantages of Computer networking.

Ans.

The main advantages of networking are the following:

- **Reduced Cost:** Using network you can share peripheral and software. You need to load software only on the file server all interconnected users used these software form server. This technique saves time and cost compared to installing and tracking files on independent computers. Using network you can also share several resources, such as printers, scanners, fax machines and modems. That reduces hardware cost.

- **File sharing:** Using network you do not need any USB drive or other media to transfer files from one computer to another computer. You can directly share the files using a network.

- **Email:** Using Internet you can send any information, greeting and much more all over the world.

2. What is a Client/Server System? Explain

Ans.

Railway inquiry system is a good example of client/server system. When you use your computer to check the schedule time about any train, the client program that runs in your computer forwards the request to a server program runs at the railway computer. The server program retrieves the information from railway server and returns back to your personal computer. Your personal computer displays the schedule time of requested train. In the client-server system, client is a computer application that runs on a local computer and requests service from a remote computer. Server is a computer application that runs on a remote computer and provides the requested service to a client. The client-server system can be used by programs running on a single computer, and different computers which are located on different locations.

Advantage

The main advantage of a client-server networking system is that you can perform administration or configuration of your entire network from a single location.

Disadvantage

Client-server networking model is very costly because it requires more hardware and the server operating system, such as Windows Server 2008 for the server.

3. Write short note on Workstation computers.

Ans.

Workstation is a computer which is designed for technical or scientific applications. The term workstation has also been used to refer to a mainframe computer terminal or a personal computer connected to a network.

A workstation may have the following features:

- A larger number of memory sockets
- Multiple processor sockets
- Multiple displays
- Support for ECC (Error Correcting Code) memory

4. What is a function of Internet Protocol?

Ans.

The main functions of Internet protocol are

- Firstly, the information is decomposed into packets of standardized size and then reassembled at the destination.
- It also routes a packet through networks, from the source to the destination which is identified by its IP address.

5. What is the use of Data Link Layer?

Ans.

A Data link layer has following use:

- The main purpose is to interpret the information in the physical layer.
- Any error is detected here in this layer.
- It is responsible for data encapsulation, where the data is encapsulated in the form of packets.

Learning Objectives : In this chapter, students will learn about:
- ✓ Some of the latest development in the field of IT

CHAPTER SUMMARY

The Global Positioning System or the GPS is a satellite-based navigation system. It is made up of a network of 24 satellites. It is placed into orbit by the U.S. Department of Defense. This technology was originally intended for military applications, but the government made the system available for commercial use eventually. GPS works 24 hours a day in any part of the world and in any weather condition. There are no subscription fees or setup charges to use GPS.

The 24 satellites that make up the GPS satellite orbits the earth about 12,000 miles above us. They make two complete orbits in less than 24 hours and are in constant motion. They travel at a speed of roughly 7,000 miles an hour. GPS satellites are powered by solar energy. They have backup batteries installed in them in case of solar eclipses. Small rocket boosters on each of these satellites keep them encircling in the right orbit.

Here are some other interesting facts about the GPS satellites

- ■ The official name for GPS is NAVSTAR.
- ■ The first GPS satellite was launched in 1978.

- ■ A full constellation of 24 satellites was achieved in 1994.
- ■ Each satellite is built to last about 10 years. Replacements are constantly being built and launched into orbit.
- ■ A GPS satellite weighs approximately 2,000 pounds and is about 17 feet in length with its solar panels extended.

Pinterest

Pinterest was founded by Bill Silbermann. It is a web and mobile application where the user can upload, manage, sort and delete images. Pinterest acts as a personalized media platform. The user can browse their own as well as other pages. They can then save individual pins to one of their own boards using the "Pin It" button.

One has to register to use Pinterest. A "board" is where the user's pins are located. Users can have several boards for various items such as quotes, travel or, most popularly, weddings. The images are known as pins.

Pinboards can be used by educators to plan lessons. Teachers can pin sites for later referral. Students can pin and organize sources and collaborate on projects.

Botnet

A botnet or a zombie army is a number of Internet computers that have been set up to forward transmissions to other computers on the Internet. The user or owner of such computers are unaware that their computer while connected to the internet is being used for such hazardous transmission.

Any such computer is referred to as a zombie or bot that serves the wishes of some virus originator. Most computers compromised in this way are home-based. According to a report from Russian-based Kaspersky Labs, botnets – not spam, viruses, or worms—currently pose the biggest threat to the Internet.

Computers that have been recruited to serve in a zombie army are those that fail to provide firewalls and other safeguards. A bot is created through an Internet port that has been left open and through which a small Trojan program can be left for future activation.

There is a hacker attack every 39 seconds.

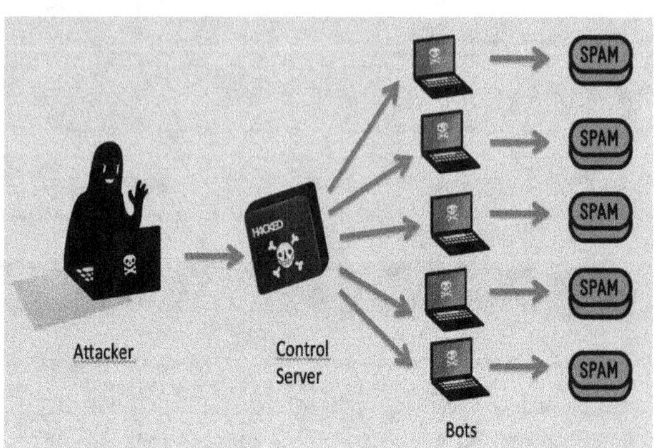

- ➡ GPS works 24 hours a day in any part of the world and in any weather condition.
- ➡ A GPS satellite weighs approximately 2,000 pounds and is about 17 feet in length with its solar panels extended.
- ➡ A botnet or a zombie army is a number of Internet computers that have been set up to forward transmissions to other computers on the Internet.

1. In computer terminology, which of the following statements define a Dorkbot?
   (a) A family of malware worms.
   (b) Dorkbot typically spreads through instant messaging and USB removable drives.
   (c) Dorkbot spreads through social media channels like Facebook and Twitter.
   (d) All of these

2. A Botnet is a ______.
   (a) Type of bot running on smart phones, attempting to gain complete control of the device
   (b) Type of bot running on an IRC network and created by a Trojan
   (c) SMC attack
   (d) Mobile VoIP

3. Barcrafts are centred on what video game?
   (a) Mine craft
   (b) World of warcraft
   (c) War craft III
   (d) Star craft II

4. Which of the following is the most widespread Botnet in history?
   (a) Hekaton
   (b) Dorkbot
   (c) Ransomware
   (d) Zeus

5. What is an Instagram?
   (a) An android app that let you store your photo and videos.
   (b) It supports various built-in filter effect.
   (c) Allows instant sharing on facebook, twitter, flicker and Tumblr.
   (d) All of these

6. Which of the following is the latest release of Samsung's popular Galaxy smart phone unveiled in February 2023?
   (a) Samsung Galaxy Tab
   (b) Samsung Galaxy S4
   (c) Samsung Galaxy S6
   (d) Samsung Galaxy S23

7. Which of the following is a windows notebook with a lid that pops off to become a standalone state?
   (a) HP Essential
   (b) HP Probook
   (c) HP Envy x2 Hybrid PC
   (d) HP Elite Book

8. What is the name of the feature in Mac OS X that displays a tray of icons?
   (a) File Vault   (b) Dock
   (c) Mission control   (d) Spotlight

9. The latest touch series of notebooks from ASUS are called ______.
   (a) Lamborghini
   (b) Taichi
   (c) Vivo Book
   (d) Transformer Book

10. Which of the following is not present in iphone?
    (a) Multitouch   (b) Edge
    (c) ios6   (d) Radio

11. The list shows new and changed features of OSX Mavericks.
    (i) icloud keychain Sync
    (ii) Added new ibook application
    (iii) App Nap
    (iv) SMB 4 is the default protocol for sharing files

    Which of the following features are true?
    (a) (i), (ii), (iv)   (b) Both (ii) and (iii)
    (c) Only (iv)   (d) (i), (ii), and (iii)

12. What is Pinterest?
    (a) A pinboard-style photo sharing website that allows user to create and manage theme based image collection.
    (b) A pinboard-style Bookmark website that allows user to track favourites.
    (c) Social news and entertainment website where users submit content in the form of pinboards.
    (d) An interesting note-taking site.

13. Video glasses are also knows as ______.
    (a) Head mounted display
    (b) Personal media viewers
    (c) Google Goggle
    (d) Both (a) and (b)

14. Which of the following is basically an impression of depth and is used to describe the brain's ability to put separate images together in order to form one 3-D image?
    (a) Stereopsis
    (b) Binocular fusion
    (c) Binocular disparity
    (d) Strabismus

15. Identify the following:
    It is an online social networking service and micro blogging service.
    Its users can send and read text based messages of up to 140 characters called tweets. It was created by Jack Dorsey in March 2006.
    (a) Facebook   (b) Twitter
    (c) Linked in   (d) YAHOO

16. GPS devices can pinpoint locations by ______.
    (a) Satellites
    (b) Lasers
    (c) Radioactive Waves
    (d) All of these

17. Which hugely popular Nintendo 64 game was rumoured to have a secret location accessible in its very first level?
    (a) Golden Eye 007
    (b) Mario 64
    (c) The legend of Zelda: Ocarina of time
    (d) The prince of Persia

18. The Black phone runs on which version of Android?
    (a) PrivatOS   (b) Kitkat
    (c) Honey comb   (d) Jelly Bean

19. Semantic Web term was coined by ______.
    (a) Jack Dorsey
    (b) Tim Berners-Lee
    (c) Dick Costolo
    (d) Noah Glass

20. Altec Lansing V2621 is a model name for a ______.
    (a) Graphics Card
    (b) Speaker
    (c) Optical Drive
    (d) Sound Card

21. Roccat kone XTD is a model name for a ______ used in High End Gaming RIGS.
    (a) Mouse   (b) Speaker
    (c) Keyboard   (d) Sound card

22. Which technology is making the web machine-readable by annotating data on the web based on its meaning?
    (a) Semantic Web
    (b) Answer machines
    (c) Virtual reality
    (d) Both (a) and (b)

23. Which of the following is not an edition of Windows 8.1?
    (a) Windows RT8.1
    (b) Windows 8.1 pro
    (c) Windows 8.1 Enterprise
    (d) Windows 8.1 Extreme

24. Who is the founder of Wikileaks?
    (a) Tarun Tejpal
    (b) Julian Assange
    (c) Matthew Charles 'Matt' Mullenweg
    (d) Niklaus Wirth

25. What is an Agribot?
    (a) A robot deployed for agricultural purposes
    (b) A robot deployed for plant nursing
    (c) A robot working cooperatively
    (d) A robot involved in robotic harvesting

1. Select the correct statement about the given logo.

parc

   (a) It stands for Palo Alto Research Center Incorporated.
   (b) It is a research and development company in California.
   (c) It is well known for important development as laser printing, ethernet and GUI.
   (d) All of these

2. Identify the following.
   ■ It is a match-three puzzle video game.
   ■ It was released in 2012.
   ■ Its characters are Tiffi, Mr. Toffee and Easter Bunny.
   (a) Candy Crush Saga
   (b) Angry Birds
   (c) Flow Puzzle
   (d) Flow Loops

3. Mountain Lion, Mavericks and Yosemite are versions of operating system, associated with ___________ computers, developed by Apple Inc.
   (a) Windows
   (b) Macintosh
   (c) Super
   (d) Both (a) and (c)

4. Smart Covers in tablet computers are used to __________.
   (a) Protect the touchscreen and save energy
   (b) Fix the device to a wall
   (c) Type and input text
   (d) Provide internet connectivity

5. __________ is a peer-to-peer file transfer protocol for sharing large amount of data over the internet, in which each part of a file downloaded by a user is transferred to other users.
   (a) Torrent
   (b) BitTorrent
   (c) ClipTorrent
   (d) DownTorrent

SECTION 2
LOGICAL REASONING

Analogy

Learning Objectives : In this chapter, students will learn about:
- ✓ Tips to solve analogy questions

CHAPTER SUMMARY

Analogy means similarity. In this type of questions, two objects related in some way are given. A third object is also given with four or five alternatives. You have to find out which one of the alternatives bears the same relation with the third objects as first and second objects are related.

Tips to Solve Questions

1. Recognise the kind of the relationship between the pair of words given.
2. Have a glance at the alternatives, for pairs of word with a similar relationship.
3. Eliminate the alternatives that do not appear to be the fittest answer.
4. After that, if more than one pair of words seems to fit, then again see the question pair.
5. Then redefine and interpret the relationship in the question pair.
6. For correct answer, always return to the question pair.
7. The parts of speech must be the same in the related words/phrases.

Example 1: Curd : Milk :: Shoe : ?

  (a) Leather   (b) Cloth

  (c) Jute   (d) Silver

Sol. (a)

As curd is made from milk similarly shoe is made from leather.

Example 2: Malaria : Mosquito :: ? : ?

  (a) Poison : Death

  (b) Cholera : Water

  (c) Rat : Plague

  (d) Medicine : Disease

Sol. (b)

As malaria is caused due to mosquito similarly cholera is cause due to water.

Example 3: ABC : ZYX :: CBA : ?

  (a) XYZ   (b) BCA

  (c) YZX   (d) ZXY

Sol. (a)

CBA is the reverse of ABC similarly XYZ is the reverse of ZYX.

1. Which one of the following letters is exactly midway between 6th letter and 14th letter in the English alphabet?
   (a) J
   (b) H
   (c) G
   (d) N

2. If the letters of the English alphabets is written in the reverse order and every alternate letter starting from W, is deleted, which letter will be exactly in the middle?
   (a) M
   (b) O
   (c) N
   (d) M or O

3. If the second half of the English alphabet is written in reverse order which letter will be 6th to the left of the letter which is 10th from the right?
   (a) J
   (b) K
   (c) L
   (d) M

4. In English, every alternate letter starting from A is written in small letters and the remaining letters is written in capital how is the word 'Academy' written?
   (a) ACADEMY
   (b) ACAdEMY
   (c) acaDemy
   (d) aCaDEmY

5. If every fifth letter in the English alphabet, from your left is replaced by the day of week respectively starting from Sunday which letter will represent 'Wednesday'?
   (a) J
   (b) O
   (c) T
   (d) Y

Directions (6-9): Study the given set of alphabets carefully and answer the following questions.

S N T A O U B F P V C G Q W D H R X E Z

6. If only the letters O to X are written in reverse order, which letter is 4th to the right of the letter which is 9th from the right?
   (a) R
   (b) B
   (c) X
   (d) U

7. If starting from S every alternate letter is deleted, which letter will be 2nd to the right of the letter which is 8th from the right?
   (a) T
   (b) X
   (c) G
   (d) V

8. If 1st, 3rd, 5th, and 9th letter of the given arrangement form a meaningful word, which of the following is the 3rd letter from the right of the word?
   (a) F
   (b) O
   (c) T
   (d) P

9. If the letters in the odd places of the given arrangement are deleted and the remaining letters are written in reverse order, which is the 6th letter from the right?
   (a) H
   (b) V
   (c) G
   (d) X

10. If all the vowels are deleted from the English alphabet, which letter will be 7th to the right of the letter which is 11th from your right?
    (a) W
    (b) X
    (c) F
    (d) H

11. If the letters in the place of multiple of 3 are deleted, from the English alphabet how more vowels are left?
    (a) 4
    (b) 2
    (c) 3
    (d) 1

12. Which of the following words cannot be made from the letters of the word MECHANICS?
    (a) CHAIN
    (b) CHANCE
    (c) CERAMICS
    (d) CANE

13. Which of the following words cannot be made from the letters of the word DIMENSIONAL?
    (a) MANSION
    (b) NOISE
    (c) SOME
    (d) SEASON

14. Which of the words cannot be made from the letters of the word COMPATIBLE?
    (a) PLATE
    (b) TABLET
    (c) MATE
    (d) POET

15. What is the maximum number of four letters meaningful words that are possible to be made using the letter of word TRAINER?
    (a) > 20
    (b) between 3 and 20
    (c) < 3
    (d) = 10

16. Three of the following four groups of letters are alike according to their position in the English alphabet and so from a group. Which is the one that does not belong to that group?
    (a) GIQ
    (b) BOW
    (c) IKP
    (d) FHS

17. Identify the series in which the number of letters skipped in between adjacent letters decrease by one.
    (a) AGMRV
    (b) HNSWA
    (c) NSXCH
    (d) SYDHK

18. Identify the series in which the number of letters skipped in between adjacent letters is always same.
    (a) HKNGSW
    (b) RVZDFG
    (c) RVZDHL
    (d) SUXADF

19. Identify the series in which the number of letters skipped in between adjacent letters is not decrease by one.
    (a) BFIK
    (b) LPSU
    (c) GKNP
    (d) TXAB

20. Identify the series in which the number of letters skipped in between adjacent letters is not the same.
    (a) LNPR
    (b) RTUW
    (c) WYAB
    (d) NQSU

21. The letters of the word NUMKITP are in disorder. If they are arranged in proper order, the name of a vegetable is formed. What is the last letter of the word so formed?
    (a) K
    (b) M
    (c) N
    (d) P

Directions (22–25): Answer the following questions based on the given arrangements:

Y W @ 2 1 & C N 3 P L B 9 β = D * E 2 £ M V $ 7 # F G 5

22. How many such symbols are there in the given arrangement which are not immediately preceded by a number and also not immediately followed by a letter?
    (a) Zero
    (b) One
    (c) Five
    (d) Three

23. If the numbers immediately preceding the symbols are doubled and attached together, then what will be the sum of the values of all such numbers?
    (a) 22
    (b) 26
    (c) 36
    (d) 38

24. Three of the following four are a like in a certain way based on the above arrangement and hence form a group. Which one does not belong to the group?
    (a) * V 2 M
    (b) β 2 D E
    (c) L D B =
    (d) V $ 7 4

25. If Y W @ 2 are written in the reverse order & C N 3 are written in the reverse order and so on, then in the new arrangement which of the following will be exactly in the middle between 9 and $?
    (a) E
    (b) =
    (c) D
    (d) 700

Directions (26–35): In each of the following questions find out the alternative which will replace the question mark.

26. 14 : 9 :: 26 : ?
    (a) 12
    (b) 13
    (c) 31
    (d) 15

27. MO : 13 11 :: HJ : ?
    (a) 19 17
    (b) 18 16
    (c) 8 10
    (d) 16 18

28. 123 : 132 :: 235 : ?
    (a) 232
    (b) 352
    (c) 253
    (d) 252

29. 8 : 28 :: 27 : ?
    (a) 28   (b) 8
    (c) 64   (d) 65
30. 3 : 12 :: 5 : ?
    (a) 25   (b) 35
    (c) 30   (d) 15
31. MXN : 13 x 14 :: FXR : ?
    (a) 14 x 15   (b) 5 x 17
    (c) 6 x 18   (d) 7 x 19
32. 16 : 56 :: 32 : ?
    (a) 96   (b) 112
    (c) 120   (d) 128
33. 4 : 19 :: 7 : ?
    (a) 52   (b) 49
    (c) 28   (d) 68
34. 24 : 60 :: 120 : ?
    (a) 160   (b) 220
    (c) 300   (d) 108
35. 335 : 216 :: 987 : ?
    (a) 868   (b) 867
    (c) 872   (d) 888

Odd One Out   2

Learning Objectives : In this chapter, students will learn about:
- ✓ Concept of Odd one out

CHAPTER SUMMARY

In these kinds of problems, a person, place animal or thing differs from all other members of a particular group or set in some way. Each question has 4 options and the candidate has to find answer related to that question.

Example 1: 74, 24, 82, 61, 10, 4. Find out the Odd One.

    (a) 61   (b) 24

    (c) 10   (d) 82

Sol. (a)

Here, each of the mentioned figures are even only 61 is Odd.

Now generally, Odd one out series questions are divided into three main sections. They are:

- Letters
- Numbers
- Words

Example 2: Find the odd one out.

    331, 482, 551, 263, 383, 362, 284

    (a) 263   (b) 383

    (c) 331   (d) 551

Sol. (b)

In each number except 383, the product of first and third digits is the middle one.

Example 4: Find the odd one out.

    AE GM MQ VZ LP

Sol. GM

Gap between G,H,I,J,K,L,M is 5, where other Alphabet's gaps are 3 like A,B,C,D,E

Here are some shortcuts solving out one out questions based on the English alphabet.

1. Vowel Comparision
2. Alphabetical order of given letters
3. Gap between the given letters

Following questions will give you better idea.

Example 5: Ram, Sham, Mohan, Seeta

Sol.

In this question, it can be seen the odd one would be Seeta on the basis of gender.

Example 6: Car, Jeep, Helicopter, Bus.

Sol.

In this question, the odd object would be airplane, because the rest three move on the road, but the airplane flies in the air. This is odd on the basis of the elementary feature.

Example 7: 13, 17, 83, 45.

Sol.

In this question, the odd would be 45, which is not a prime number and the rest are prime numbers.

Example 8: Book, Paper, Pencil and Sharpener.

Sol.

Here all the items given are stationery items except book, therefore book is the answer.

1. Find the odd one out.
   (a) Cup (b) Plate
   (c) Page (d) Spoon

2. Find the odd one out.
   (a) Darjeeling
   (b) Gangtok
   (c) Dispur
   (d) Lucknow

3. Find the odd one out.
   4 8 16 32 62
   (a) 4 (b) 8
   (c) 16 (d) 62

4. Find the odd one out.
   (a) Mouse (b) Keyboard
   (c) Monitor (d) Computer

5. Find the odd one out.
   (a) Bottle (b) Plate
   (c) Can (d) Jug

6. Find the odd one out.
   (a) Tea (b) Coffee
   (c) Soup (d) Beer

7. Find the odd one out.
   (a) Pencil (b) Pen
   (c) Stationery (d) Eraser

8. Find the odd one out.
   (a) Sugar (b) Salt
   (c) Sand (d) Milk Powder

9. Find the odd one out.
   (a) Physics (b) Chemistry
   (c) History (d) Biology

10. Find the odd one out.
    (a) Hills (b) Plains
    (c) Valleys (d) Land

11. Find the odd one out.
    (a) Style (b) Format
    (c) Colour (d) Size

12. Find the odd one out.
    (a) Word (b) HTML
    (c) Excel (d) PowerPoint

13. Find the odd one out.
    (a) Telephone (b) Smartphone
    (c) Cell phone (d) iPad

14. Find the odd one out.
    (a) iPad (b) iPod
    (c) Mac Air (d) iWatch

15. Find the odd one out.
    (a) Fan (b) Cooler
    (c) Heater (d) Air Conditioner

Alphabet Test   3

Learning Objectives : In this chapter, students will learn about:
- ✓ Alphabet series concepts

Alphabetical Series form an important part of the reasoning section in various competitive examinations.

Solved Examples

Example 1: In the following letter series, some of the letters are missing, which are given in such order as one of the alternatives below it. Choose the correct alternative.

$$\_ \text{tu} \_ \text{rt} \_ \text{s} \_\_ \text{usrtu} \_$$

  (a) rtusru   (b) rsutrr

  (c) rsurtr   (d) rsurts

Sol. (d)

The series rtus/rtus/rtus/rtus. Thus, the pattern 'rtus' is repeated.

Directions

In each of the following questions, various terms of an alphabet series are given with one or more terms missing as shown by (?). Choose the missing terms out of the given alternatives.

Example 1: A, G, L, P, S, ?

  (a) U   (b) W

  (c) X   (d) Y

Sol. (a)

$$A \xrightarrow{+6} G \xrightarrow{+5} L \xrightarrow{+4} P \xrightarrow{+3} S \xrightarrow{+2} \boxed{U}$$

Example 2: ajs, gpy, ?, sbk, yhq

  (a) dmv   (b) mve

  (c) oua   (d) qzi

Sol. (b)

1st letter: $\quad a \xrightarrow{+6} g \xrightarrow{+6} \boxed{m} \xrightarrow{+6} s \xrightarrow{+6} y$

2nd letter: $\quad j \xrightarrow{+6} p \xrightarrow{+6} \boxed{v} \xrightarrow{+6} b \xrightarrow{+6} h$

3nd letter: $\quad s \xrightarrow{+6} y \xrightarrow{+6} e \xrightarrow{+6} k \xrightarrow{+6} q$

Example 3: AB, DEF, HIJK, ?, STUVWX

  (a) LMNO   (b) LMNOP

  (c) MNOPQ   (d) QRSTU

Sol. (c)

The number of letters in terms of the given series increases by one at each step.

The first letter of each term is two steps ahead of the last letter of the preceding term.

However, each term consists of consecutive letters in order.

Example 4: Y, B, T, G, O, ?

  (a) N   (b) M

  (c) L   (d) K

Sol. (c)

The given sequence is a combination of two series:

    I. Y, T, O and II. B, G, ?

I consists of 2nd, 7th and 12th letters from the end of the English alphabet

II consists of 2nd, 7th and 12th letters from the beginning of the English alphabet.

So, the missing letter in II is the 12th letter from the beginning of the English alphabet, which is L.

Directions (1-10): In each of the following letter series, some of the letters are missing, which are given in such order as one of the alternatives below it. Choose the correct alternative.

1. _ op _ mo _ n _ _ pnmop _.
   - (a) mnpmon
   - (b) mpnmop
   - (c) mnompn
   - (d) mnpomn

2. _bcc _ ac _ aabb _ ab _ cc
   - (a) aabca
   - (b) abaca
   - (c) bacab
   - (d) bcaca

3. m _ nm _ n _ an _ a _ ma _
   - (a) aamnan
   - (b) ammanm
   - (c) aammnn
   - (d) amammn

4. ab __ d __ aaba __ na _ badna _ b
   - (a) andaa
   - (b) babda
   - (c) badna
   - (d) dbanb

5. bca _ b _ aabc __ a __ caa
   - (a) acab
   - (b) bcbb
   - (c) cbab
   - (d) ccab

6. ab _ _ baa _ _ ab _
   - (a) aaaaa
   - (b) aabaa
   - (c) aabab
   - (d) baabb

7. _ bc _ ca _ aba _ c _ ca
   - (a) abcbb
   - (b) bbbec
   - (c) bacba
   - (d) abbec

8. ba _ cb _ b _ bab _
   - (a) acbb
   - (b) bacc
   - (c) bcaa
   - (d) cabb

9. c _ bba _ cab _ ac _ ab _ ac
   - (a) abebe
   - (b) acbcb
   - (c) babec
   - (d) bcacb

10. _ aa _ ba _ bb _ ab _ aab
    - (a) aaabb
    - (b) babab
    - (c) bbaab
    - (d) bbbaa

Directions (11–25): In each of the following questions, an alphabet series is given with one missing term. Choose correct alternative that will continue the same pattern and fill in the blank spaces.

11. QAR, RAS, SAT, TAU, ______
    - (a) UAV
    - (b) UAT
    - (c) TAS
    - (d) TAT

12. DEF, DEF_2, DE_2F_2, ______, $D_2E_2F_3$
    - (a) DEF_3
    - (b) D_3EF_3
    - (c) D_2E_3F
    - (d) $D_2E_2F_2$

13. P_5QR, P_4QS, P_3QT, ______, P_1QV
    - (a) PQW
    - (b) PQV_2
    - (c) P_2QU
    - (d) PQ_3U

14. FAG, GAF, HAI, IAH, ______
    - (a) JAK
    - (b) HAL
    - (c) HAK
    - (d) JAI

15. CMM, EOO, GQQ, ______, KUU
    - (a) GRR
    - (b) GSS
    - (c) ISS
    - (d) ITT

16. ELFA, GLHA, ILJA, ______, MLNA
    - (a) OLPA
    - (b) KLMA
    - (c) LLMA
    - (d) KLLA

17. ejo tyd ins xch ?
    - (a) nrw
    - (b) mrw
    - (c) msx
    - (d) nsx

18. JAK, KBL, LCM, MDN, ______
    - (a) OEP
    - (b) NEO
    - (c) MEN
    - (d) PFQ

19. BCB, DED, FGF, HIH, ______
    - (a) JKJ
    - (b) HJH
    - (c) IJI
    - (d) JHJ

20. A, B, N, C, D, O, E, F, P, ?, ?, ?
    - (a) G, H, I
    - (b) G, H, J
    - (c) G, H, Q
    - (d) J, K, L

21. A, B, B, D, C, F, D; H, E, ?, ?
    - (a) E, F
    - (b) F, G
    - (c) F, I
    - (d) J, F

22. AB, DEF, HIJK, ?, STUVWX
    - (a) LMNO
    - (b) LMNOP
    - (c) MNOPQ
    - (d) QRSTU

23. Y, B, T, G, O, ?
    - (a) N
    - (b) M
    - (c) L
    - (d) K

24. b e d f ? h j ? l
    - (a) i m
    - (b) m i
    - (c) i n
    - (d) j m

25. ZA_5, Y_4B, XC_6, W_3D, ______
    - (a) E_7V
    - (b) V_2E
    - (c) VE_5
    - (d) VE_7

Blood Relation Test

Learning Objectives : In this chapter, students will learn about:
- ✓ Different types of blood relation

CHAPTER SUMMARY

To answer these types of questions, you should have a sound knowledge of the blood relation. To remember easily, the relations may be divided into two sides as given below:

I. Relations of Paternal side:
1. Father's father → Grandfather
2. Father's mother → Grandmother
3. Father's brother → Uncle
4. Father's sister → Aunt
5. Children of uncle → Cousin
6. Wife of uncle → Aunt
7. Children of aunt → Cousin
8. Husband of aunt → Uncle

II. Relations of Maternal side:
1. Mother's father → Maternal grandfather
2. Mother's mother → Maternal grandmother
3. Mother's brother → Maternal uncle
4. Mother's sister → Aunt
5. Children of maternal uncle → Cousin
6. Wife of maternal uncle → Maternal aunt

Relations from one generation to next

Generation I	Grandfather, grandmother, maternal grandfather, maternal grandmother

↓

Generation II	Mother, father, uncle, aunt, maternal uncle, maternal aunt

↓

Generation III	Self, sister, sister-in-law, brother, brother-in-law

↓

Generation IV	Son, daughter, nephew, niece

Example 1: If A + B means A is the mother of B; A × B means A is the father of B; A \$ B means A is the brother of B and A @ B means A is the sister of B then which of the following means P is the son of Q?

(a) Q + R @ P @ N
(b) Q + R * P @ N
(c) Q × R \$ P @ N
(d) Q × R \$ P \$ N

Sol. (D)

$Q \times R$ = Q is the mother of R [–Q, ±R]

$R \$ P$ = R is the brother of P [+R, ±P]

$P \$ N$ = P is the brother of N [+P, ±N]

Therefore P is the son of Q.

Example 2: A has 3 children. B is the brother of C and C is the sister of D, E who is the wife of A is the mother of D. There is only one daughter of the husband of E. what is the relation between D and B?

Sol.

With the chart

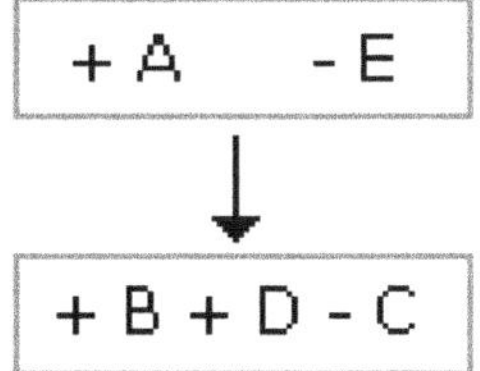

Therefore, D is a boy because there is only one daughter of E.

Hence, B is the brother of D.

Example 3: Pointing to a photograph, Rekha says to Lalli, "The girl in the photo is the second daughter of the wife of only son of the grandmother of my younger sister." How this girl of photograph is related to Rekha?

Sol.

First Method – By Generating Charts:

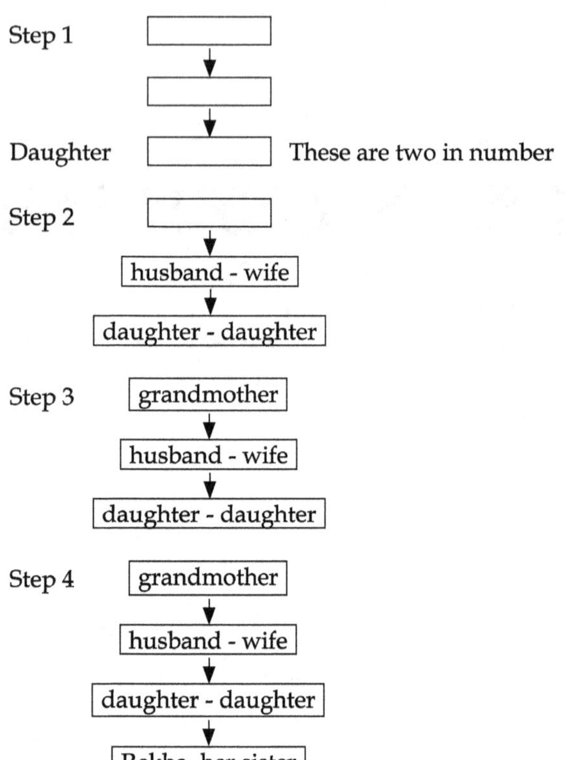

Second method:

1. Grandmother of younger sister of Rekha → Grandmother of Rekha
2. Wife of only son of grandmother → Mother of Rekha
3. Younger daughter of the mother → Younger sister

Note: While solving the question (+) can be used for male and (–) can be used for female.

Directions: Each of these questions is based on the following information:

A + B means A is the mother of B.

A – B means A is the sister of B.

A * B means A is the father of B.

A β B means A is the brother of B.

1. Which of the following means Q is the grandfather of P?
   (a) P + N * M * Q
   (b) Q * N * M + P
   (c) Q β M β N * P
   (d) None of these

2. Which of the following means that N is the maternal uncle of M?
   (a) N β P – L + E – M
   (b) N – Y + A β M
   (c) M – Y * P – N
   (d) N β C + F * M

3. Pointing to a photograph of a boy Sanjay said, "He is the son of the only daughter of my father." How is Sanjay related to that boy?
   (a) Sister   (b) Uncle
   (c) Cousin   (d) Father

4. If A is the brother of B; B is the sister of C; and C is the father of D, how D is related to A?
   (a) Brother
   (b) Sister
   (c) Nephew
   (d) Cannot be determined

5. Introducing a boy, a girl said, "He is the son of the daughter of the father of my uncle." How is the boy related to the girl?
   (a) Brother   (b) Nephew
   (c) Uncle   (d) Son-in-law

6. Pointing to Gagan, Neena says, "I am the daughter of the only son of his grandfather." How Neena is related to Gagan?
   (a) Niece
   (b) Daughter
   (c) Sister
   (d) Cannot be determined

7. Ajay's son Babloo is married with Chanchal whose sister Divya is married to Rahul the brother of Babloo. How Divya is related to Ajay?
   (a) Sister
   (b) Daughter's-in-law
   (c) Sister-in-law
   (d) Cousin

8. Pointing to a girl Sandeep said, "She is the daughter of the only sister of my father." How is Sandeep related to the girl?
   (a) Uncle   (b) Cousin
   (c) Father   (d) Grandfather

9. Pointing to Vivek, Madhu said, "I am the only daughter of one of the sons of his father." How is Vivek related to Madhu?
   (a) Nephew
   (b) Uncle
   (c) Father or Uncle
   (d) Father

10. Introducing a man, Satish said, "He is the father of the only daughter of my son." How that man is related to Satish?
    (a) Son   (b) Brother-in-law
    (c) Husband   (d) Son-in-law

11. Pointing to a man on the stage, Ritu said, "He is the brother of the daughter of the wife of my husband." How is the man on the stage related to Ritu?
    (a) Husband   (b) Cousin
    (c) Nephew   (d) Son

12. A party consists of grandmother, father, mother, four sons and their wives and one son and two daughters to each of the sons. How many females are there in all?
    (a) 14   (b) 19
    (c) 12   (d) 25

13. Lata and Mona are Ravi's wives. Shalu is Mona's Step-daughter. How is Lata related to Shalu?
    (a) Sister   (b) Mother-in-Law
    (c) Mother   (d) Step-mother

14. Deepak has a brother Amit. Deepak is the son of Chaya. Binod is Chaya's father. In terms of relationship, what is Amit of Binod?

(a) Son   (b) Grandson

(c) Brother   (d) Grandfather

15. Disha's mother is the only daughter of Mona's father. How is Mona's husband related to Disha?

(a) Uncle   (b) Father

(c) Grandfather (d) Brother

16. If

(i) M is brother of N

(ii) B is brother of N

(iii) M is brother of D

then which of the following statements is definitely true?

(a) N is brother of B

(b) N is brother of D

(c) M is brother of B

(d) D is brother of M

17. Daya is brother of Raj. Rita is sister of Amit. Raj is son of Rita. How is Daya related to Rita?

(a) Son   (b) Brother

(c) Nephew   (d) Father

18. A is B's sister. C is B's mother. D is C's father. E is D's mother. Then, how is A related to D?

(a) Grandmother

(b) Grandfather

(c) Daughter

(d) Grand daughter

19 Given that:

(i) A is brother of B

(ii) C is father of A

(iii) D is brother of E

(iv) E is daughter of B

The uncle of D is

(a) A   (b) B

(c) C   (d) E

20. Pointing to Lalit in the photograph, Rajan said, "His mother has only one grandchild whose mother is my sister."How is Rajan related to Lalit?

(a) Brother

(b) Brother-in-law

(c) Father-in-law

(d) Data inadequate

Direction Sense Test

Learning Objectives : In this chapter, students will learn about:
- ✓ Different directions and their concept

CHAPTER SUMMARY

There are four main directions - *East, West, North* and *South* as shown below:

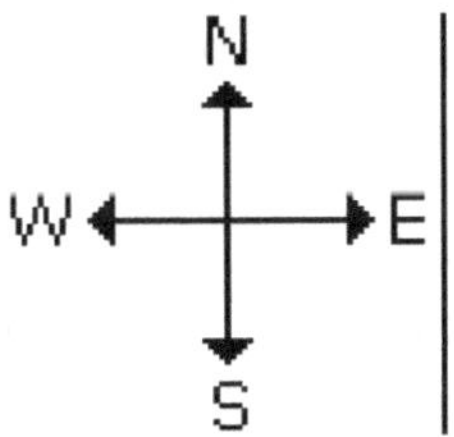

There are four Intermediate directions - *North-East (N-E)*, *North-West (N-W)*, *South-East (S-E)*, and *South-West (S-W)* as shown below:

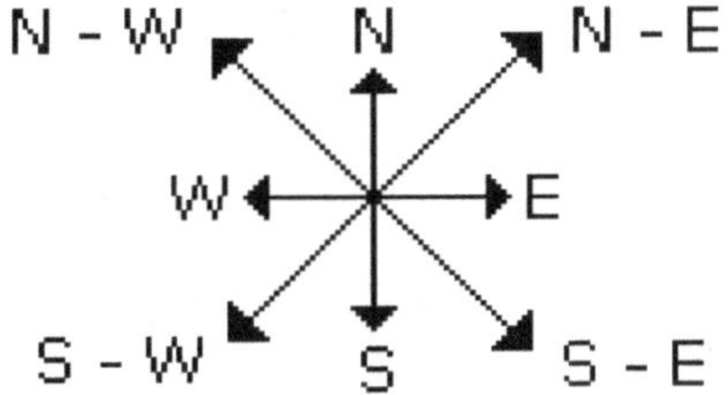

Few points to know for direction sense:

1. At the time of sunrise, if a man stands facing the east, his shadow will be towards west.

2. At the time of sunset, the shadow of an object is always in the east.

3. If a man stands facing the North, at the time of sunrise his shadow will be towards his left and at the time of sunset it will be towards his right.

4. At 12:00 noon, the rays of the sun are vertically downward hence there will be no shadow.

Example 1: Golu starting from his house, goes 4 Km in the East, then he turns to his right and goes 3 Km. What minimum distance will be covered by him to come back to his house?

Sol.

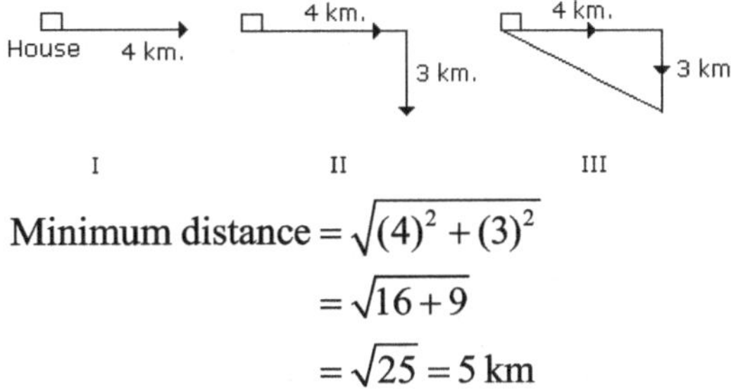

$$\text{Minimum distance} = \sqrt{(4)^2 + (3)^2}$$
$$= \sqrt{16 + 9}$$
$$= \sqrt{25} = 5 \, \text{km}$$

Example 2: One morning after sunrise Ashu while going to school met Ankit at Crossing Republic road. Ankit's shadow was exactly to the right of Ashu. If they were face to face, which direction was Ashu facing?

Sol.

In the morning sunrises in the east.

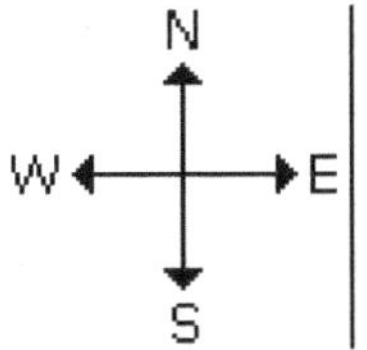

So in morning the shadow falls towards the west.

Now Ankit's shadow falls to the right of the Ashu. Hence Ashu is facing South.

1. One morning after sunrise, Shraddha and Shubhra were standing in a chowk in Rai Bareily with their back towards each other. Shraddha shadow fell exactly towards her right hand side. Which direction was Shubhra facing?
   (a) East   (b) West
   (c) North   (d) South

2. A girl was going towards east. She turns left than turned 90°. A girl was going towards east. She turned left and then turned 90° in anti-clockwise direction. In which direction was she going now?
   (a) East   (b) West
   (c) North   (d) South

3. Golu walks 1 km Southwards takes a left turns, walks 6 km, then turns left, walks 5 km and again turning right, walks 5 km. In which direction is he now from the starting point?
   (a) East   (b) North
   (c) West   (d) South

4. Ankit starts from his house and walks Westwards. He takes a left turn and right turn, before each turn he walks 7 km. In which direction is he walking now?
   (a) North   (b) South
   (c) West   (d) East

5. Rajesh went 50 km towards East, turned right and went 50 m. Rajesh again turned right and went 5 km. He then took a 450 turn towards his right and went straight. In which direction is he walking now?
   (a) West
   (b) North-East
   (c) North-West
   (d) North

6. Rakesh walks 50 km towards East. He then turns right and then walk 15 km. He again turns right and 50 km. Further, he moves 10 km after turning to the right. How far he is from his original position?
   (a) 15 km   (b) 30 km
   (c) 20 km   (d) 5 km

7. After his office in the afternoon Ronak goes facing the sun. He turns to his left, then to his right and then turn to his right and again to his left. In which direction is he moving?
   (a) North   (b) West
   (c) East   (d) South

8. Sahil starting from his house, goes 10 km towards East, turns to his left and goes 6 km. Finally he turns to his left and goes 10 km. How far is he from his house?
   (a) 6 km   (b) 4 km
   (c) 10 km   (d) 8 km

9. Mohan starting from his house, goes 8 km in the East, turns to his right and goes 6 km. What minimum distance will be covered by him to come back to his house?
   (a) 5 km   (b) 6 km
   (c) 8 km   (d) 10 km

10. If South-East becomes North, North-East becomes West and so on, what will West become?
    (a) North-East   (b) North-West
    (c) South-East   (d) South-West

11. A man walks 15 km towards South and then turns to the right. After walking 7 km he turns to the left and walk 9 km. In which direction is he from the starting place?
    (a) West   (b) South
    (c) North-East   (d) South-West

12. Starting from the point X, Suraj walks 20 m towards west. He turns left and walked 25 m. He then turned left and walked 20 m. After this he turns to his right and walked 18 m. How far now Suraj from X?
    (a) 43 m   (b) 47 m
    (c) 48 m   (d) 32 m

13. One evening before sunset Tulsi and Hasini were talking to each other face to face. If Hasini's shadow was exactly to her right, in which direction was Tulsi facing?
    (a) North
    (b) South
    (c) East
    (d) Data is inadequate

14. Rohan rode his bicycle Northwards, turned left and rode 2 km and again turned left and rode 3 km. He found himself 2 km west of his starting point. How far did he ride northwards initially?

(a) 1 km   (b) 2 km

(c) 3 km   (d) 5 km

15. Golu walks 5 km towards North. He turns to east and walks 20 km. After this he turns to North and walks 5 km. Again he turns towards East and walks 5 km. In which direction is he from the starting point?

(a) North   (b) North-East

(c) West   (d) South-West

Seating Arrangement

6

Learning Objectives : In this chapter, students will learn about:
- ✓ Row seating arrangement
- ✓ Circle seating arrangement

CHAPTER SUMMARY

Seating/Sitting arrangement is one of the important parts of verbal reasoning. There are two types of seating arrangements:

- Row seating arrangement
- Circle seating arrangement

Row Seating Arrangement

Here are a few points to remember in row seating arrangements.

- Find and draw a line of direction. (North, South, East, West)
- Note down right side and left side in the top of the line which you draw
- Arrange the seats.

Example 1: A, B, C, D and E are sitting on a bench. A is sitting next to B, C is sitting next to D, D is not sitting with E who is on the left end of the bench. C is on the second position from the right. A is to the right of B and E. A and C are sitting together. In which position A is sitting?

Sol.

Now, we have a platform to put seating arrangements of any questions to be answered. Let us solve this question by the method explained below:

- Draw a line and find out who is on the last, in this question "E" is at the left end of the bench.
- Another placement would be of "A" which is right of "B" and "E".

$$L \underline{\hspace{4cm}} R$$
$$E \quad B \quad A \quad C \quad D$$

Circle Seating Arrangements

Here are a few points to remember incircle seating arrangements.

- Draw a circle.
- Find out who is on the right and who is on left.
- You will find your answer.

Directions (1-4): Five girls are sitting on a bench to be photographed. Shraddha is to the left of Rani and to the right of Tina. Sheetal is to the right of Rani. Reeta is between Rani and Sheetal.

1. Who is sitting immediate right to Reeta?
   (a) Tina
   (b) Rani
   (c) Sheetal
   (d) Shraddha

2. Who is in the middle of the photograph?
   (a) Tina
   (b) Rani
   (c) Reeta
   (d) Shraddha

3. Who is second from the right?
   (a) Sheetal
   (b) Rani
   (c) Reeta
   (d) Tina

4. Who is second from the left in the photograph?
   (a) Reeta
   (b) Sheetal
   (c) Tina
   (d) Shraddha

Directions (5-8): Pramod, Amit, Ravi, Sam, Tom, Udit, Vinay and Vineet are sitting round the circle and are facing the centre:

Pramod is second to the right of Tom who is the neighbour of Ravi and Vinay.

Sam is not the neighbour of Pramod.

Vinay is the neighbour of Udit.

Amit is not between Sam and Vineet. Vineet is not between Udit and Sam.

5. Which two of the following are not neighbours?
   (a) Ravi and Vinay
   (b) Udit and Vinay
   (c) Ravi and Pramod
   (d) Amit and Vineet

6. Who is on the immediate right to Vinay?
   (a) Pramod
   (b) Udit
   (c) Ravi
   (d) Tom

7. Which of the following is correct?
   (a) Pramod is to the immediate right of Amit.
   (b) Ravi is between Udit and Vinay.
   (c) Amit is to the immediate left of Vineet.
   (d) Udit is between Vineet and Sam.

8. What is the position of Sam?
   (a) Between Udit and Vinay
   (b) Second to the right of Pramod
   (c) To the immediate right of Vineet
   (d) Data inadequate.

Directions (9-10): Six friends are sitting in a circle and are facing the centre. Daisy is between Prakash and Rahul. Sonia is between Meenu and Lokesh. Prakash and Meenu are opposite to each other.

9. Who is sitting right to Prakash?
   (a) Meenu
   (b) Daisy
   (c) Rahul
   (d) Lokesh

10. Who are the neighbours of Meenu?
    (a) Prakash and Daisy
    (b) Daisy and Pamela
    (c) Sonia and Rahul
    (d) Lokesh and Sonia

Syllogism

Learning Objectives : In this chapter, students will learn about:
- ✓ Concept of statements and their logical conclusion

CHAPTER SUMMARY

The questions of this type contain two or more statements and these statements are followed by two or more conclusions. You have to find out which of the conclusions logically follow from the given statements. The statements have to be taken true even if they seem to be at variance from the commonly known facts.

For such questions, you can take the help of Venn Diagrams. On the basis of the given statements, you should draw all the possible diagrams, and then derive the solution from each of these diagrams separately. Finally, the answer common to the all the diagrams is taken.

Example 1:

Statements:
1. All dogs are asses.
2. All asses are bulls.

Conclusions:
1. Some dogs are not bulls.
2. Some bulls are dogs.
3. All bulls are dogs.
4. All dogs are bulls.

Sol.

On the basis of both statements, the following one diagram is possible.

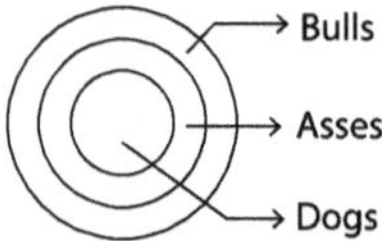

From the diagram it is clear that (2) and (4) conclusions logically follow.

Example 2:

Statements:
1. Some dogs are asses.
2. Some asses are bulls.

Conclusions:
1. Some asses are not dogs.
2. Some dogs are bulls.

Sol.

From these given statements the following diagrams are possible:

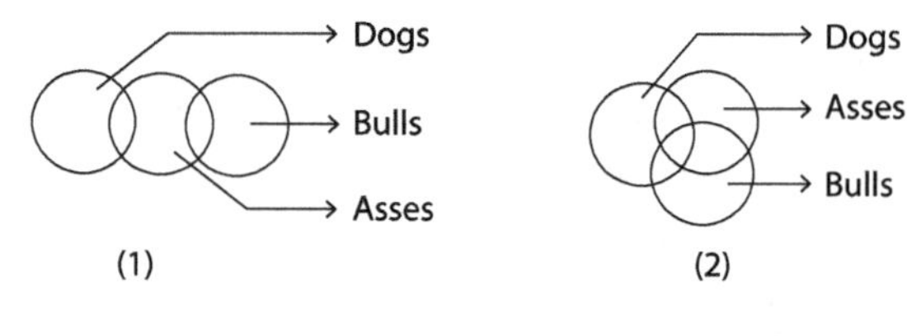

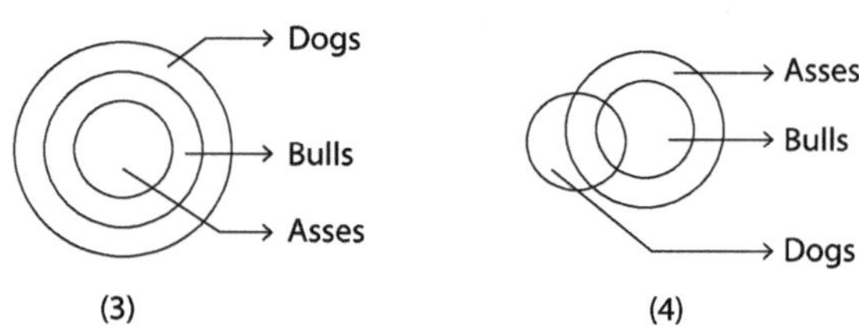

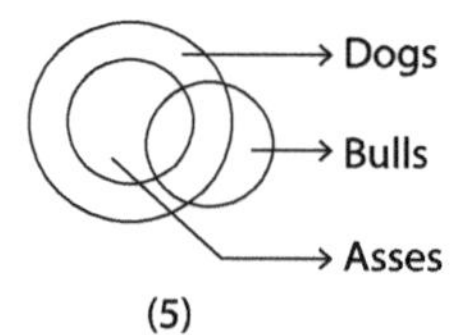

From the diagram neither (1) nor (2) conclusions follow.

Say if you are confused on statements and you do not find any answers of syllogism by Venn diagram, then follow the below discussed technique.

In all the statements of syllogism questions, first-term is called the subject and the second is called predicate.

Statement	Subject	Predicate
all pigs are ducks	pigs	ducks
all BJPs are AAPs	BJPs	AAPs
all bowlers are batsman	bowlers	batsman
all readers are commentators	readers	commentators

Now see that each statement has 4 variables like we mentioned below.

Things	Subject	is/are (not)	Predicate
all	dogs	are	cats
some	readers	are not	commentators

Types of statements in syllogism

Statement	Type	Code name
All pigs are ducks	Universal Positive	UP
Some Pigs are Ducks	Particular Positive	PP
No Pig is a Duck	Universal Negative	UN
Some Pigs are not Ducks	Particular Negative	PN

Classify which statement is universal or particular:

All, every, any, none, not a single, only	Universal
Some, many, a few, quite a few, not many, very little, most of, almost, generally, often, frequently	Particular

Conversation of statements

Code-Name	Conversation
UP	Only PP
UN	PN or UN
PP	Only PP
PN	We cannot convert it

UP + UP = UP
UP + UN = UN
UN + (UP/PP) = PN
PP + (UP/UN) = PP or PN

Here is the easy way to understand the upper chart:

All + All = All

All + No = No

All + Some = No Conclusion

Some + All = Some

Some + Some = No Conclusion

Some + No = Some Not

No + No = No Conclusion

No + All = Some not reversed

No + Some = Some not reversed

Let us solve a question using this technique.

Statement:

All mothers are parents. (UP)

Some women are not mothers. (PN)

Conclusion:

(a)   All mothers are women

(b)   Some mothers are parents.

(c)   All parents are mothers.

(d)   None of the above

Now you can see ALL + Some have no conclusion so that means our answer would be (D)

Directions (1–5): In each of the following questions two statements are given. Which are followed by four conclusions (1), (2), (3) and (4). Choose the conclusions which logically follow from the given statements.

1. **Statements:** No door is dog. All the dogs are cats.

   Conclusions:
   (1) No door is cat.
   (2) No cat is door.
   (3) Some cats are dogs.
   (4) All the cats are dogs.
   (a) Only (2) and (4)   (b) Only (1) and (3)
   (c) Only (3) and (4)   (d) Only (3)

2. **Statements:** All green are blue. All blue are white.

   Conclusions:
   (1) Some blue are green.
   (2) Some white are green.
   (3) Some green are not white.
   (4) All white are blue.
   (a) Only (1) and (2)   (b) Only (1) and (3)
   (c) Only (1) and (4)   (d) Only (2) and (4)

3. **Statements:** All men are vertebrates. Some mammals are vertebrates.

   Conclusions:
   (1) All men are mammals.
   (2) All mammals are men.
   (3) Some vertebrates are mammals.
   (4) All vertebrates are men.
   (a) Only (4)   (b) Only (2)
   (c) Only (3)   (d) Only (1)

4. **Statements:** All the phones are scales. All the scales are calculators.

   Conclusions:
   (1) All the calculators are scales.
   (2) All the phones are calculators
   (3) All the scales are phones.
   (4) Some calculators are phones.
   (a) Only (1) and (4)   (b) Only (3) and (4)
   (c) Only (2) and (4)   (d) Only (1) and (2)

5. **Statements:** Some tables are T.V. Some T.V. are radios.

   Conclusions:
   (1) Some tables are radios.
   (2) Some radios are tables.
   (3) All the radios are T.V.
   (4) All the T.V. are tables.
   (a) Only (2) and (4)   (b) Only (1) and (3)
   (c) Only (4)   (d) None of these

Directions (6–10): In the following figure small square represents the persons who know English, triangle to those who know Marathi, big square to those who know Telugu and circle to those who know Hindi. In the different regions of the figures from 1 to 12 are given.

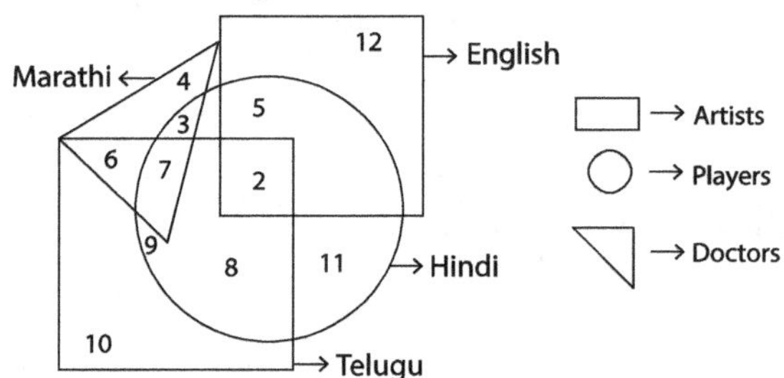

6. How many persons can speak English and Hindi both the languages only?
   (a) 5   (b) 8
   (c) 7   (d) 18

7. How many persons can speak Marathi and Telugu both?
   (a) 10   (b) 11
   (c) 13   (d) None of these

8. How many persons can speak only English?
   (a) 9   (b) 12
   (c) 7   (d) 19

9. How many persons can speak English, Hindi and Telugu?
   (a) 8   (b) 2
   (c) 7   (d) None of these

10. How many of them speak only Marathi?
    (a) 8   (b) 12
    (c) 4   (d) None of these

Embedded Figures 8

CHAPTER SUMMARY

A figure 'A' is called embedded in a figure B, if figure B contains figure A as its part. Many types of problems can be formed on embedded figures.

In such type of problems, we have a problem figure represented by X followed by four alternatives figures A, B, C and D. One has to locate the correct alternative in which figure X is embedded. The following examples will clarify.

Example 1:

Problem Figure   Alternative Figures

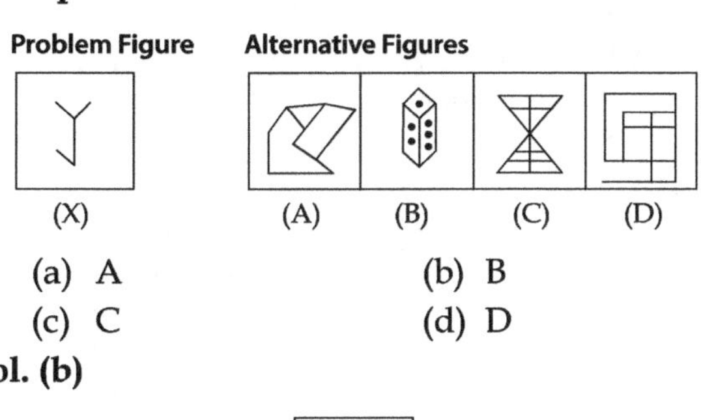

(X)   (A)   (B)   (C)   (D)

(a) A   (b) B
(c) C   (d) D

Sol. (b)

Example 2: Find out the alternative figure which contains figure (X) as its part.

Problem Figure   Alternative Figures

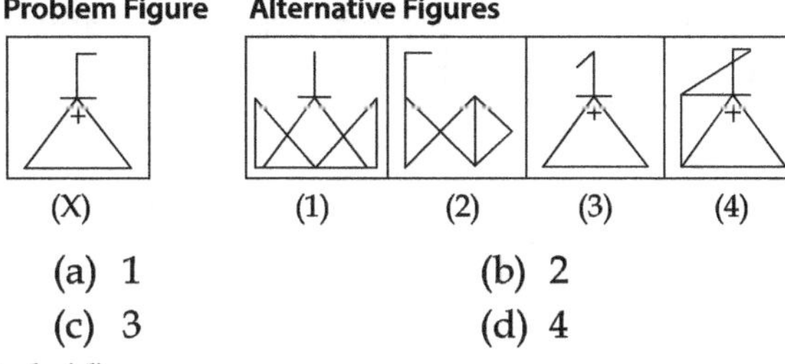

(X)   (1)   (2)   (3)   (4)

(a) 1   (b) 2
(c) 3   (d) 4

Sol. (d)

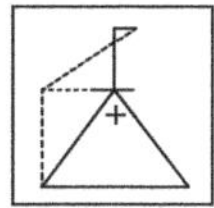

Directions (1-30): In each of the following questions, you are given a figure (X) followed by four alternative figures (A), (B), (C) and (D) such that figure (X) is embedded in one of them. Find out the alternative figure which contains fig. (X) as its part.

1. Find out the alternative figure which contains figure (X) as its part.

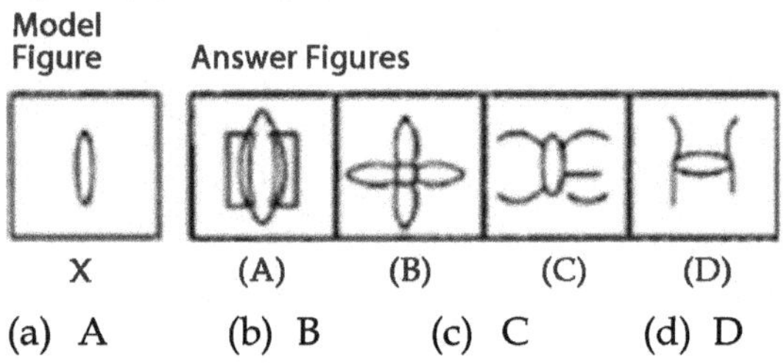

Model Figure   Answer Figures

X   (A)   (B)   (C)   (D)

(a) A   (b) B   (c) C   (d) D

2. Find out the alternative figure which contains figure (X) as its part.

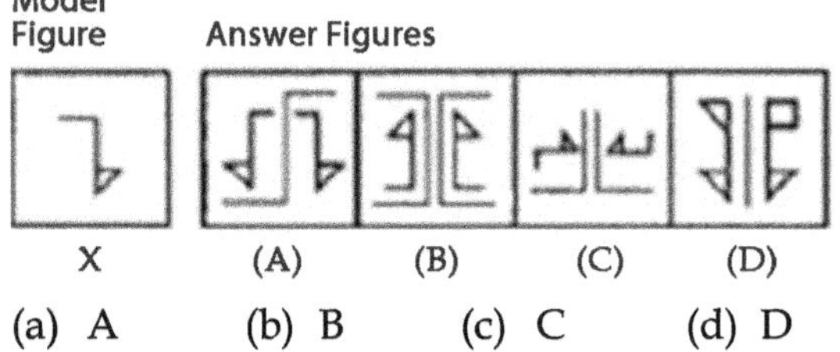

Model Figure   Answer Figures

X   (A)   (B)   (C)   (D)

(a) A   (b) B   (c) C   (d) D

3. Find out the alternative figure which contains figure (X) as its part.

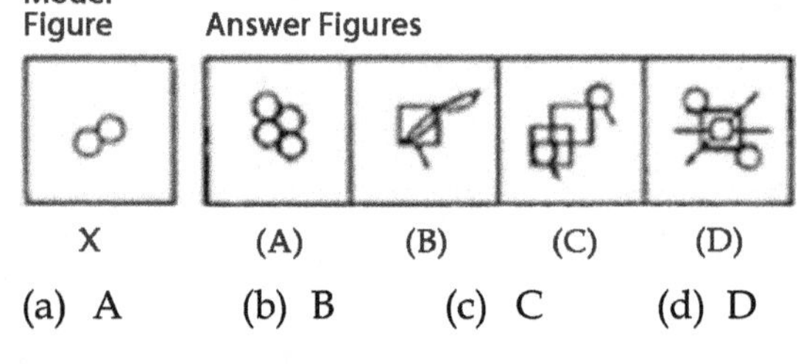

Model Figure   Answer Figures

X   (A)   (B)   (C)   (D)

(a) A   (b) B   (c) C   (d) D

4. Find out the alternative figure which contains figure (X) as its part.

Model Figure   Answer Figures

X   (A)   (B)   (C)   (D)

(a) A   (b) B   (c) C   (d) D

5. Find out the alternative figure which contains figure (X) as its part.

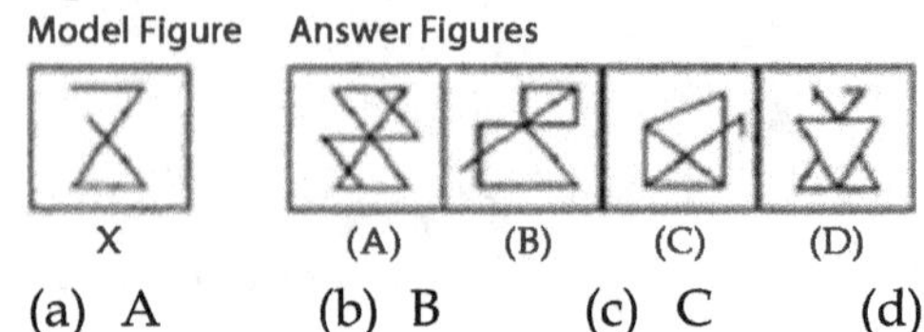

Model Figure   Answer Figures

X   (A)   (B)   (C)   (D)

(a) A   (b) B   (c) C   (d) D

6. Find out the alternative figure which contains figure (X) as its part.

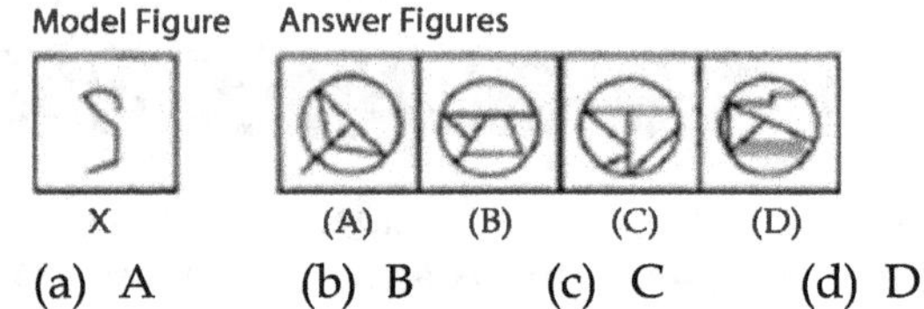

Model Figure   Answer Figures

X   (A)   (B)   (C)   (D)

(a) A   (b) B   (c) C   (d) D

7. Find out the alternative figure which contains figure (X) as its part.

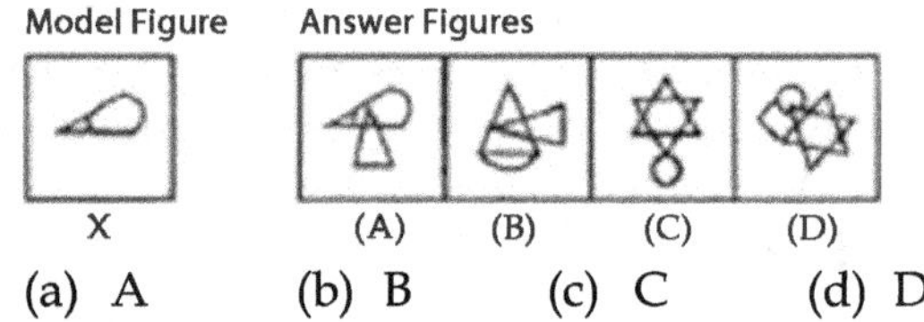

Model Figure   Answer Figures

X   (A)   (B)   (C)   (D)

(a) A   (b) B   (c) C   (d) D

8. Find out the alternative figure which contains figure (X) as its part.

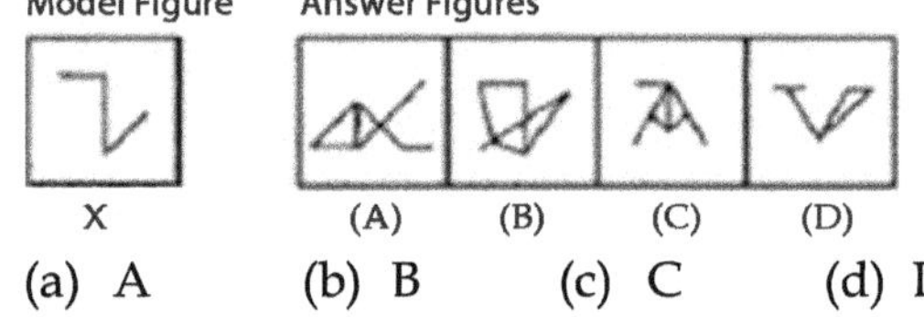

Model Figure   Answer Figures

X   (A)   (B)   (C)   (D)

(a) A   (b) B   (c) C   (d) D

9. Find out the alternative figure which contains figure (X) as its part.

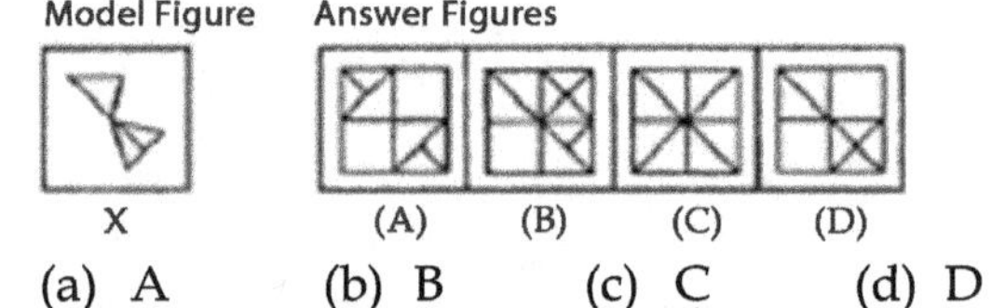

Model Figure   Answer Figures

X   (A)   (B)   (C)   (D)

(a) A   (b) B   (c) C   (d) D

10. Find out the alternative figure which contains figure (X) as its part.

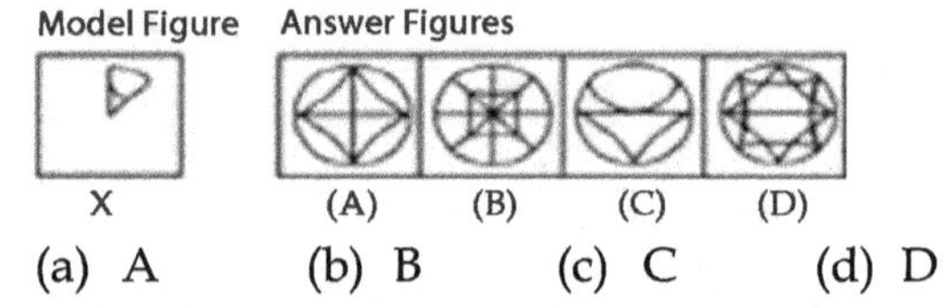

Model Figure   Answer Figures

X   (A)   (B)   (C)   (D)

(a) A   (b) B   (c) C   (d) D

11. Find out the alternative figure which contains figure (X) as its part.

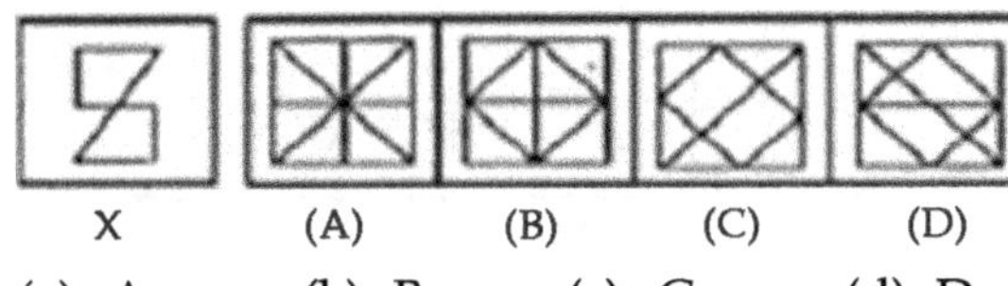

(a) A (b) B (c) C (d) D

12. Find out the alternative figure which contains figure (X) as its part.

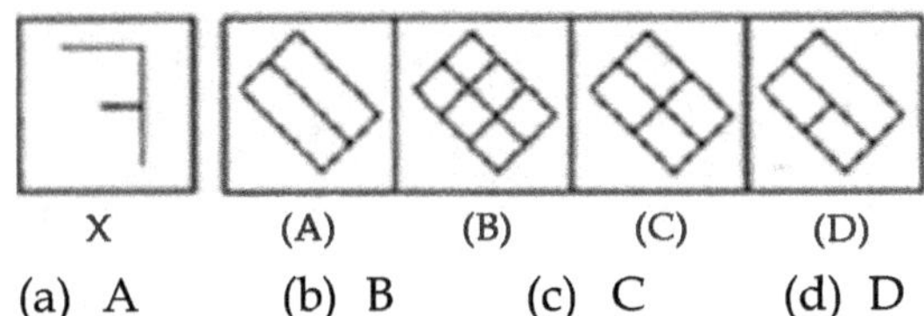

(a) A (b) B (c) C (d) D

13. Find out the alternative figure which contains figure (X) as its part.

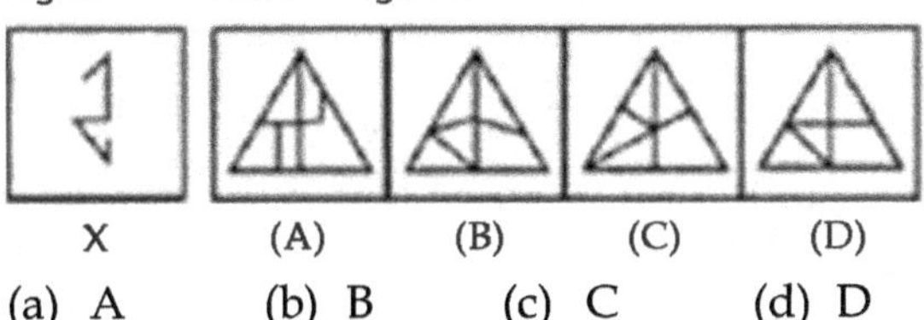

(a) A (b) B (c) C (d) D

14. Find out the alternative figure which contains figure (X) as its part.

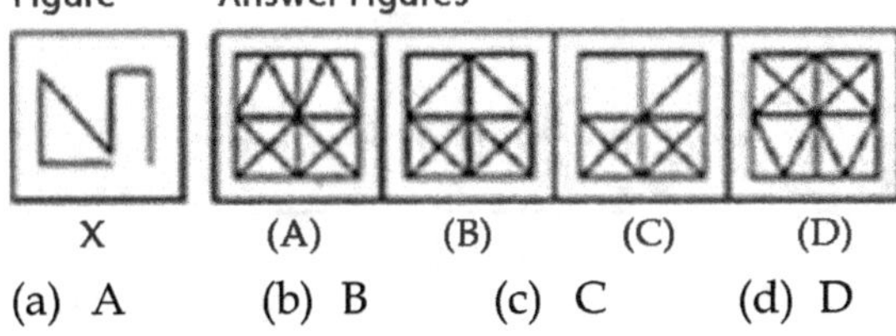

(a) A (b) B (c) C (d) D

15. Find out the alternative figure which contains figure (X) as its part.

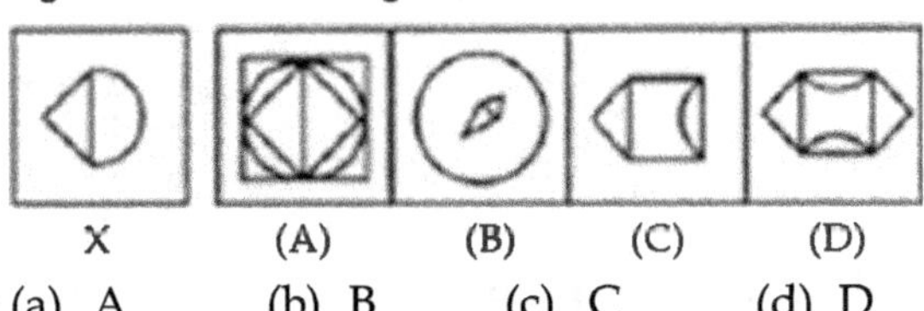

(a) A (b) B (c) C (d) D

16. Find out the alternative figure which contains figure (X) as its part.

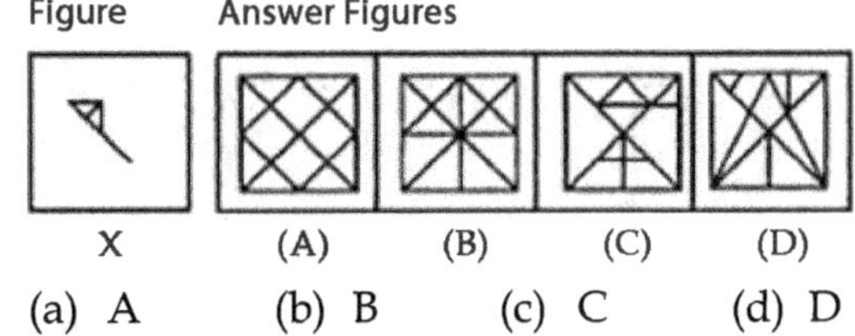

(a) A (b) B (c) C (d) D

17. Find out the alternative figure which contains figure (X) as its part.

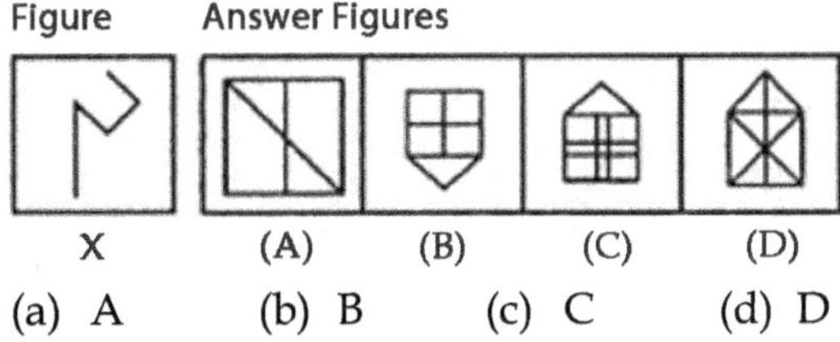

(a) A (b) B (c) C (d) D

18. Find out the alternative figure which contains figure (X) as its part.

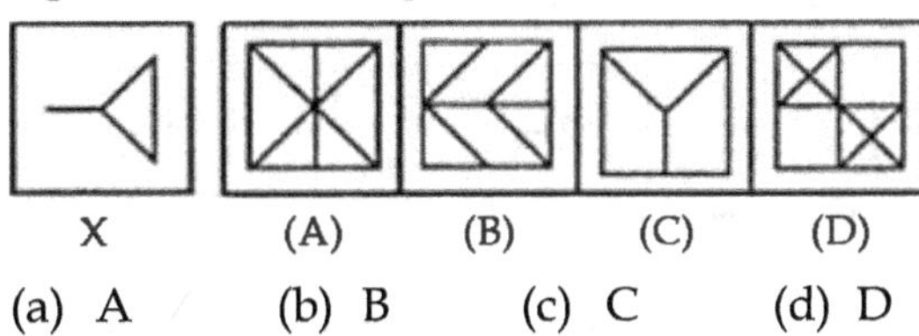

(a) A (b) B (c) C (d) D

19. Find out the alternative figure which contains figure (X) as its part.

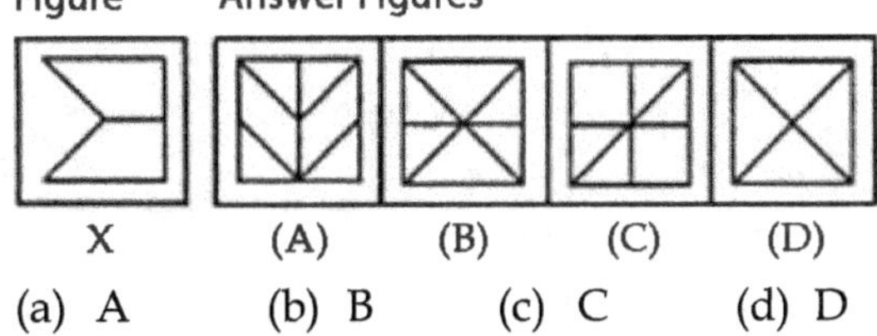

(a) A (b) B (c) C (d) D

20. Find out the alternative figure which contains figure (X) as its part.

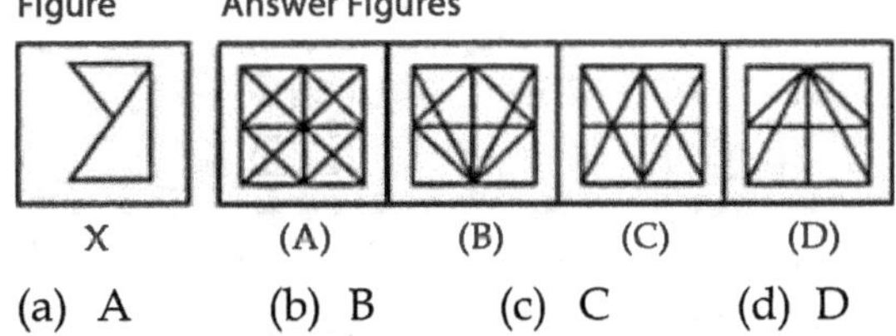

(a) A (b) B (c) C (d) D

21. Find out the alternative figure which contains figure (X) as its part.

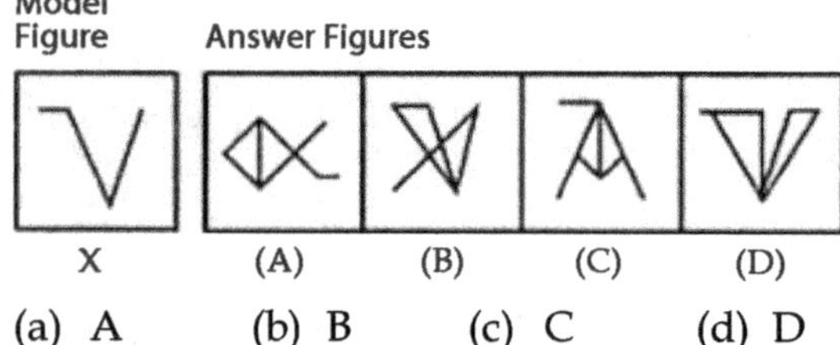

(a) A (b) B (c) C (d) D

22. Find out the alternative figure which contains figure (X) as its part.

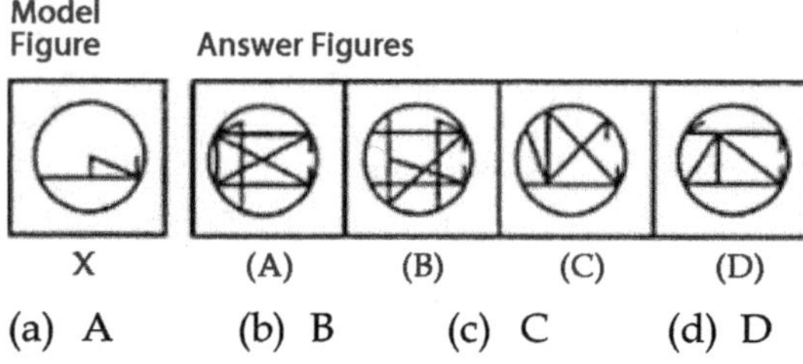

(a) A (b) B (c) C (d) D

23. Find out the alternative figure which contains figure (X) as its part.

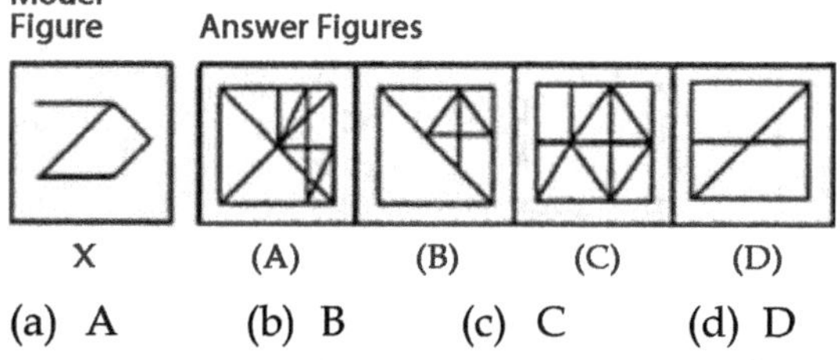

(a) A (b) B (c) C (d) D

24. Find out the alternative figure which contains figure (X) as its part.

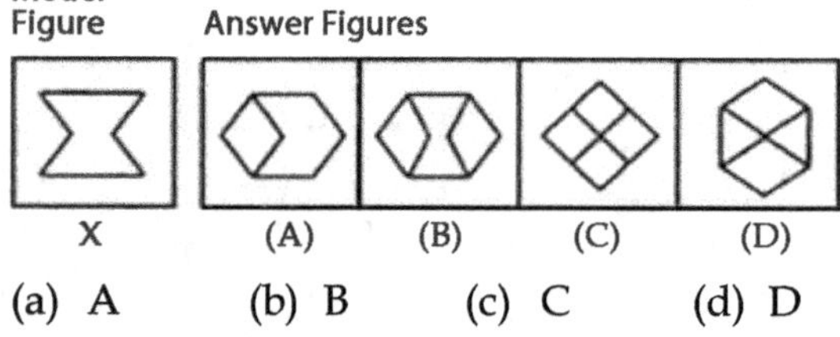

(a) A (b) B (c) C (d) D

25. Find out the alternative figure which contains figure (X) as its part.

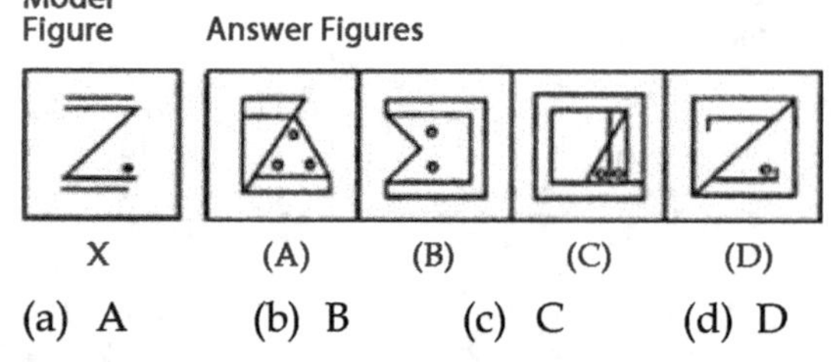

(a) A (b) B (c) C (d) D

26. Find out the alternative figure which contains figure (X) as its part.

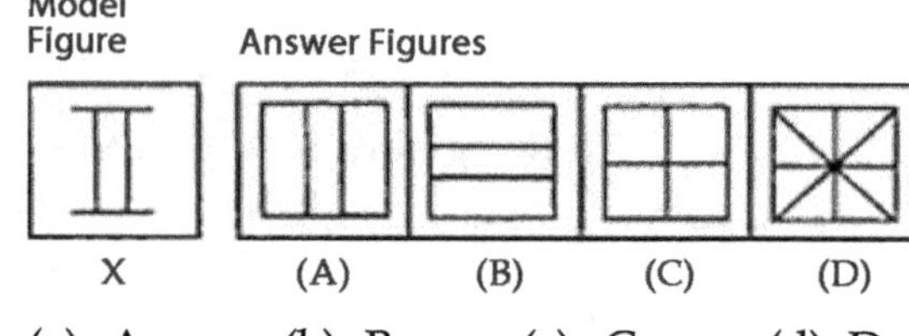

(a) A (b) B (c) C (d) D

27. Find out the alternative figure which contains figure (X) as its part.

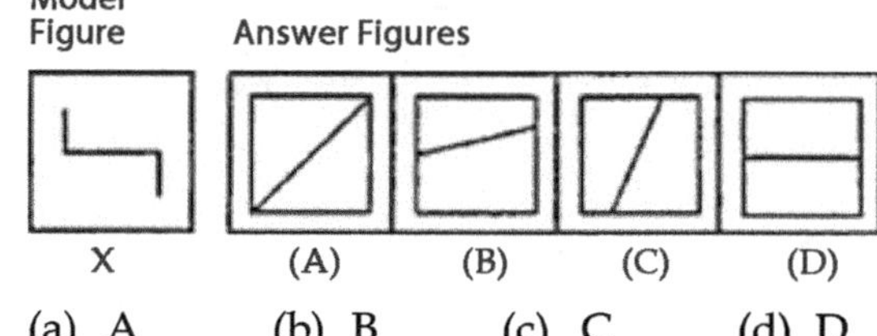

(a) A (b) B (c) C (d) D

28. Find out the alternative figure which contains figure (X) as its part.

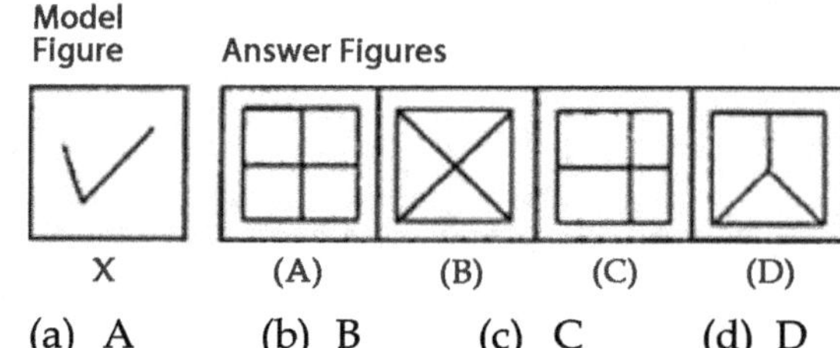

(a) A (b) B (c) C (d) D

29. Find out the alternative figure which contains figure (X) as its part.

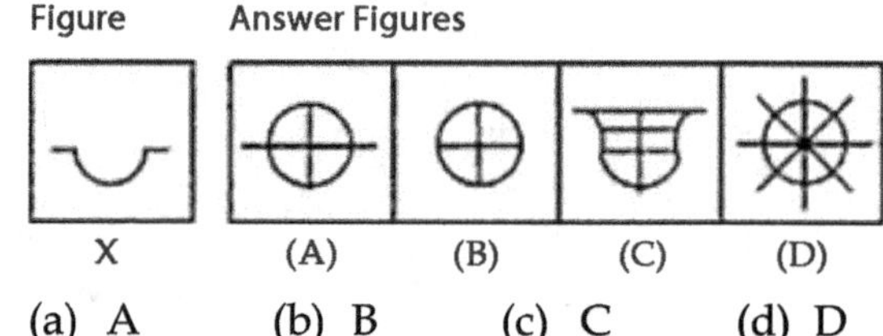

(a) A (b) B (c) C (d) D

30. Find out the alternative figure which contains figure (X) as its part.

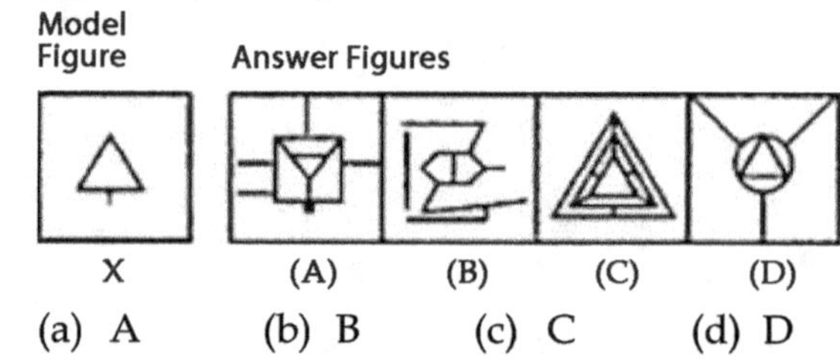

(a) A (b) B (c) C (d) D

Figure Puzzles

Learning Objectives : In this chapter, students will learn about:
- ✓ Questions on mathematical operations and number puzzles

CHAPTER SUMMARY

Questions on mathematical operations and number puzzles are designed to test candidate's skill at mathematical operations and numbers. In mathematical operations, usual mathematical symbols are converted into another form by either interchanging the symbols or using different symbols in place of original symbols in order to make simpler calculation tedious. On the other hand, in questions of number puzzles, a few numbers are inserted into a figure which follows a particular rule for the placement of different numbers at different places of the figures. Students are asked to select a missing number, following the rule of placement of numbers, from the given options.

Example 1: Which number will replace the question mark?

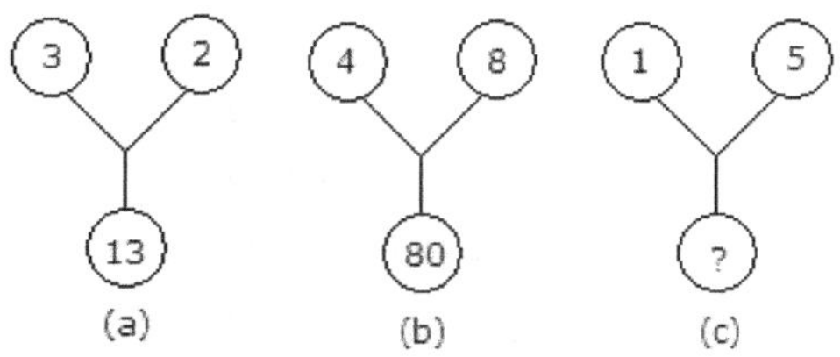

Sol.

From fig. a: $(3)^2 + (2)^2 = 13$
From fig. b: $(4)^2 + (8)^2 = 80$
From fig. c: $? = (1)^2 + (5)^2$
$? = 1 + 25$
$? = 26$

Hence the number 26 will replace the question mark.

Example 2: Which number will replace the question mark?

9	17	16
5	4	?
5	4	8
9	17	8

Sol.

From column I: $(9 \times 5) \div 5 = 9$
From column II: $(17 \times 4) \div 4 = 17$
From column III: $(16 \times ?) \div 8 = 8$
$16 \times ? = 64$
$? = 4$

Hence the number 4 will replace the question mark.

Example 3: Which number will replace the question mark?

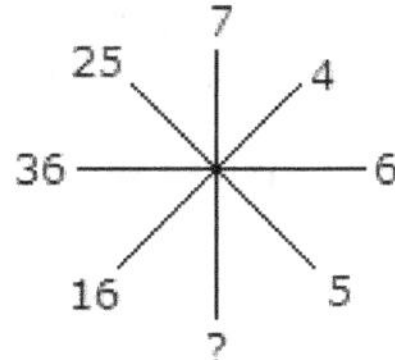

Sol.

$(5)^2 = 25$
$(6)^2 = 36$
$(4)^2 = 16$
$(7)^2 = 49$

Hence the number 49 will replace the question mark.

MULTIPLE CHOICE QUESTIONS

Directions (1–25): In this type of questions, a figure or a matrix is given in which some numbers are filled according to a rule. A place is left blank. You have to find out a character (a number or a letter) from the given possible answers which may be filled in the blank space.

1. Which one will replace the question mark?

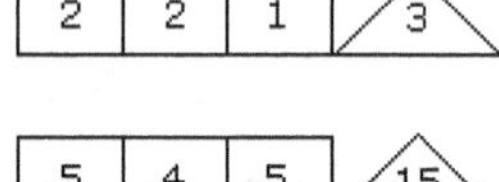

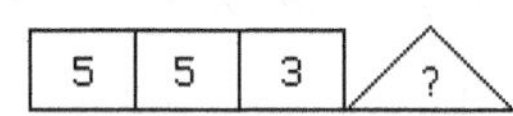

(a) 11   (b) 19
(c) 15   (d) 22

2. Which one will replace the question mark?

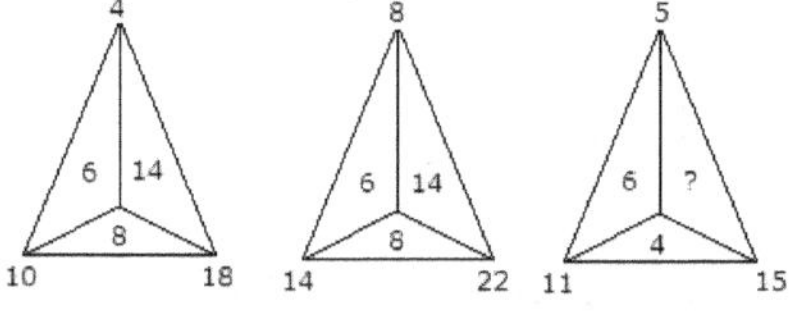

(a) 8   (b) 14
(c) 10   (d) 6

3. Which one will replace the question mark?

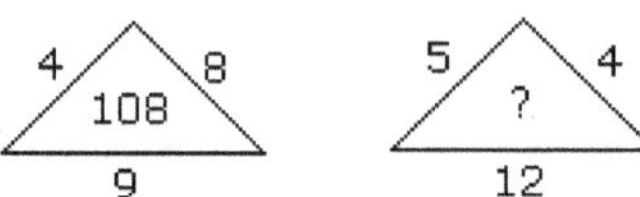

(a) 80   (b) 114
(c) 108   (d) None of these

4. Which one will replace the question mark?

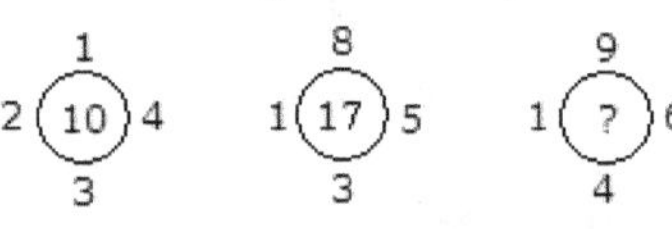

(a) 18   (b) 20
(c) 21   (d) 19

5. Which one will replace the question mark?

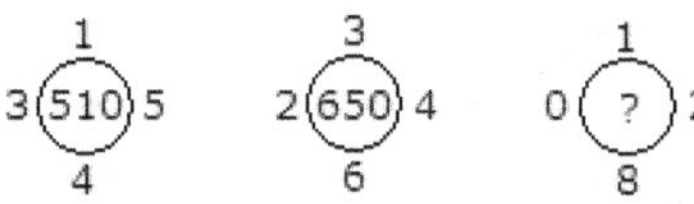

(a) 660   (b) 670
(c) 610   (d) 690

6. Which one will replace the question mark?

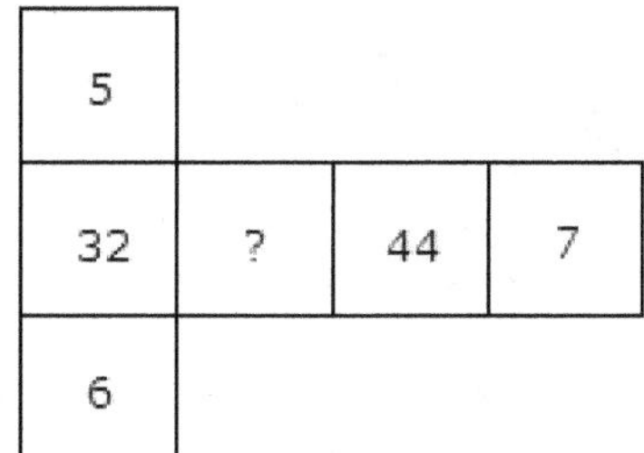

(a) 6   (b) 7
(c) 8   (d) 9

7. Which one will replace the question mark?

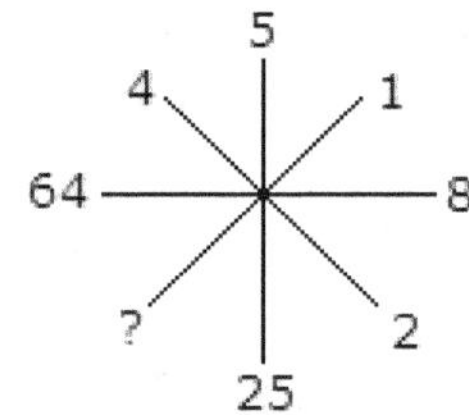

(a) 33   (b) 38
(c) 32   (d) 37

8. Which one will replace the question mark?

(a) 1   (b) 2
(c) 3   (d) 4

9. Which one will replace the question mark?

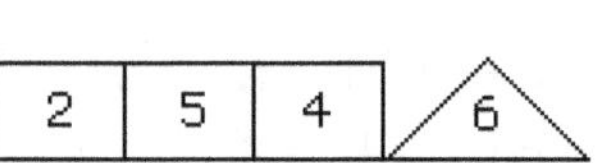

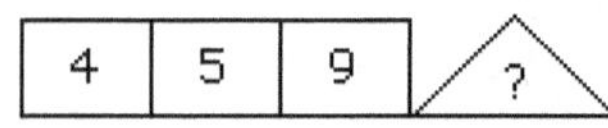

(a) 8   (b) 9
(c) 10   (d) 11

10. Which one will replace the question mark?

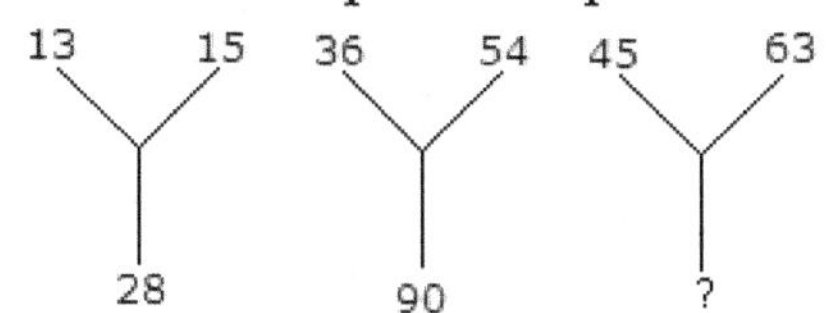

(a) 18   (b) 90
(c) 108   (d) 28

11. Which one will replace the question mark?

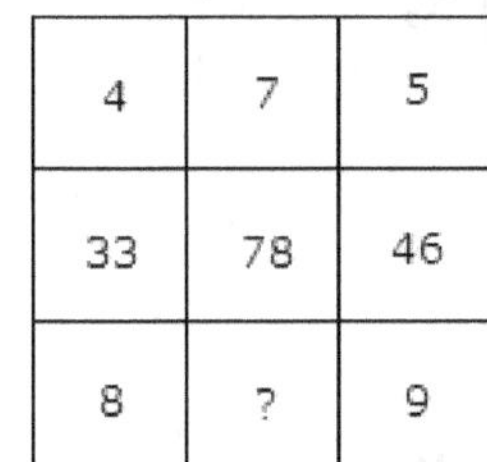

(a) 14   (b) 22
(c) 32   (d) 320

12. Which one will replace the question mark?

4	7	5
33	78	46
8	?	9

(a) 12   (b) 13
(c) 11   (d) 10

13. Which one will replace the question mark?

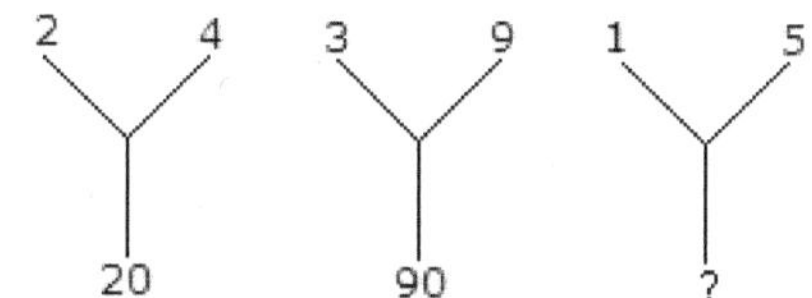

(a) 20   (b) 26
(c) 25   (d) 75

14. Which one will replace the question mark?

3	?	5
5	4	7
4	4	4
60	96	140

(a) 4   (b) 6
(c) 9   (d) 8

15. Which one will replace the question mark?

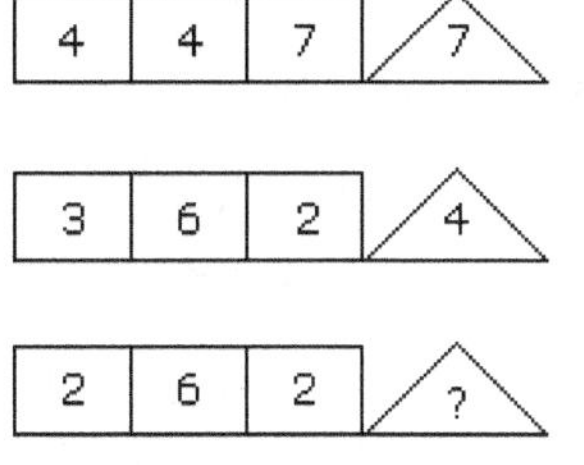

(a) 2   (b) 4
(c) 6   (d) 8

16. Which one will replace the question mark?

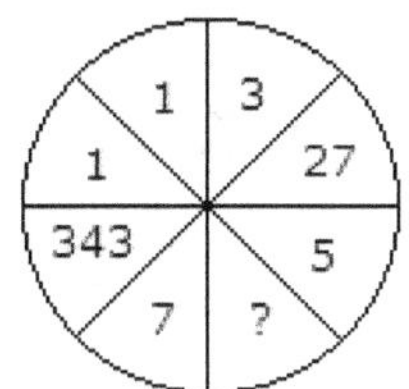

(a) 25   (b) 625
(c) 125   (d) 50

17. Which one will replace the question mark?

4	9	2
3	5	7
8	1	?

(a) 9   (b) 6
(c) 15   (d) 14

18. Which one will replace the question mark?

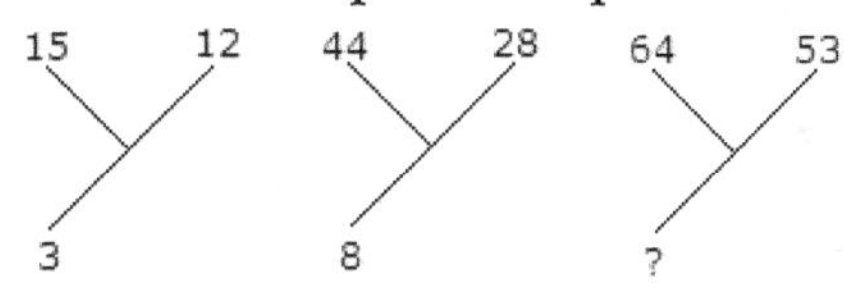

(a) 30   (b) 13
(c) 70   (d) 118

19. Which one will replace the question mark?

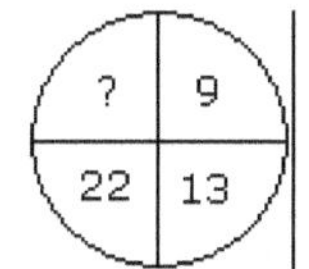

(a) 40   (b) 38
(c) 44   (d) 39

20. Which one will replace the question mark?

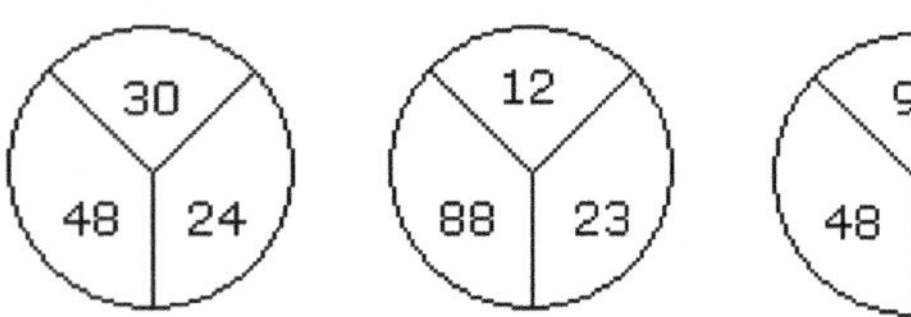

(a) 60   (b) 46
(c) 86   (d) 75

21. Which one will replace the question mark?

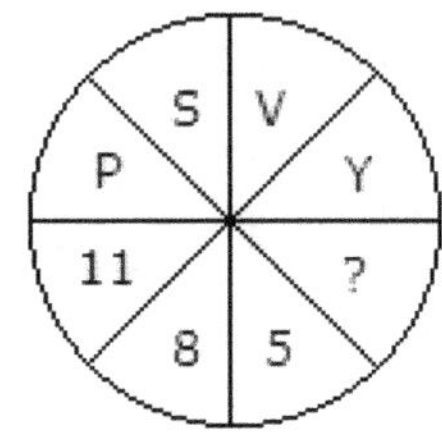

(a) 3   (b) 2
(c) 7   (d) 6

22. Which one will replace the question mark?

5	6	5
8	9	7
10	7	?
400	378	315

(a) 9   (b) 5
(c) 7   (d) 3

23. Which one will replace the question mark?

1	$\frac{1}{2}$	$\frac{3}{2}$
2	$\frac{2}{3}$	$\frac{8}{3}$
3	?	$\frac{19}{5}$

(a) 1/2   (b) 2/3
(c) 3/4   (d) 4/5

24. Which one will replace the question mark?

7	4	5
8	7	6
3	3	?
29	19	31

(a) 3   (b) 5
(c) 4   (d) 6

25. Which one will replace the question mark?

4	5	6
2	3	7
1	8	3
21	98	?

(a) 94   (b) 76
(c) 16   (d) 73

Learning Objectives : In this chapter, students will learn about:
- ✓ Different types of Venn diagram

CHAPTER SUMMARY

Venn diagrams are illustrations that are used in the branch of mathematics known as set theory. They are used to show the mathematical or logical relationship between different groups of things (sets). A Venn diagram shows all the logical relations between the sets.

The use of Venn diagram is made to test the aptitude of candidates regarding the relationship between some items of a group. A candidate can easily solve the problem if he/she has good understanding of the diagram.

Some critical examples are given below:

Example 1: If all the words are of different groups, then they will be shown by the diagram as given below.

Dog, Cow, Horse

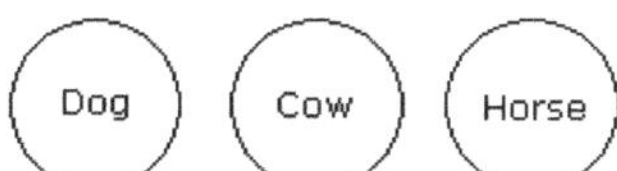

All these three are animals but of different groups, there is no relation between them. Hence they will be represented by three different circles.

Example 2: If the first word is related to second word and second word is related to third word. Then they will be shown by diagram as given below.

Unit, Tens, Hundreds

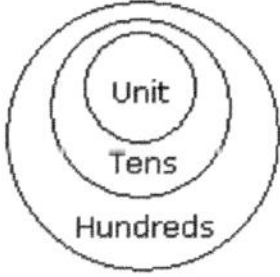

Ten units together make one Tens or in one tens, whole unit is available and ten tens together make one hundreds.

Example 3: If two different items are completely related to third item, they will be shown as below.

Pen, Pencil, Stationery

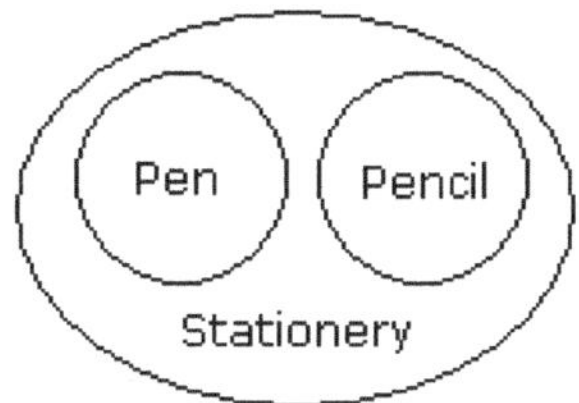

Example 4: If there is some relation between two items and these two items are completely related to a third item they will be shown as given below.

Women, Sisters, Mothers

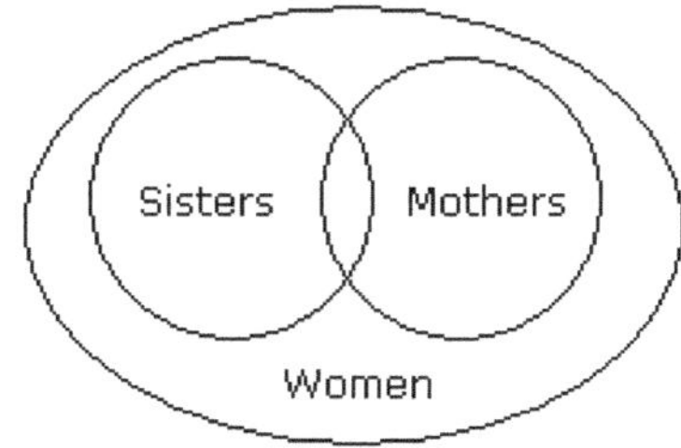

Some sisters may be mothers and vice-versa. Similarly some mothers may not be sisters and vice-versa. But all the sisters and all the mothers belong to the women group.

Example 5: Two items are related to a third item to some extent but not completely and first two items totally different.

Students, Boys, Girls

The boys and girls are different items while some boys may be students. Similarly among girls some may be students.

Example 6: All the three items are related to one another but to some extent not completely.

Boys, Students, Athletes

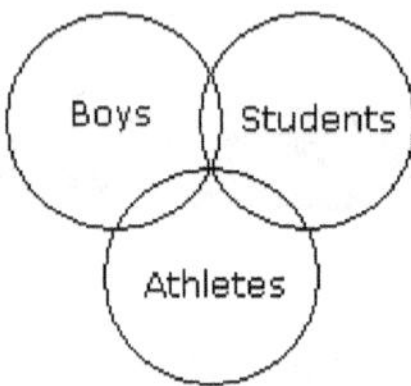

Some boys may be students and vice-versa. Similarly some boys may be athletes and vice-versa. Some students may be athletes and vice-versa.

Example 7: Two items are related to each other completely and third item is entirely different from first two.

Lions, Carnivorous, Cows

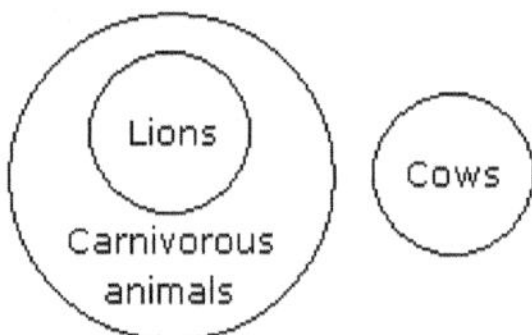

All the lions are carnivorous but no cow is lion or carnivorous.

Example 8: First item is completely related to second and third item is partially related to first and second item.

Dogs, Animals, Flesh-eaters

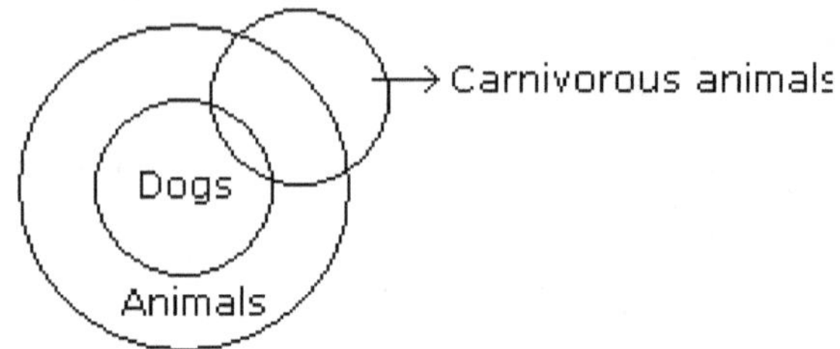

All the dogs are belonging to animals but some dogs are flesh eater but not all.

Example 9: First item is partially related to second but third is entirely different from the first two.

Dogs, Flesh-eaters, Cows

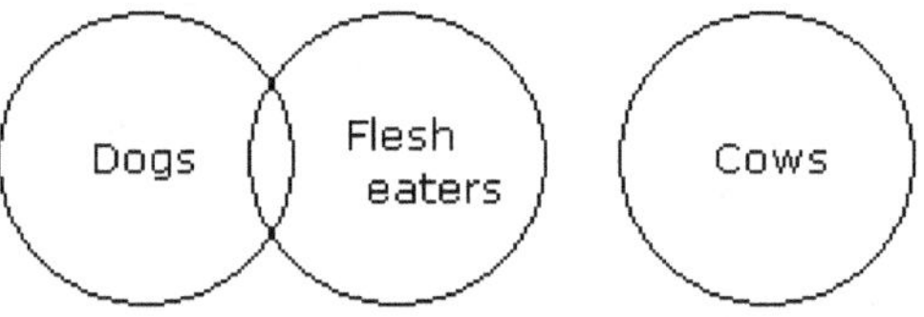

Some dogs are flesh-eaters but not all while any dog or any flesh-eater cannot be cow.

MULTIPLE CHOICE QUESTIONS

Directions (1-30): Each of these questions given below contains three elements. These elements may or may not have some inter linkage. Each group of elements may fit into one of these diagrams at (A), (B), (C), (D). You have to indicate the group of elements which correctly fits into the diagrams.

1. Which of the following diagrams indicates the best relation among Author, Lawyer and Singer?

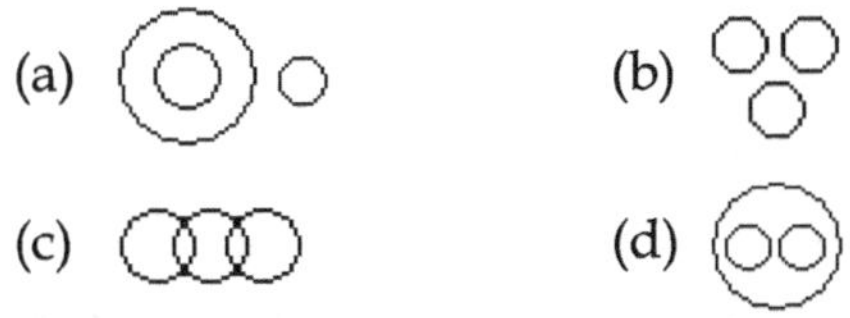

   (a)   (b)   (c)   (d)

2. Which of the following diagrams indicates the best relation among Factory, Product and Machinery?

   (a)   (b)   (c)   (d)

3. Which of the following diagrams indicates the best relation among Women, Mothers and Engineers?

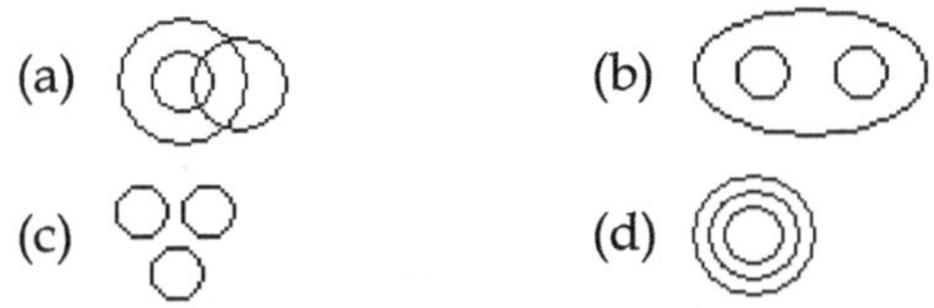

   (a)   (b)   (c)   (d)

4. Which of the following diagrams indicates the best relation among Paper, Stationery and Ink?

   (a)   (b)   (c)   (d)

5. Which of the following diagrams indicates the best relation among Teacher, Men and Women?

   (a)   (b)   (c)   (d)

6. Which of the following diagrams indicates the best relation among Oil, Wick and Lamp?

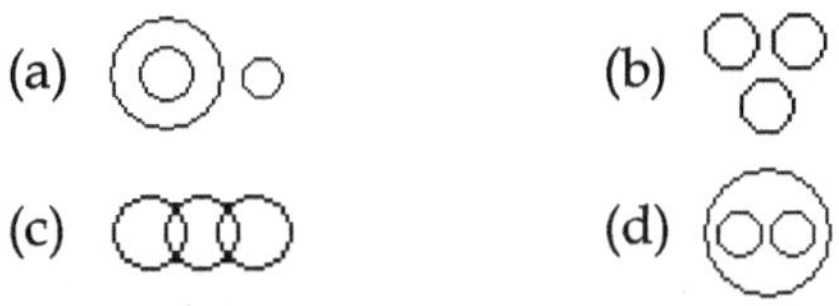

   (a)   (b)   (c)   (d)

7. Which of the following diagrams indicates the best relation among Football, Player and Field?

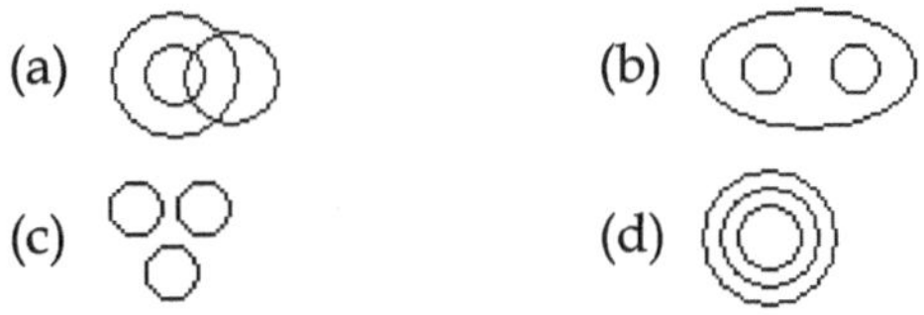

   (a)   (b)   (c)   (d)

8. Which of the following diagrams indicates the best relation among Sweets, Rasgulla and Apple?

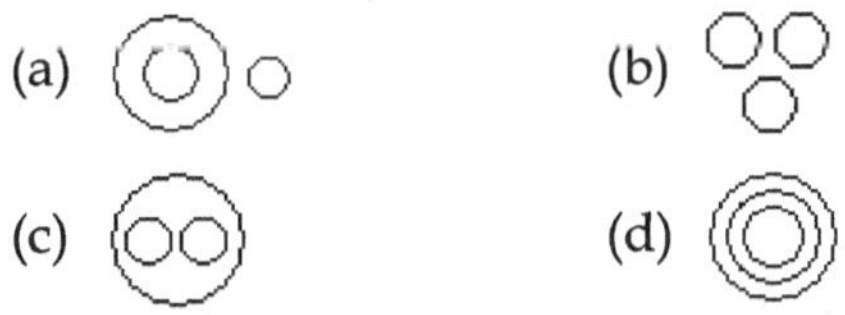

   (a)   (b)   (c)   (d)

9. Which of the following diagrams indicates the best relation among Mammal, Cow and Bat?

   (a)   (b)   (c)   (d)

10. Which of the following diagrams indicates the best relation among dogs, pet animals and animals?

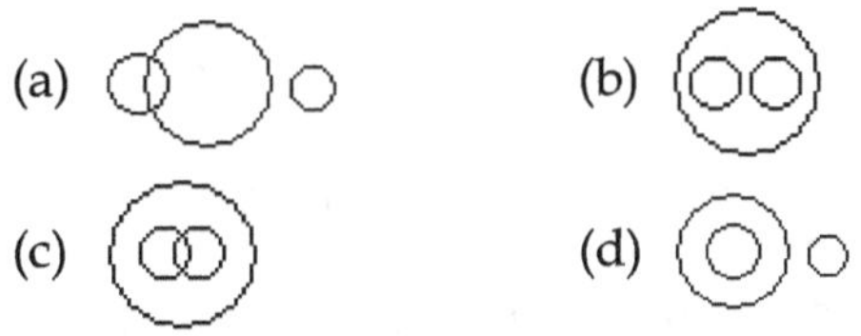

    (a)   (b)   (c)   (d)

11. Which of the following diagrams indicates the best relation among Sailor, Ship and Ocean?

    (a)   (b)   (c)   (d)

12. Which of the following diagrams indicates the best relation among Gold, Metal and Zinc?

(a)　　(b)

(c)　　(d)

13. Which of the following diagrams indicates the best relation among Professors, Doctors and Men?

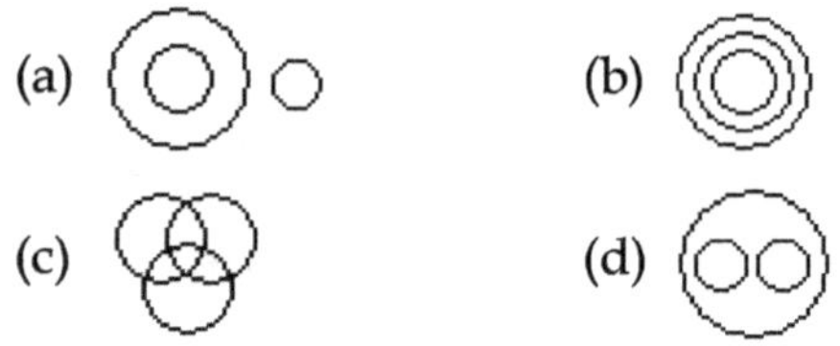

(a)　　(b)

(c)　　(d)

14. Which of the following diagrams indicates the best relation among Ass, Pet and Horse?

(a)　　(b)

(c)　　(d)

15. Which of the following diagrams indicates the best relation among Page, Chapter and Book?

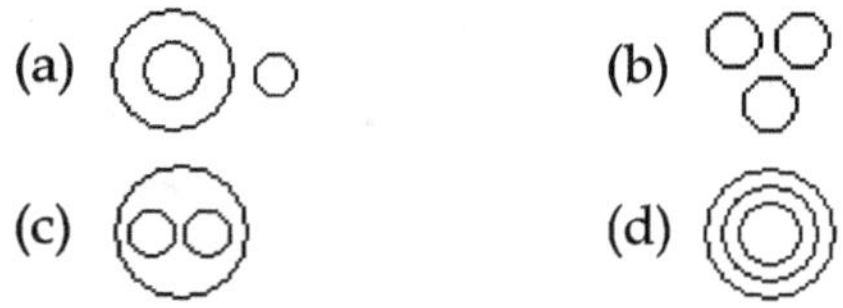

(a)　　(b)

(c)　　(d)

16. Which of the following diagrams indicates the best relation among Parents, Mother and Father?

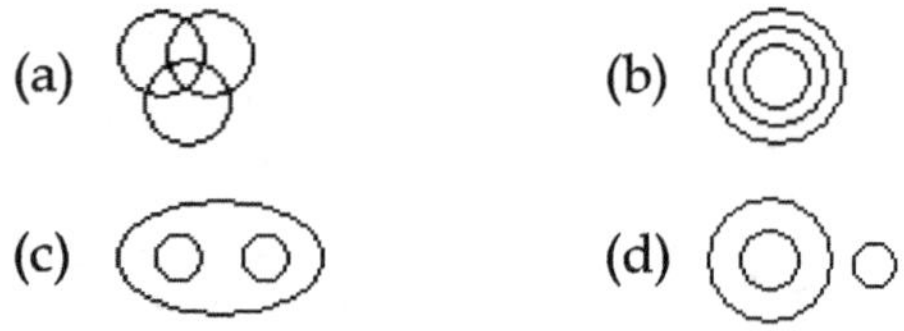

(a)　　(b)

(c)　　(d)

17. Which of the following diagrams indicates the best relation among Men, Rodents and Living beings?

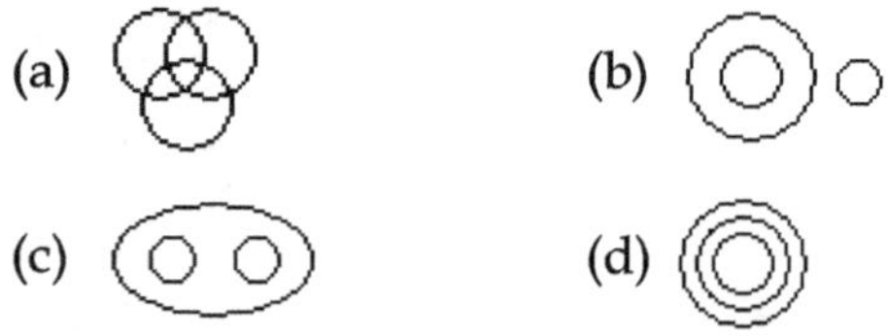

(a)　　(b)

(c)　　(d)

18. Which of the following diagrams indicates the best relation among Elephants, Wolves and Animals?

(a)　　(b)

(c)　　(d)

19. Which of the following diagrams indicates the best relation among Furniture, Chairs and Tables?

(a)　　(b)

(c)　　(d)

20. Which of the following diagrams indicates the best relation among Elephant, Carnivorous and Tiger?

(a)　　(b)

(c)　　(d)

21. Which of the following diagrams indicates the best relation among Class, Blackboard and School?

(a)　　(b)

(c)　　(d)

22. Which of the following diagrams indicates the best relation among Rabi-Crop, Paddy and Wheat?

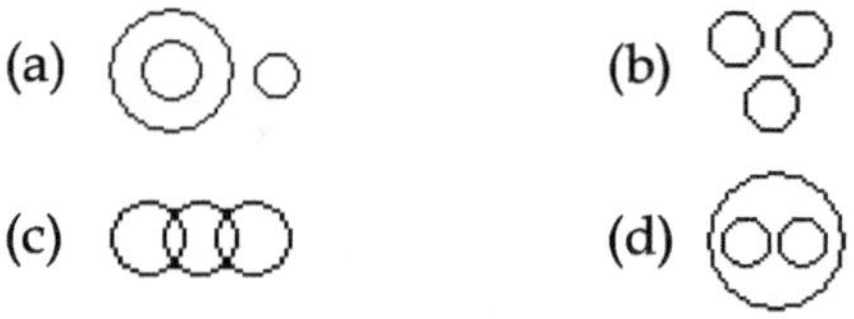

(a)　　(b)

(c)　　(d)

23. Which of the following diagrams indicates the best relation among Hospital, Nurse and Patient?

(a)　　(b)

(c)　　(d)

24. Which of the following diagrams indicates the best relation among Mercury, Zinc and Metal?

(a) 　(b) 　(c) 　(d)

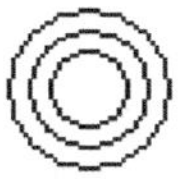

25. Which of the following diagrams indicates the best relation among Teacher, Writer and Musician?

(a) 　(b) 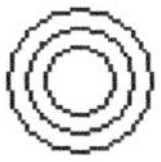　(c) 　(d)

26. Which of the following diagrams indicates the best relation among Iron, Lead and Nitrogen?

(a) 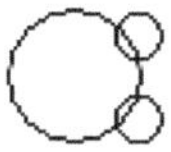　(b) 　(c) 　(d)

27. Which of the following diagrams indicates the best relation among Examination, Questions and Practice?

(a) 　(b) 　(c) 　(d)

28. Which of the following diagrams indicates the best relation among Bulb, Lamp and Light?

(a) 　(b) 　(c) 　(d)

29. Which of the following diagrams indicates the best relation among Lion, Dog and Snake?

(a) 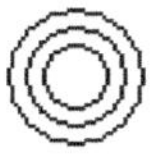　(b) 　(c) 　(d)

30. Which of the following diagrams indicates the best relation among Moon, Sun and Earth?

(a) 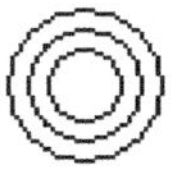　(b) 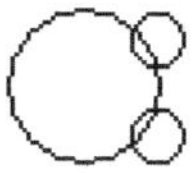　(c) 　(d)

Directions (31–34): Study the following figure and answer the questions given below.

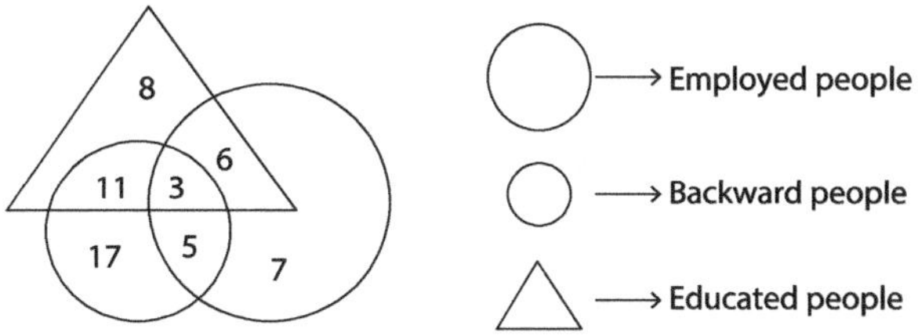

31. How many educated people are employed?
(a) 9　　(b) 18
(c) 20　　(d) 15

32. How many backward people are educated?
(a) 9　　(b) 28
(c) 14　　(d) 6

33. How many backward uneducated people are employed?
(a) 14　　(b) 5
(c) 7　　(d) 11

34. How many backward people are not educated?
(a) 3　　(b) 14
(c) 22　　(d) 25

Directions (35–38): Study the following figure and answer the questions given below.

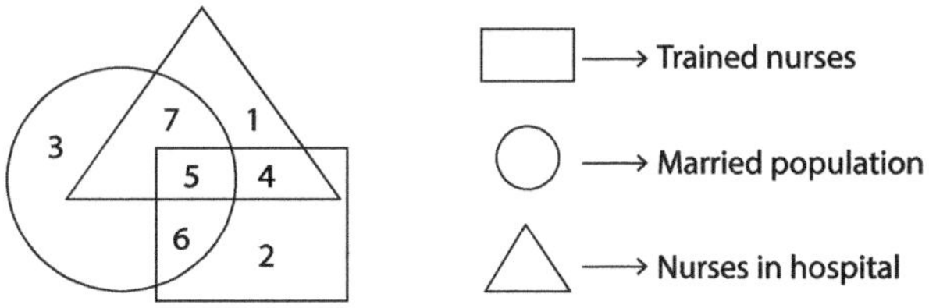

35. If the hospital management requires only married trained nurses for operation theatre, which number of diagram should be chosen by it?
(a) 7　　(b) 4
(c) 5　　(d) 6

36. By which number, married but untrained nurses in the hospital are represented?

(a) 4   (b) 6

(c) 7   (d) 5

37. By which numbers trained nurses are represented?

(a) 3, 6   (b) 7, 5

(c) 5, 6   (d) 1, 5

38. What is represented by the number 7?

(a) Married nurses in the hospital

(b) Trained nurses

(c) Unmarried trained nurses

(d) Married trained nurses

Directions (39–40): Study the following figure and answer the questions given below.

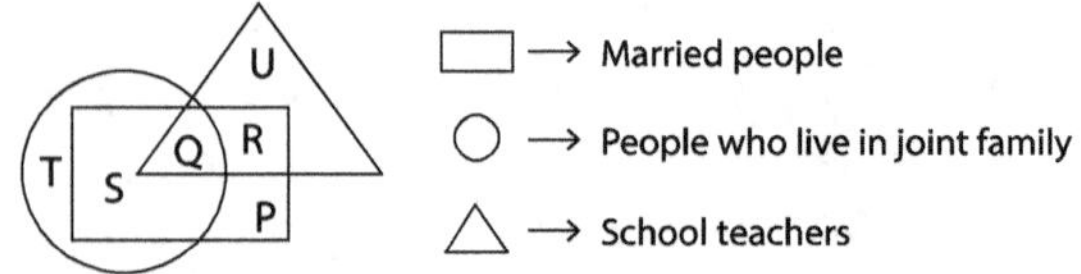

39. By which letter, the married teachers who live in joint family are represented?

(a) R   (b) Q

(c) S   (d) P

40. By which letter, the married people who live in joint family but not are school teachers are represented?

(a) R   (b) U

(c) S   (d) P

Analytical Reasoning 11

Learning Objectives : In this chapter, students will learn about:
- ✓ Concept of analytical reasoning questions

CHAPTER SUMMARY

Analytical reasoning comes under non verbal reasoning and is designed to test the deduction ability of an individual based on the set of given facts. The given facts maybe unrelated to law and hypothetical most of the times.

Analytical Reasoning questions assess the ability to consider a group of facts and rules. The specific scenarios associated with these questions are unrelated to law and may not be true. In analytical reasoning questions, you are asked to follow the science of deduction on a set of statements and rules or principles that describe relationships among persons, things, or events.

The passage providing information for analytical reasoning describes common ordering relationships or grouping relationships, or a combination of both types of relationships. Examples include scheduling employees for work shifts, assigning instructors to class sections, ordering tasks according to priority, and distributing grants for projects.

Analytical Reasoning questions test a range of deductive reasoning skills. They are:

- Comprehending the structure of a set of relationships by determining the solution to the problem posed
- Reasoning with conditional statements and recognizing logically equivalent formulations of such statements
- Inferring what must be true from given information
- Recognizing when two statements are logically equivalent in context by identifying a condition that could replace one of the original conditions.

1. Amit is 15th from the left end of a row of 25 boys and Sumit is 15th from the right end in same row. How many boys are there between them in the same row?

   (a) 4   (b) 7

   (c) 3   (d) 8

2. If you are 9th in the queue starting either end, how many are there in the queue?

   (a) 17   (b) 9

   (c) 10   (d) 15

3. Hyderabad is larger than Delhi. Mumbai is larger than Chennai. Bangalore is not as larger as Delhi but larger than Mumbai. Which is the smallest city?

   (a) Delhi   (b) Hyderabad

   (c) Mumbai   (d) Chennai

4. Rakesh is taller than Hari. Mohit is taller than Rakesh. Dev is taller than Mohit. Surya is the tallest. If they arranged according to their heights, who will be in the middle?

   (a) Rakesh   (b) Dev

   (c) Hari   (d) Mohit

5. P is older than Q but younger than R. S is younger than T but older than P. If R is younger than S, who is the oldest?

   (a) R   (b) T

   (c) S   (d) P

6. Tony knows more than Rekha, Mona knows as much as Neha. Shikha knows less than Vibha. Rekha knows more than Neha. Who is the best knowledgeable person?

   (a) Tony   (b) Mona

   (c) Rekha   (d) Vibha

7. Monu, Miku, Sonu and Aman appeared in an examination. Marks obtained by Monu were less than the marks obtained by Miku. Sonu marks were more than those of Miku, but not more than the marks obtained by Aman. Who get the second highest marks?

   (a) Monu   (b) Aman

   (c) Miku or Sonu   (d) Sonu

Direction (8–12): Study the following figure and answer the questions given below.

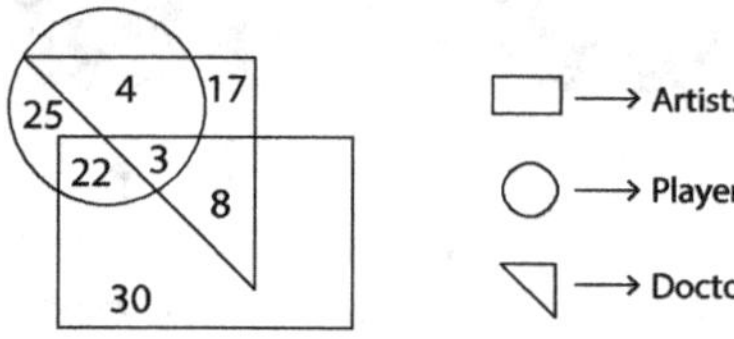

8. How many doctors are neither artists nor players?

   (a) 17   (b) 5

   (c) 10   (d) 30

9. How many doctors are both players and artists?

   (a) 22   (b) 8

   (c) 3   (d) 30

10. How many artists are players?

    (a) 5   (b) 8

    (c) 25   (d) 16

11. How many players are neither artists nor doctors?

    (a) 25   (b) 17

    (c) 5   (d) 10

12. How many artists are neither players nor doctors?

    (a) 10   (b) 17

    (c) 30   (d) 15

SECTION 3
ACHIEVER'S SECTION

Achiever's Section

Some Useful General apps for the Students

1. xTiles

- **Best for:** Notes, research papers, student planning
- **Devices:** Web, Windows, macOS, Android, iPhone

xTiles (https://xtiles.app/) is a flexible tool for arranging all kinds of students' tasks, educational content, and student planning in one user-friendly workspace with the ability to create a personal knowledge base and share it. A polished yet simple interface allows combine images, links, and text in one space. It is one of the best app for students.

The versatility of ready-to-use templates gives you many different possibilities: 1) Create your dashboard will contain all the information about your life, education, and work 2) Collect, organize, and store information for any of your research. 3) Systematize your notes during lectures.

xTiles gives a start version to everyone and provides a free unlimited plan for students for five years.

2. Evernote

- **Best for:** Notes, Exam Prep, Planning
- **Devices:** Android, iPhone, and iPad

Evernote (https://evernote.com/) is among the best **useful apps for students**. Whether you're in high school or pursuing a degree, Evernote makes student life easier, as it organizes all of your courses and assignments so you can quickly locate what you're searching for. With this, students can stay organized and on schedule. The best part is its free basic plan lets you take notes in different formats, including text, sketches, photos, audio, and video. You can easily sync your notes between devices and share them with others.

3. RefME – Referencing Made Easy

- **Best for:** Citations, Reference
- **Devices:** Android, iPhone and iPad

RefMe (available on Playstore) is an award-winning app that automates the referencing process, allowing students to quickly construct references, citations, and bibliographies by searching (for book/journal title, DOI, ISBN, or ISSN) or copying or pasting URLs. If you are writing a research paper, this app will create a reference for you. You can then easily export your references by email to yourself or Evernote.

4. PDF Reader Pro

- **Best App for:** Reading notes, lesson plans, research papers, dissertations
- **Devices:** Android, iPhone and iPad

PDF Reader (available on Playstore) is an excellent tool for students. They can even view PDFs as slideshows in the classroom presentation. It includes numerous incredible features, such as commenting, online document filling, electronic signature input, and the most up-to-date OCR technology. It's ideal for students who want to combine documents online, split files, secure files, process files, and convert documents, among other things.

5. myHomework Student Planner

- **Best for:** Student Planning
- **Devices:** Android, iPad and iPhone

myHomework (https://myhomeworkapp.com/) Student Planner is a **digital-planning app for students** that allows them to organize their coursework, forthcoming tasks, and daily routine. Users only need to enter their class information into the calendar. Adding homework explanations is as simple as clicking a button. Users set the due dates and times and the priority level (high, medium, or low). They can also set reminders.

Some Useful Educational Apps for Students

1. OXFORD DICTIONARY

- **Best for:** Language
- **Devices:** Android, iPhone and iPad

With over 150 years of scholarship behind it, the Oxford Dictionary of English is widely regarded as the top authority in studying and referencing the English language. ODE is a useful resource for anyone who uses English in an academic or professional setting. Students are preparing for the ACT, SAT, IELTS, or TOEFL exams, Academics and professionals who actively use English.

As well as everyone else who requires a contemporary English dictionary that is both comprehensive and authoritative at work or home.

2. CueBrain

- **Best for:** Learn language vocabulary
- **Devices:** Android, iPhone and iPad

Students learning a new language will like this app, which teaches foreign language vocabulary on the fly with interactive flashcards and quiz sessions. It supports numerous languages, including French, Portuguese, German, and Italian, and allows students to track their progress in the cloud.

3. Grammarly

- **Best for:** Personal learning
- **Devices:** Android, iPhone and iPad

Grammar and spelling in English are a mess. Even if you've been speaking and writing in the language your entire life, it's still possible to misspell a term (not to mention make a typo). While reviewing your work thoroughly can identify most errors, it is time-consuming.

Grammarly can help you catch more errors faster. It evaluates your work for common grammar, spelling, and usage mistakes. It flags errors and even explains what you should write instead when it detects them. It's not flawless, but it's lightyears better than any word processor's built-in spelling/grammar checker.

4. Mathway

- **Best App for:** Solving homework headaches
- **Devices:** Android, iPhone and iPad

Mathway is one of the **best apps for students** who are likely to encounter number crunching and other Mathematics equations during their studies. It helps you answer problems and explains how you get to the solution.

All you have to do is enter your problem (or upload a picture of it) into the app, and Mathway will solve it. You can also read the detailed step-by-step instruction, which will help you learn how to solve similar equations in the future.

This is one of the most rewarding features. The app's explanation part is like having a virtual instructor with you all the time, explaining the workings of any mathematics you have trouble understanding.

5. Coggle

- **Best for:** Mind-Mapping
- **Devices:** Android, iPhone and iPad

Coggle is a mind-mapping and brainstorming software worth considering. Its clean and simple interface speaks volumes of its intelligent design concept. With this software, you will be able to collaborate with your groupmates in real-time, making it ideal for group assignments and projects, especially if you are learning online. You may also use this software to save changes to your work automatically! Regardless of how many photographs you need to save, you may do it with Coggle's drag-and-drop feature; no need to worry about memory constraints or flowing text.

Model Test Paper 1

Mental Ability

1. How many of the following numbers are divisible by 132?

   264, 396, 462, 792, 968, 2178, 5184, 6336

   (a) 4　　　(b) 5　　　(c) 6　　　(d) 7

2. How many digits will be there to the right of the decimal point in the product of 95.75 and 0.02554?

   (a) 5　　　(b) 6　　　(c) 7　　　(d) 1

3. From a group of boys and girls, 15 girls leave. There are then left 2 boys for each girl. After this, 45 boys leave. There are then 5 girls for each boy. Find the number of girls in the beginning.

   (a) 65　　　　　　　(b) 54

   (c) 25　　　　　　　(d) 40

4. If 76 is divided into four parts proportional to 7, 5, 3, 4, then the smallest part is ______.

   (a) 10　　　　　　　(b) 15

   (c) 16　　　　　　　(d) 19

5. A dice is tossed. Find the probability of getting a multiple of 2.

   (a) 1/2　　　　　　　(b) 2/3

   (c) 1/3　　　　　　　(d) 1/4

6. The marks (out of 100) obtained by a group of students in science test are 85, 74, 90, 85, 39, 48, 56, 95, 80 and 78. Find the mean marks obtained by the group.

   (a) 56　　　　　　　(b) 79

   (c) 72　　　　　　　(d) 73

7. Which square must be shaded so that the figure has a line of symmetry?

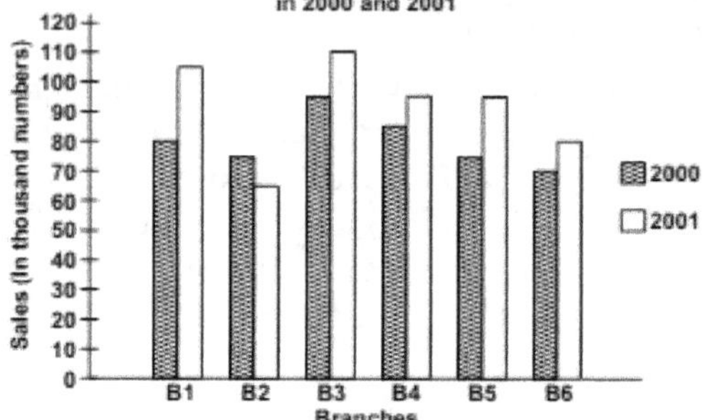

   (a) P　　　(b) Q　　　(c) R　　　(d) S

8. The given bar-graph shows the sales of books (in thousand numbers) from six branches (B1-B6) of a publishing company during two consecutive years 2000 and 2001. Answer the question based on this bar-graph.

   What is the ratio of the total sale of branch B2 for both years to the total sale of branch B4 for both years?

   (a) 2 : 3　　　　　　　(b) 3 : 5

   (c) 4 : 5　　　　　　　(d) 7 : 9

9. 3 is a factor of x and 24 is a multiple of x. What could be the value of x?

   (a) 8　　　　　　　(b) 12

   (c) 56　　　　　　　(d) 72

10. 18810 rounded off to the nearest hundred is ______.

   (a) 18700　　　　　　　(b) 18800

   (c) 18850　　　　　　　(d) 18900

Logical And Analytical Reasoning

11. A, B, C, D and E are sitting on a bench. A is sitting next to B, C is sitting next to D, D is not sitting with E who is on the left end of the bench. C is on the second position from the right. A is to the right of B and E. On which position A is sitting?

   (a) Between B and D

   (b) Between B and C

   (c) Between E and D

   (d) Between C and E

12. Four faces of a die is shown below. How many points will be on the face opposite to the face which contains 3 points?

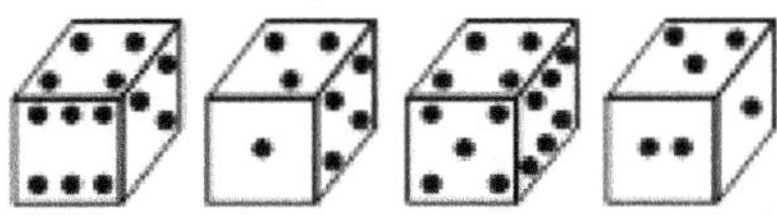

(a) 2   (b) 4
(c) 5   (d) 6

13. Find the next number in the given series
66, 36, 18, ___?
(a) 7   (b) 8
(c) 9   (d) 5

14. A piece of sheet is folded and cut and then unfolded as shown in the image given below. Select the figure from the given four options which exactly resembles the unfolded paper.

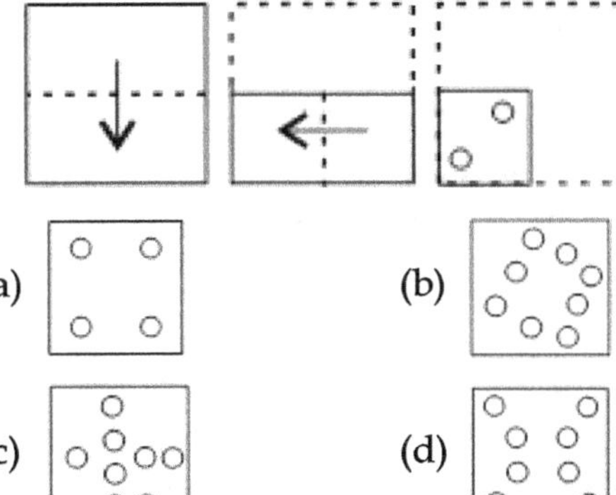

(a)   (b)

(c)   (d)

15. If '→' stands for 'addition'; '←' stands for 'subtraction'; '↑' stands for 'division'; '↓' stands for 'multiplication' and '↗' stands for 'equal to', then which of the following options is correct?

(a) $2 ↓ 5 ← 6 → 2 ↗ 6$

(b) $5 → 7 ← 3 ↑ 2 ↗ 4$

(c) $3 ↓ 6 ↗ 2 → 3 ← 6 ↗ 5$

(d) $7 → 42 ↑ 6 ↗ 5$

16. Reena walked from A to B 10 m in the east. Then she turned to the right and walked 3 m. Again she turned to the right and walked 14 m. How far is she from A?
(a) 4 m   (b) 5 m
(c) 24 m   (d) 25 m

17. Choose the mirror-image of the Fig. (X) if mirror is placed along MR.

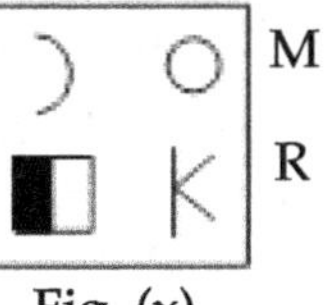

Fig. (x)

(a) 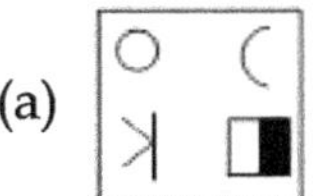   (b) 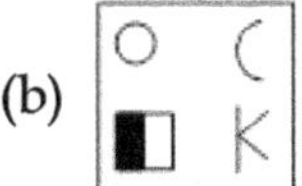

(c) 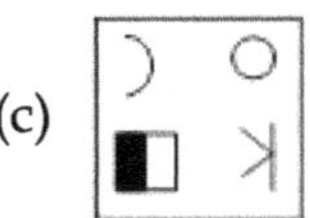   (d) 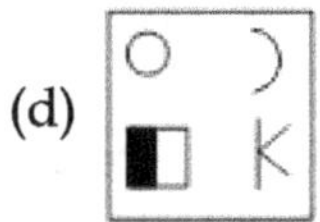

18. If TOGETHER is written as RQEGRJCT, how will PAROLE be written?
(a) NCPQJG   (b) NCQPJG
(c) RCPQJK   (d) RCTQNG

19. The two problem figures have some common characteristics. Select the figure from the options which has the same commonality.

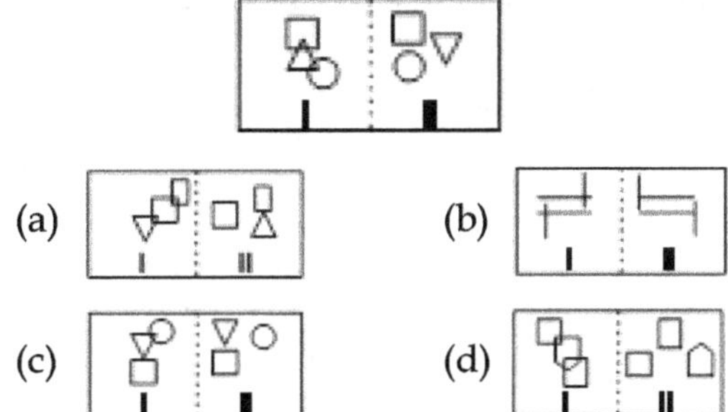

(a)   (b)

(c)   (d)

20. Find the missing number.

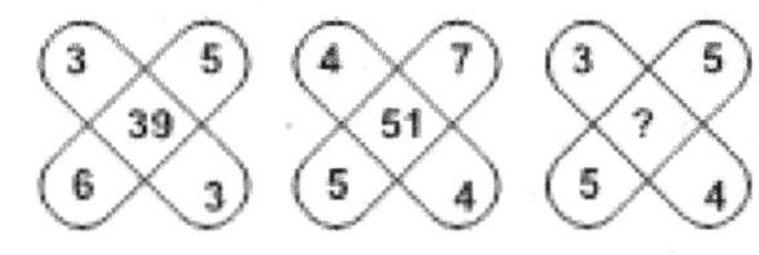

(a) 47   (b) 45
(c) 37   (d) 35

Computers And Information Technology

21. In QBASIC, "CLASS VII" is a _____.
(a) String constant
(b) Numeric constant
(c) String Variable
(d) Numeric Variable

22. Match the following.

Column-I	Column-II
(i) CLS	a. To add comments
(ii) PRINT	b. Used to gather input from user
(iii) LET	c. To print text, numbers or a line space
(iv) INPUT	d. To assign a value to a variable
(v) REM	e. Clear screen

(a) I – e, II – c, III – b, IV – d, V – a
(b) I – e, II – d, III – b, IV – c, V – a
(c) I – e, II – c, III – a, IV – b, V – d
(d) I – e, II – c, III – d, IV – b, V – a

23. For the given piece of code in QBASIC, the output will be _______.

PRINT "Best";

PRINT "ofLuck"

(a) Best of Luck
(b) BestofLuck
(c) BEST OF LUCK
(d) best of luck

24. _______ sets the default layout and formatting for all the slides in a presentation.
(a) Slide placeholder
(b) Slide Sorter
(c) Slide Master
(d) Summary Slide

25. _________ on the internet are equivalent to 24-hour coffee shops with people eager to communicate anytime you want.
(a) Online library
(b) Chat rooms
(c) Electronic post offices
(d) Blogs

26. In MS Excel, to select the entire column in which the cell pointer is positioned press __________.

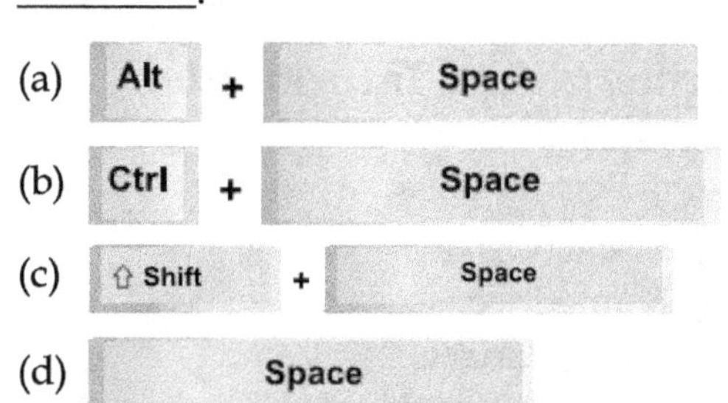

27. For the given piece of code in QBASIC, the output will be _______,

FOR I = 1 to 5
PRINT I
NEXT I

(a) 1 2 3 4 5
(b) 1 2 3 4
(c) 5 4 3 2 1
(d) 0 1 3 5 4

28. Which of the following is responsible for supplying power to various components of the PC?
(a) SMPS
(b) RJ 45
(c) RAM
(d) USB

29. _______ are extra unwanted browser windows of commercials that open automatically as you browse web pages.
(a) Websites
(b) Windows
(c) Attachments
(d) Popups

30. In MS Excel, which tab can be used to insert charts in a worksheet ?
(a) Insert
(b) Data
(c) Review
(d) View

31. In MS Excel, how formula to calculate the Simple Interest should be put in cell E2 – such that it works for any valid value? The formula for calculating Simple Interest is given below:

Interest = (Principal * Rate of Interest * Time)/100

	A	B	C	D	E
1	Principal	Rate of Interest	Time Duration		Interest
2	200	12	2		?
3					

(a) = (A1*B1*C1)/100
(b) = (A2*B2*C2)/100
(c) = (2000*12*2)/100
(d) A2*B2*C2/100

32. Which of the following is not found in Insert tab of MS PowerPoint?

(a)    (b) 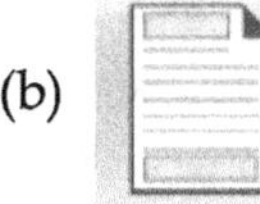

(c) 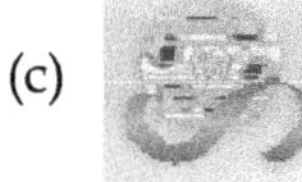   (d) 

33. MBR – stands for ______.
(a) Mega Boot Record
(b) Master Boot Record
(c) Major Boot Record
(d) Machine Boot Record

34. A daisy wheel printer is a type of ______.
(a) Impact Printer
(b) Laser Printer
(c) Dot Matrix Printer
(d) Non-Impact Printer

35. The given figure in MS PowerPoint represents __________.

(a) Elbow Arrow Connector
(b) Arrow
(c) Down arrow
(d) Elbow Connector

36. In MS Word, to insert a PAGE BREAK select the ________ Tab.
(a) Home   (b) Mailings
(c) Insert   (d) View

37. Which of the following is an internet standard for electronic mail transmission across IP network?
(a) SMTP   (b) FTP
(c) TCP/IP   (d) Gopher

38. The given figure shows some records entered in MS excel worksheet. What will happen in the selected cell if you press Alt + = (ALT + Equal) key followed by enter key?

	A	B	C	D	E
1	English	Hindi	Maths		Total
2	44	32	48		?
3					

(a) Sum of cell A2, B2, C2 will appear as a result
(b) Some error will be displayed
(c) Nothing will happen
(d) Average of cell A2, B2, C2 will appear as a result

39. The image here shows

(a) The list of design themes that you can choose for your slides.
(b) The list of slide layouts that can be used in a presentation.
(c) The list of slides in the active presentation.
(d) The list of transitions to the current slide.

40. Which of the following is a list of slide objects in MS PowerPoint?
(a) Organization charts, Graphs, Diagrams and Drawings
(b) Text
(c) Clip art, Images and Multimedia elements
(d) All of these are slide objects

41. Which feature of MS Word can be used to create special text effect as shown in the given image?

Science Olympiad Foundation

(a) WordArt
(b) Clip Art
(c) AutoShapes
(d) Format Painter

42. Which MS Word feature has been used here?

> **A**n operating System acts as an intermediate between the user and the machine.

(a) WordArt   (b) Foot notes
(c) Drop Cap   (d) Tab Stop

43. Aditya has been using his computer for many years. Over time, the performance of the computer has deteriorated. What should he do to improve the performance of his computer?

(a) Run Scan Disk

(b) Run the Disk Defragmenter

(c) Go to Windows Control Panel

(d) Completely format his system

44. E-mails that usually contain bogus warnings intended to frighten or mislead people are called ________.

(a) Spams   (b) Junk

(c) Hoaxes   (d) None of these

45. Which of the following charts is not available in MS Excel?

(a) Stock   (b) Bar

(c) Radar   (d) YZ Graph

46. Write the following expression in appropriate formula in QBASIC.

A·B − R·S + R2

(a) $A * B - R * S + R \wedge 2$

(b) $A \times B - R \times S - R \times R$

(c) $A * B - R * S + R \times R$

(d) $A·B - R·S + R \times 2$

47. While working on MS PowerPoint, how can one view the slides in the format shown in the image?

(a) Insert → Shapes → Basic shapes

(b) View → Handout Master → Slides Per Page → 6 slides

(c) Review → Handout Master → 6 slides

(d) Slide show → Use presenter view

48. The ribbon shown in the given image is ________ tab of MS Word.

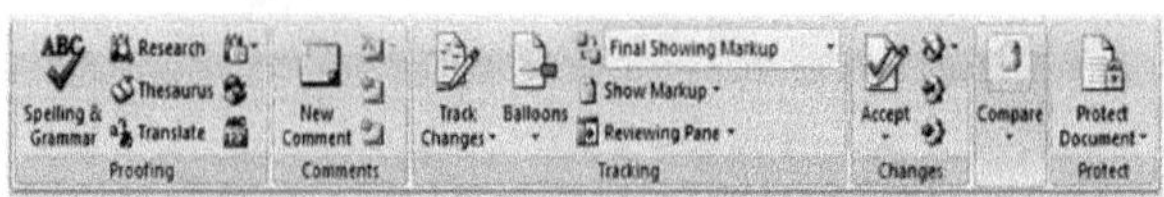

(a) Insert   (b) Review

(c) Mailings   (d) View

49. What is a BUS in a computer?

(a) BUS is the connection between two or more components inside a computer.

(b) BUS is an external device connected through cables.

(c) BUS is an internal communication among mouse and keyboard.

(d) BUS is the video memory linked through external devices.

50. It is physically composed of series of flat, magnetically coated platters stacked on a spindle. The spindle turns while the head moves between the platters. It is ________.

(a) Hard disk   (b) CD

(c) Floppy   (d) Mouse

Mental Ability

1. If AE || BF, find the value of x and y respectively.

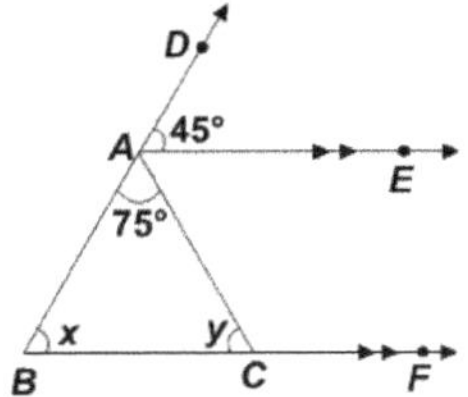

   (a) 45°, 65°   (b) 60°, 45°

   (c) 35°, 75°   (d) 45°, 60°

2. Raj bought a glass of mixed juice in which orange, carrot and beet root were present in the ratio 2 : 3 : 1, respectively. If 400 ml of juice accounts for only orange and carrot juices, find the quantity of different juices.

   (a) Orange - 160 ml   (b) Orange - 80 ml
       Carrot - 80 ml   Carrot - 160 ml
       Beet root - 80 ml   Beet root - 240 ml

   (c) Orange - 160 ml   (d) Orange - 240 ml
       Carrot - 240 ml   Carrot - 160 ml
       Beet root - 80 ml   Beet root - 80 ml

3. Five years ago, a father was seven times as old as his daughter. If the present age of the father is 47 years, find the present age of the daughter.

   (a) 11 years   (b) 6 years

   (c) 13 years   (d) 40 years

4. According to a survey the number of books read by 20 students during the past three months is as follows:

2, 4, 5, 1, 3, 2, 5, 6, 1, 2, 4, 3, 6, 10, 12, 10, 2, 8, 6, 7

Find the mean of the given data. Also find the number of students who read less than the mean number of books.

   (a) 5, 11

   (b) 4.95, 10

   (c) 3.95, 8

   (d) 6.25, 5

5. The temperature at 12 noon was 10°C above zero. If it decreases at the rate of 2°C per hour until midnight, at what time would the temperature be 8°C below zero? What would be the temperature at midnight?

   (a) 10 P.M., −10°C   (b) 3 P.M., −8°C

   (c) 8 P.M., −12°C   (d) 9 P.M., −14°C

6. Find the value of x and y respectively in the given figure.

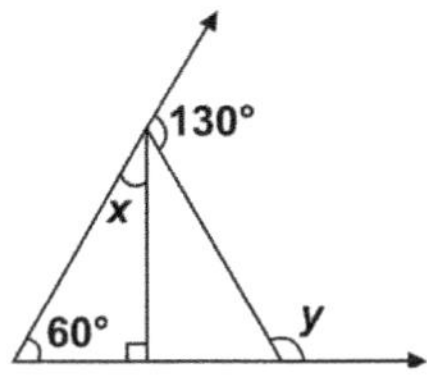

   (a) 30°, 150°   (b) 20°, 120°

   (c) 30°, 110°   (d) 60°, 130°

7. Raju sold a TV for ₹8100 suffering a loss of 10%. At what price should he have sold it to gain 10% profit?

   (a) ₹9900   (b) ₹9801

   (c) ₹9810   (d) ₹9090

8. Find the value of

$$32.78 - 15.43 + \left\{ \frac{855.114}{12.35} - 8.325 \right\}$$

   (a) 87.865   (b) 78.265

   (c) 63.518   (d) 395.02

9. Rehan got a prize of ₹75,000 in a TV contest. He paid 1/10 of the prize as income tax. Out of the remaining, he gave 1/3 to his son, 1/5 to his daughter, 1/10 to the Red Cross Society and the rest to his wife. How much money did Rehan's wife get?

   (a) ₹33,750   (b) ₹67,500

   (c) ₹24,750   (d) ₹37,500

10. Rajan borrowed a sum from the bank for 5 years at the rate of 4% p.a. After 5 years, he returned ₹4500. Find the amount borrowed by him.

   (a) ₹2735   (b) ₹2505

   (c) ₹2475   (d) ₹3750

Logical And Analytical Reasoning

11. Raj is shorter than Mohit. Amit is taller than Raj. Abhishek is taller than Mohit but shorter than Kabir. Mohit is taller than Amit. Who will be in the 4th position if they stand in a row according to their heights in descending order?

    (a) Abhishek   (b) Mohit

    (c) Amit   (d) Raj

12. If 'INDIA' is coded as 'KLFGC', then how will 'JAPAN' be coded?

    (a) KYRYP   (b) HYRYP

    (c) LYRYP   (d) LYRYQ

13. Priya walks 1 Km to east and then she turns to South and walks 4 Km. Again she turns to east and walks 2 Km. After this she turns to north and walks 8 Km. How far is she from her starting point?

    (a) 4 Km   (b) 5 Km

    (c) 8 Km   (d) 10 Km

14. If '+' means '×', '−' means '÷', '×' means '−' and '÷' means '+', then value of $16 \div 64 - 8 \times 4 + 2$ is ______.

    (a) 20   (b) 18

    (c) 16   (d) 7

15. Pointing to a man in a photograph, Sumit said, "that man's only daughter is my mother". How is Sumit related to that man?

    (a) Cousin   (b) Brother

    (c) Nephew   (d) Grandson

16. Tanmay remembers that his sister's birthday falls after 7th July but before 12th July while his brother Tarun remembers that his sister's birthday falls after 10th July but before 15th July, on what date does Tanmay's sister birthday fall?

    (a) 10th July   (b) 11th July

    (c) 12th July   (d) 15th July

17. Which of the following Venn diagrams correctly represents the relation among 'Uncles, Parents, Friends'?

    (a) 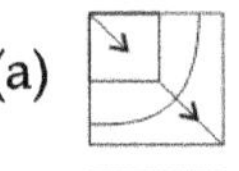   (b) 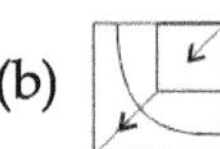

    (c) 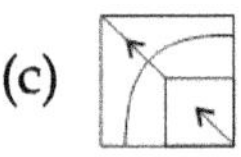   (d) 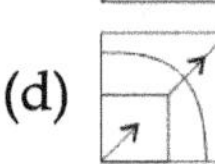

18. The following question is based on the following set of numbers.

    153   364   279   536   298

    What is the difference between the middle digits of the highest and the lowest of the above five numbers?

    (a) 2   (b) 3   (c) 4   (d) 5

19. Select a figure from amongst the options which will complete Fig. (X).

    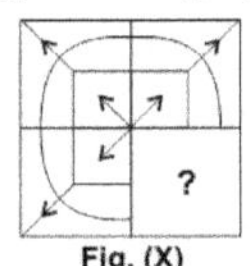

    Fig. (X)

    (a)   (b)

    (c)   (d)

20. How many unit cubes were removed from the solid on the left to obtain the solid on the right?

    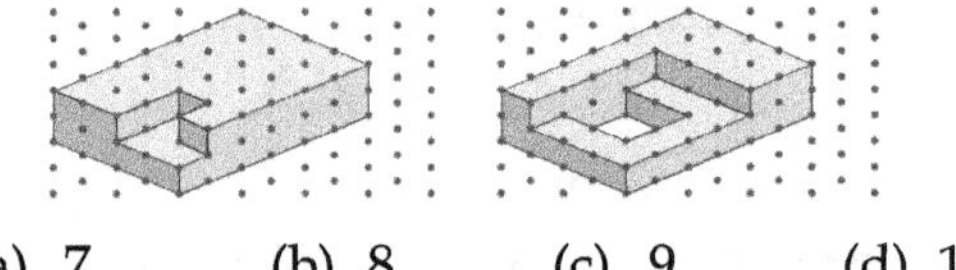

    (a) 7   (b) 8   (c) 9   (d) 10

Computers and Information Technology

21. How is the MS Word tab shown in the image below displayed?

    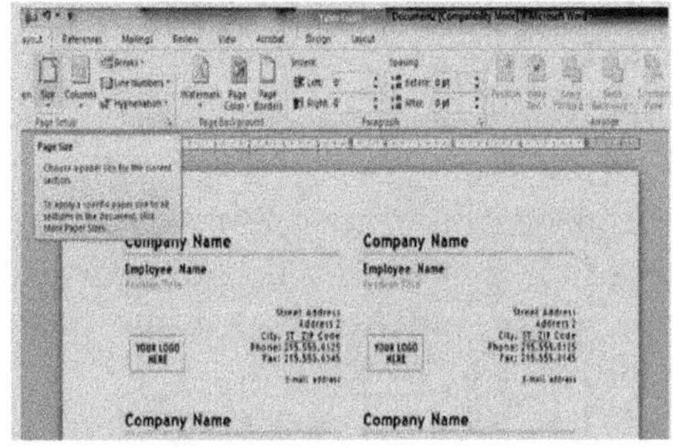

    (a) When you create a file from a pre-defined business card template.

    (b) When you click on an image, the tools for formatting the image are displayed.

    (c) When you create a business card format without using a template.

    (d) This is the Home tab of MS Word.

22. Which of the following virus is not a Polymorphic virus?
    (a) Melissa   (b) Satan Bug
    (c) Tuareg   (d) Elkern
23. The given image is present in ______ tab of MS Excel.

    (a) Insert   (b) Home
    (c) Data   (d) View
24. Find the odd one out.
    (a) Thumb drive   (b) Hard drive
    (c) Pen drive   (d) Jump drive
25. This is a format for compressing video with audio at broadcast quality resolution. The output is used for playback in a higher data transfer rate environment. Used usually in the professional market, USB, DVDs and other Video CDs. Identify the most appropriate format.
    (A) MPEG-1   (B) MPEG-2
    (C) MP3   (D) WAV
26. You have been editing a large MS Word document. Your edits are mainly concentrated around 3-4 locations in the document. Which of the following shortcut keys will quickly take you through all the 3-4 edit points in the document?

    (a)    (b) 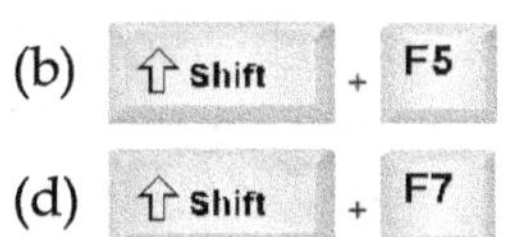

    (c) Shift + F12   (d) Shift + F7
27. ______ is a method to acquire sensitive information like usernames, passwords and banking details – like credit card PINS, etc.
    (a) Phishing   (b) Spying
    (c) Infecting   (d) Sprucing
28. In image scanners, which of the following device is not used to record how much light is being reflected of an item being scanned?
    (a) Cathode Ray Tube
    (b) Contact image sensor
    (c) Photo multiplicr tubes
    (d) Charge-coupled devices

29. Which of the following is not a second generation machine?
    (a) CDC 1604   (b) PDP-8
    (c) Honeywell 400   (d) IBM 7030
30. What will be the output of the following formula in MS Excel?

    =SUM(A1:A5, B3:B6)

	A	B
1	1	11
2	2	12
3	3	13
4	4	14
5	5	15
6	6	16
7		

    (a) 80   (b) 73
    (c) 79   (d) 102
31. Match the following.

    Column-I   **Column-II**
    (i)   Organize and store   (a) Prezi
          employee information
    (ii) Edit a book or a   (b) Safari
          manuscript
    (iii) Play video games   (c) Microsoft
          with a friend in   excel
          another country
    (iv) Create budget   (d) Word Perfect
    (v)   Create a tutorial   (e) Oracle

    (a) (i)–(e), (ii)–(d), (iii)–(c), (iv)–(b), (v)–(a)
    (b) (i)–(e), (ii)–(d), (iii)–(b), (iv)–(c), (v)–(a)
    (c) (i)–(d), (ii)–(e), (iii)–(b), (iv)–(c), (v)–(a)
    (d) (i)–(a), (ii)–(e), (iii)–(b), (iv)–(c), (v)–(d)
32. Find the odd one out.

    (a)    (b) 

    (c) 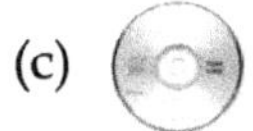   (d) 

33. ______ was the world's first commercially released CD player. It was launched by ____.
    (a) CDP-101, Sony
    (b) DPC-6800, Panasonic
    (c) PT 82, Casio
    (d) Zing 89, Yamaha

34. In a computer network, which one of the following network connection devices decides the best path for data transmission from the data source to the destination?
   (a) Router   (b) Bridge
   (c) Switch   (d) Hub

35. Which of the following computers had a unique feature among other well-known early computers of providing separate processes for handling input/output and processing functions?
   (a) EDSAC   (b) UNIVAC
   (c) ENIAC   (d) EDVAC

36. ______ scanners are also known as film scanners as they can easily scan the original image of the film.
   (a) Handheld   (b) Flatbed
   (c) Drum   (d) Slide

37. Which of the following types of processing is used in controlling robots?
   (a) Interactive
   (b) Real time
   (c) Batch
   (d) None of these

38. Which of the following is not a mobile communication technology?
   (a) GSM   (b) EDGE
   (c) 3G   (d) VoIP

39. Which of the following is the first Phablet of Acer recently launched in June 2013?
   (a) Liquid S1
   (b) P3
   (c) Liquid mini
   (d) Liquid Metal

40. Identify the following.
   - A social networking site.
   - Founded by Michael and Xochi Birch in January 2005.
   - The site was acquired by AOL which turned out to be a worst deal.
   (a) Facebook   (b) Twitter
   (c) Bebo   (d) Tumblr

41. In MS Word, this button is used to ____.
   (a) Insert an image into the document
   (b) Apply text wrapping to an image
   (c) Crop an image to it the document
   (d) Insert a caption to a picture of other image

42. The following icon represents ______ and is found under ______ tab in MS PowerPoint.
   (a) Action, Insert
   (b) Hyperlink, Insert
   (c) Custom animation, Animation
   (d) Action, Home

43. In MS PowerPoint, which of the following options is used to share the presentation with remote users who can watch in a web browser?
   (a)   (b)
   (c)   (d)

44. Which keyboard shortcut allows you to create an embedded chart of the data in the current range in MS excel?
   (a) Alt + F1   (b) F11
   (c) F12   (d) F1

45. Homegroup option is found under ______ category of Control Panel in Windows 7.
   (a) Ease of Access
   (b) Network and Internet
   (c) System and Security
   (d) Appearance and Personalization

Achievers Section

46. What is the output of the given QBASIC code?
```
S = 1
FOR I = 1 TO 15 STEP 2
IF I > 12 THEN EXIT FOR
S = S * I
NEXT I
PRINT I
```
   (a) 13   (b) 17
   (c) 9   (d) 7

47. Identify the system.
- It was an electromechanical device.
- It used over 3000 electrically actuated switches.
- It could perform addition, subtraction, multiplication, division and table reference on as large as 23 digit numbers.

(a) Electronic Delay Storage Automatic Calculator

(b) Electronic Numerical Integrator and Calculator

(c) Universal Automatic Computer One

(d) Mark I Computer

48. Identify the following.
- A type of port invented by Apple.
- It transfers large amount of data at very fast speed.
- It connects camcorders and video equipments to the computer.

(a) Ethernet Port

(b) FireWire port

(c) VGA port

(d) PS/2 port

49. When a text is selected and marked as Index entry, MS Word adds a special Xe field that includes the marked main entry and ______ information.

(a) Hyperlink

(b) Bookmark

(c) Cross-reference

(d) Index

50. A ______ is a small screen (CRT or LCD) in an aircraft surrounded by multiple buttons that can be used to display information to the pilot in numerous configurable ways.

(a) CFD   (b) MFD

(c) AFD   (d) TFD

Answer Keys

Scan the QR Code to see the Hints and Solutions

Access Content Online on Dropbox: https://www.dropbox.com/scl/fi/x1il8nzpuzwm1qyz8yycu/NSO-01-Science-Olympiad-Hints-and-Solutions.pdf?rlkey=kzkx1753ie7dfs4rlkt3yo4pa&dl=0

SECTION 1: COMPUTERS AND IT

1. FUNDAMENTALS OF COMPUTER

Answer Key									
1. (a)	2. (d)	3. (b)	4. (d)	5. (b)	6. (c)	7. (a)	8. (d)	9. (a)	10. (d)
11. (c)	12. (b)	13. (d)	14. (a)	15. (c)	16. (d)	17. (a)	18. (b)	19. (b)	20. (a)
21. (b)	22. (c)	23. (d)	24. (d)	25. (c)	26. (b)	27. (a)	28. (b)	29. (c)	30. (b)
31. (d)	32. (a)	33. (c)	34. (b)	35. (c)	36. (c)	37. (a)	38. (d)	39. (b)	40. (a)

HOTS				
1. (a)	2. (b)	3. (a)	4. (b)	5. (b)

2. EVOLUTION OF COMPUTERS

Answer Key									
1. (b)	2. (b)	3. (c)	4. (d)	5. (c)	6. (c)	7. (b)	8. (d)	9. (d)	10. (a)
11. (d)	12. (b)	13. (d)	14. (b)	15. (a)	16. (b)	17. (b)	18. (c)	19. (b)	20. (d)

HOTS				
1. (c)	2. (b)	3. (b)	4. (c)	5. (b)

3. MS WORD

Answer Key									
1. (b)	2. (a)	3. (c)	4. (a)	5. (b)	6. (c)	7. (b)	8. (b)	9. (d)	10. (a)
11. (d)	12. (c)	13. (a)	14. (d)	15. (b)	16. (b)	17. (a)	18. (c)	19. (a)	20. (b)

HOTS				
1. (c)	2. (b)	3. (d)	4. (d)	5. (a)

4. MS EXCEL

Answer Key

1. (a)	2. (c)	3. (b)	4. (c)	5. (c)	6. (c)	7. (c)	8. (d)	9. (d)	10. (c)
11. (a)	12. (b)	13. (d)	14. (a)	15. (a)	16. (b)	17. (c)	18. (c)	19. (a)	20. (b)
21. (d)	22. (d)	23. (d)	24. (d)	25. (a)					

HOTS

1. (b)	2. (a)	3. (b)	4. (a)	5. (d)

5. MS POWERPOINT

Answer Key

1. (b)	2. (d)	3. (c)	4. (c)	5. (a)	6. (c)	7. (d)	8. (b)	9. (b)	10. (a)
11. (d)	12. (d)	13. (a)	14. (a)	15. (d)	16. (c)	17. (c)	18. (b)	19. (b)	20. (b)
21. (c)	22. (c)	23. (d)	24. (b)	25. (a)					

HOTS

1. (b)	2. (b)	3. (b)	4. (c)	5. (b)

6. PROGRAMMING IN QBASIC

Answer Key

1. (d)	2. (a)	3. (a)	4. (a)	5. (c)	6. (a)	7. (b)	8. (a)	9. (d)	10. (a)
11. (a)	12. (d)	13. (a)	14. (d)	15. (c)	16. (d)	17. (d)	18. (b)	19. (d)	20. (b)
21. (a)	22. (a)	23. (c)	24. (a)	25. (b)	26. (d)	27. (c)	28. (c)	29. (c)	30. (a)
31. (b)	32. (d)	33. (b)	34. (d)	35. (c)	36. (c)	37. (c)	38. (d)	39. (d)	40. (b)
41. (a)	42. (b)	43. (b)	44. (b)	45. (c)					

HOTS

1. (a)	2. (b)	3. (d)	4. (d)	5. (a)

7. INTERNET AND VIRUSES

Answer Key

1. (d)	2. (d)	3. (d)	4. (d)	5. (b)	6. (b)	7. (b)	8. (c)	9. (c)	10. (d)
11. (d)	12. (b)	13. (d)	14. (a)	15. (a)	16. (a)	17. (b)	18. (a)	19. (c)	20. (d)
21. (c)	22. (d)	23. (b)	24. (d)	25. (b)	26. (c)	27. (a)	28. (b)	29. (d)	30. (b)
31. (a)	32. (a)	33. (d)	34. (d)	35. (b)	36. (c)	37. (a)	38. (b)	39. (b)	40. (a)
41. (b)	42. (c)	43. (a)	44. (c)	45. (d)	46. (b)	47. (d)	48. (d)	49. (c)	50. (b)

HOTS

1. (c)	2. (d)	3. (c)	4. (b)	5. (b)

8. NETWORKING

Answer Key

1. (c)	2. (b)	3. (d)	4. (a)	5. (b)	6. (d)	7. (c)	8. (d)	9. (b)	10. (c)
11. (b)	12. (b)	13. (a)	14. (a)	15. (c)	16. (c)	17. (d)	18. (b)	19. (a)	20. (a)

HOTS

1. (b)	2. (d)	3. (d)	4. (c)	5. (b)

9. LATEST DEVELOPMENTS IN IT

Answer Key

1. (d)	2. (b)	3. (d)	4. (d)	5. (d)	6. (d)	7. (c)	8. (b)	9. (c)	10. (d)
11. (d)	12. (a)	13. (d)	14. (a)	15. (b)	16. (a)	17. (a)	18. (a)	19. (b)	20. (b)
21. (a)	22. (d)	23. (d)	24. (b)	25. (a)					

HOTS

1. (d)	2. (a)	3. (b)	4. (a)	5. (b)

SECTION 2: LOGICAL REASONING

1. ANALOGY

Answer Key									
1. (a)	2. (b)	3. (b)	4. (c)	5. (c)	6. (b)	7. (d)	8. (c)	9. (c)	10. (a)
11. (b)	12. (c)	13. (d)	14. (b)	15. (b)	16. (b)	17. (d)	18. (c)	19. (d)	20. (b)
21. (c)	22. (c)	23. (d)	24. (c)	25. (a)	26. (d)	27. (b)	28. (c)	29. (d)	30. (c)
31. (c)	32. (b)	33. (a)	34. (c)	35. (a)					

2. ODD ONE OUT

Answer Key									
1. (c)	2. (d)	3. (d)	4. (d)	5. (b)	6. (d)	7. (c)	8. (c)	9. (c)	10. (d)
11. (b)	12. (b)	13. (d)	14. (c)	15. (c)					

3. ALPHABET TEST

Answer Key									
1. (a)	2. (c)	3. (c)	4. (a)	5. (a)	6. (b)	7. (a)	8. (b)	9. (b)	10. (c)
11. (a)	12. (d)	13. (c)	14. (a)	15. (c)	16. (d)	17. (b)	18. (b)	19. (a)	20. (c)
21. (d)	22. (c)	23. (c)	24. (a)	25. (d)					

4. BLOOD RELATION TEST

Answer Key									
1. (d)	2. (a)	3. (b)	4. (c)	5. (a)	6. (c)	7. (b)	8. (b)	9. (c)	10. (d)
11. (d)	12. (a)	13. (c)	14. (b)	15. (b)	16. (c)	17. (a)	18. (d)	19. (a)	20. (b)

5. DIRECTION SENSE TEST

Answer Key									
1. (c)	2. (b)	3. (a)	4. (c)	5. (c)	6. (d)	7. (b)	8. (a)	9. (d)	10. (c)
11. (d)	12. (a)	13. (b)	14. (c)	15. (b)					

6. SEATING ARRANGEMENT

Answer Key

1. (c)	2. (b)	3. (c)	4. (d)	5. (a)	6. (d)	7. (c)	8. (c)	9. (d)	10. (c)

7. SYLLOGISM

Answer Key

1. (d)	2. (a)	3. (c)	4. (c)	5. (d)	6. (a)	7. (d)	8. (b)	9. (b)	10. (c)

8. EMBEDDED FIGURES

Answer Key

1. (c)	2. (c)	3. (a)	4. (a)	5. (a)	6. (c)	7. (a)	8. (b)	9. (d)	10. (b)
11. (a)	12. (c)	13. (d)	14. (d)	15. (a)	16. (b)	17. (d)	18. (b)	19. (b)	20. (a)
21. (b)	22. (d)	23. (c)	24. (b)	25. (d)	26. (a)	27. (d)	28. (b)	29. (a)	30. (c)

9. FIGURE PUZZLES

Answer Key

1. (d)	2. (c)	3. (c)	4. (b)	5. (d)	6. (a)	7. (d)	8. (a)	9. (d)	10. (c)
11. (c)	12. (c)	13. (b)	14. (b)	15. (c)	16. (c)	17. (b)	18. (b)	19. (b)	20. (c)
21. (b)	22. (a)	23. (d)	24. (b)	25. (a)					

10. VENN DIAGRAM

Answer Key

1. (b)	2. (d)	3. (a)	4. (a)	5. (d)	6. (d)	7. (c)	8. (a)	9. (b)	10. (c)
11. (b)	12. (d)	13. (c)	14. (d)	15. (d)	16. (c)	17. (c)	18. (b)	19. (c)	20. (d)
21. (c)	22. (a)	23. (c)	24. (b)	25. (a)	26. (b)	27. (c)	28. (c)	29. (c)	30. (c)
31. (a)	32. (c)	33. (b)	34. (c)	35. (c)	36. (c)	37. (c)	38. (a)	39. (b)	40. (c)

11. ANALYTICAL REASONING

Answer Key

1. (a)	2. (a)	3. (d)	4. (d)	5. (b)	6. (a)	7. (d)	8. (a)	9. (c)	10. (c)
11. (a)	12. (c)	13. (b)	14. (c)	15. (a)	16. (c)	17. (c)	18. (c)	19. (a)	20. (d)

MODEL TEST PAPER - 1

Answer Key

1. (a)	2. (b)	3. (d)	4. (a)	5. (a)	6. (d)	7. (a)	8. (d)	9. (b)	10. (b)
11. (b)	12. (c)	13. (b)	14. (d)	15. (a)	16. (b)	17. (a)	18. (a)	19. (d)	20. (c)
21. (a)	22. (d)	23. (b)	24. (c)	25. (b)	26. (b)	27. (a)	28. (a)	29. (d)	30. (a)
31. (b)	32. (d)	33. (b)	34. (a)	35. (a)	36. (c)	37. (a)	38. (a)	39. (a)	40. (d)
41. (a)	42. (c)	43. (b)	44. (c)	45. (d)	46. (a)	47. (b)	48. (b)	49. (a)	50. (a)

MODEL TEST PAPER - 2

Answer Key

1. (d)	2. (c)	3. (a)	4. (b)	5. (d)	6. (c)	7. (a)	8. (b)	9. (c)	10. (d)
11. (c)	12. (c)	13. (b)	14. (c)	15. (d)	16. (b)	17. (a)	18. (a)	19. (a)	20. (d)
21. (a)	22. (a)	23. (b)	24. (b)	25. (b)	26. (b)	27. (a)	28. (a)	29. (b)	30. (b)
31. (b)	32. (d)	33. (a)	34. (a)	35. (b)	36. (d)	37. (b)	38. (d)	39. (a)	40. (c)
41. (d)	42. (a)	43. (a)	44. (a)	45. (b)	46. (a)	47. (d)	48. (b)	49. (c)	50. (b)

Appendix

There are different organizations that conduct these examinations and covering all of them is not needed as the focus should be to understand the main type of exams conducted. They are similar for these organizations with the difference being the change in name of the exam.

Science Olympiad Foundation (SOF)		
S. No.	**Name of Exam**	**Grade**
1.	National Science Olympiad (NSO)	Class 1-10
2.	National Cyber Olympiad (NCO)	Class 1-10
3.	International Mathematics Olympiad (IMO)	Class 1-10
4.	International English Olympiad (IEO)	Class 1-10
5.	International Commerce Olympiad (ICO)	Class 1-10
6.	International General Knowledge Olympiad (IGKO)	Class 1-10
7.	International Social Studies Olympiad (ISSO)	Class 1-10
Indian Talent Olympiad (ITO)		
S. No.	**Name of Exam**	**Grade**
1.	International Science Olympiad (ISO)	Class 1-12
2.	International Math Olympiad (IMO)	Class 1-12
3.	English International Olympiad (EIO)	Class 1-12
4.	General Knowledge International Olympiad (GKIO)	Class 1-12
5.	International Computer Olympiad (ICO)	Class 1-12
6.	International Drawing Olympiad (IDO)	Class 1-12
7.	National Essay Olympiad (NESO)	Class 1-12
8.	National Social Studies Olympiad (NSSO)	Class 1-12
EduHeal Foundation		
S. No.	**Name of Exam**	**Grade**
1.	Eduheal International Cyber Olympiad (ICO)	Class 1-12
2.	Eduheal International English Olympiad (IEO)	Class 1-12
3.	National Interactive Math Olympiad (NIMO)	Class 1-12
4.	National Interactive Science Olympiad (NISO)	Class 1-12
5.	International General Knowledge Olympiad (IGO)	Class 1-12
6.	National Space Science Olympiad (NSSO)	Class 1-12

Humming Bird Education		
S. No.	Name of Exam	Grade
1.	Humming Bird Commerce Competency Olympiad (HCC)	Class 1-12
2.	Humming Bird Cyber Olympiad (HCO)	Class 1-12
3.	Humming Bird English Olympiad (HEO)	Class 1-12
4.	Humming Bird General Knowledge Olympiad (HGO)	Class 1-12
5.	Humming Bird Hindi Olympiad (HHO)	Class 1-12
6.	Humming Bird Mathematics Olympiad (HMO)	Class 1-12
7.	Humming Bird Science Olympiad (HSO)	Class 1-12
8.	Humming Bird Aptitude and Reasoning Olympiad (ARO)	Class 1-12
9.	Humming Bird Spelling Competition (Spell BEE)	Class 1-12
10.	Humming Bird Language Olympiad	Class 1-12

International Assessments for Indian Schools (IAIS) (MacMillan and EEA Collaboration)		
S. No.	Name of Exam	Grade
1.	IAIS Maths Olympiad	Class 3-12
2.	IAIS ScienceOlympiad	Class 3-12
3.	IAIS English Olympiad	Class 3-12
4.	IAIS Digital Technologies Olympiad	Class 3-12

SilverZone Foundation		
S. No.	Name of Exam	Grade
1.	International Informatics Olympiad	Class 1-12
2.	International Olympiad of Mathematics	Class 1-12
3.	International Olympiad of Science	Class 1-12

Unified Council		
S. No.	Name of Exam	Grade
1.	Unified Council Cyber Exam	Class 1-12
2.	Unified International English Olympiad.	Class 1-12
3.	Unified International Mathematics Olympiad (UIMO)	Class 1-12

Unicus		
S. No.	Name of Exam	Grade
1.	Unicus Non-Routine Mathematics Olympiad (UNRMO)	Class 1-11
2.	Unicus Mathematics Olympiad (UMO)	Class 1-11

3.	Unicus Science Olympiad (USO)	Class 1-11
4.	Unicus English Olympiad (UEO)	Class 1-11
5.	Unicus Cyber Olympiad (UCO)	Class 1-11
6.	Unicus General knowledge Olympiad (UGKO)	Class 1-11
7.	Unicus Critical Thinking Olympiad (UCTO)	Class 1-11

CREST (Online Mode)		
S. No.	**Name of Exam**	**Grade**
1.	Mathematics (CMO)	Classes KG-10
2.	Science (CSO)	Classes KG-10
3.	English (CEO)	Classes KG-10
4.	Computer (CCO)	Classes 1-10
5.	Reasoning (CRO)	Classes 1-10
6.	Spell Bee Summer (CSB)	Classes 1-8
7.	Spell Bee Winter (CSBW)	Classes 1-8
8.	Mental Maths (MMO)	Classes 1-12
9.	Green Warrior Olympiad (GWO)	Classes 1-12

How To Apply?

Anyone willing to participate in the Olympiad exam can follow these steps to apply for the exam:

☞ Log in to the official website of the conducting organization.

☞ Find the Registration Option to register

☞ Fill up the details such as Student Name, Parent Name, School Name, Class,Postal Address, E-mail Address, Password, etc.

☞ Select the subjects you want to apply for. Pay the necessary registration fees and you are done.

☞ You will receive necessary details on your email id.

There are no minimum marks required by the Olympiad conducting organizations to apply for the exam.

Awards

Based on the organization rules, students as well as schools participating in these exams are awarded with several recognitions based on the marks they score.